Lefèvre

PIONEER OF ECCLESIASTICAL
RENEWAL IN FRANCE

Philip Edgcumbe Hughes

William B. Eerdmans Publishing Company
Grand Rapids, Michigan

For my Gallic friends
†JEAN CADIER
PIERRE COURTHIAL
PIERRE MARCEL
ROGER NICOLE

Copyright © 1984 by Wm. B. Eerdmans Publishing Company
255 Jefferson Ave. S.E., Grand Rapids, Michigan 49503

Library of Congress Cataloging in Publication Data
Hughes, Philip Edgcumbe.
Lefèvre: pioneer of ecclesiastical renewal in France.

Bibliography: p. 199
Includes index.
1. Lefèvre d'Etaples, Jacques, d. 1536. 2. Christian
biography—France. I. Title.
BR350.L44H84 1984 230'.2'0924 [B] 84-13739
ISBN 0-8028-0015-7

Contents

v

Foreword

The portrait of Jacques Lefèvre d'Etaples offered in the following pages is drawn from a study of the original works and letters of Lefèvre and his contemporaries. The translations of passages from their writings, and from the writings of authors of other times, are my own, unless otherwise stated. There still remains much work to be done on Lefèvre, and it is gratifying to know that he is now increasingly receiving the scholarly attention that is due to a man of his intellectual stature and spiritual influence. It is my hope that this book may be of some worth as a contribution to the understanding of the development of Lefèvre's own convictions and to the appreciation of his place in the history of Christian thought.

P. E. H.
Rydal, Pennsylvania

Abbreviations

WORKS BY LEFÈVRE

CE—Commentary on the Catholic Epistles (*Commentarii in Epistolas Catholicas*, 1527).

CG—Commentary on the Gospels (*Commentarii initiatorii in Quatuor Evangelia*, 1522).

EG—Epistles and Gospels for the Fifty-two Sundays of the Year (*Epistres et Evangiles pour les cinquante et deux sepmaines de l'an*, 1525).

PE—Commentary on the Pauline Epistles (*Epistola ad Rhomanos. . . . Commentariorum libri quatuordecim*, 1512; I have used the second edition, published in 1515).

QP—The Fivefold Psalter (*Quincuplex Psalterium*, 1509).

WORKS BY OTHER AUTHORS

Allen—*Opus epistolarum Des. Erasmi Roterodami denuo recognitum et auctum*, ed. P. S. Allen, 11 vols. (1906–1947).

Herminjard—A. L. Herminjard, *Correspondance des réformateurs dans les pays de langue française recueillie et publiée avec d'autres lettres relatives à la Réform et des notes historiques et biographiques*, 9 vols. (1866–1897).

Renaudet—Augustin Renaudet, *Préréforme et Humanisme à Paris pendant les premières guerres d'Italie* (1916; 2d ed. 1953).

Rice—Eugene F. Rice, Jr., *The Prefatory Epistles of Jacques Lefèvre d'Etaples and Related Texts* (1972).

Introduction

Of the notable figures of the fifteenth and sixteenth centuries perhaps none has suffered neglect more unjustly than has Jacques Lefèvre d'Etaples. Now at last he is beginning to receive the attention to which he is entitled. In his own day his name was coupled with that of Desiderius Erasmus at the summit of the hierarchy of learning. His career was not stamped with the dazzling brilliance of Pico della Mirandola, the prophetic fire of Savonarola, the lofty detachment of Erasmus, the thundering impetuosity of Luther, or the polished intellectuality of Calvin, all of them his contemporaries; but, as with each of them, his genius lit up the European world. He was his own man, selflessly dedicated to the pursuit of authenticity, willing to abandon familiar and long-traveled paths when he saw that they were leading in the wrong direction, earnest in his appropriation of the truth as it was discovered, and zealous in communicating it to others. In this quest he did not hesitate to cut away the accretions of centuries by which the clear light of the truth had become occluded and, as a pioneer, to open the way for others to follow him into the enjoyment of that light.

Not only in the span of his years but also, and more particularly, in the progress of his thought, Lefèvre blazed the trail that led from Renaissance to Reformation. Confidently (and, as we shall show, not unreasonably) expecting the renewal of the church in France, and constantly laboring for it, he never left the Roman communion, though he maintained cordial friendships with some who had. During the course of a long life he witnessed a great variety of significant changes and developments, some encouraging to him, some not.

The year of his death we know: 1536—the same year in which Erasmus died. But the year of his birth is uncertain. Apparently a number of Lefèvre's contemporaries believed that he was about a hundred years old at the time of his death, and if this is correct he must have been born in 1436 or thereabouts. Thus one of his disciples, Jean Salmon (also known as Macrinus) asserted in an ode composed in honor of Lefèvre in 1537, the year after his death, that he was "close to a hundred years old."[1] A corroborating witness Hubert Thomas Leodius, secretary to the Elector Palatine Frederick II, claims that when he was in Paris during the following year (1538) he heard an account of the death of Lefèvre from the lips of Marguerite of Navarre. Marguerite was certainly well qualified to recount the facts, for Lefèvre had not only long enjoyed her friendship and patronage but also died at her home in Nérac. According to Leodius,[2] Lefèvre said shortly before his death that he was 101 years old. This evidence, however, is at variance with a statement made by Lefèvre himself in 1501: in a letter commending Charles de Bovelles' *Introduction to the Art of Opposites*[3] he wrote that he was then twice the age of Bovelles and that Bovelles was in his twentieth year. As Bovelles was born in 1479, Lefèvre was not speaking with absolute precision; but it would be reasonable to conclude from this statement that at the beginning of the sixteenth century Lefèvre was in his forties. If, moreover, the Jacobus Fabri who is recorded as having received a degree at the University of Paris in 1479 is one and the same with our Jacques Lefèvre d'Etaples (also known as Fabri, Faber, and Faber Stapulensis), it is far more likely that he was then, in 1479, a young man in his twenties than already past forty, which would be an exceptionally late age for graduation.

Everything considered, we are disposed to concur with the judgment that Lefèvre was born about 1455. This would make him some eighty years old at the time of his death—a considerable age for those days when life-expectancy was much shorter than it is now. It is, indeed, in no way surprising to find Lefèvre described as an old man in 1519 (when, according to the suggested reckoning, he was about sixty-four) and on subsequent occasions by Erasmus, who was some ten or twelve years his junior. There are also indications that a few years previously Lefèvre's health had been weakened and his appearance aged, perhaps permanently, by illness. Thus, in August 1516 he asked his former pupil, the Englishman Thomas Grey, to remember him kindly to Erasmus and to explain that illness had left him so debilitated that he was in no condition to write or even to dictate a letter, but that there had been no change in his feelings for Erasmus, whom he loved and revered and whose erudition he praised everywhere.[4] In November of the same year Guillaume Budé wrote to Erasmus of the critical state of Lefèvre's health; in his reply, sent in the middle of the following February, Erasmus expressed his own concern for one whose friendship he prized and whose qualities he admired:

---

1. *Hymnorum libri* (Paris, 1537).

2. In *Annalium de vita et rebus gestis illustrissimi principis Frederici II electoris Palatini*, written in 1555 but not published until 1624.

3. *In artem oppositorum introductio.*

4. Allen, II:287.

The news you have given me concerning Jacques Lefèvre's illness as being long lasting and virtually unremitting is excessively grievous; for this man is endowed with such godliness, such graciousness, and such learning, and because of all his studies is so deserving, that it is unworthy for him ever to grow old or die.[5]

Lefèvre was a man of small stature but of large humanity. The likeness of him in Beza's *Icones (Contemporary Portraits)* is remarkable for the firmness of the features, the determined set of the mouth, the steadiness of the gaze, and a visage bespeaking a personality that is at once perceptive, penetrating, judicious, generous, and compassionate. A native of Etaples, an undistinguished seaport in Picardy in the northwest corner of France, he came to Paris as a student and remained there for many years, winning renown as a leader in both learning and spirituality. Impatient with learning for learning's sake, he was himself living proof of his conviction that genuine wisdom, far from being merely cerebral, is always related to sanctity of life and concern for one's fellows. A man of intense application, with a phenomenal capacity for concentrated labor, he saw it as his duty to lead his generation back to the pure sources of religious and philosophical knowledge, thus putting an end to the practice of drinking from polluted academic streams that had wandered far from their origin. The influence of this quiet person, so free from self-seeking and the desire for public recognition, was altogether exceptional. "Truly the providence of God is amazing!" Beza exclaimed when writing of Lefèvre in his *Icones:*

For who would have imagined that a single individual, not particularly impressive to look at, would have succeeded in chasing barbarism from the world's most famous university where over a period of many years it had been firmly entrenched? Yet such is Jacques Lefèvre, a person of humble background and from a place of little repute, . . . but nonetheless one of the earth's noblest of men, if one takes into account his erudition, his piety, his magnanimity, and, most notable of all, the fact that he himself was brought up in the midst of this same barbarism—this man, I say, successfully carried through this lofty undertaking and put ignorance to flight.

Of Lefèvre's earlier years in Paris we know little, except that he was connected with the Collège du Cardinal Lemoine (an institution reserved for the education of scholars from his home region of Picardy), that he graduated as master of arts but for some unrevealed reason did not proceed to the doctorate in theology, that he was ordained to the priesthood, and that he taught philosophy and mathematics at this college until 1508 (though perhaps not uninterruptedly). During these years he acquired a reputation that placed him in the front rank of contemporary men of letters. In March 1506 the German scientist Heinrich Stromer lauded Lefèvre, by then

---

5. Ibid., p. 474.

acknowledged to be the leading Aristotelian authority of the day, as "a man endowed with sublime genius who has reached the peak of every branch of learning and from whose literary labors flow works of manifold scholarship, which are read with greatest eagerness by learned persons."[6]

Josse Clichtove, Lefèvre's disciple and collaborator (who later turned against him), included the following encomium of his master in his oration when he received the doctor's degree in Paris that same year:

> I ought to rejoice and be grateful for my ever venerable teacher Jacques Lefèvre d'Etaples, whose guidance and instruction it has been my good fortune to enjoy, no less than Philip the king of the Macedonians rejoiced that his son Alexander was born in the time of Aristotle, by whose teaching he was instructed.[7]

Another admirer was the learned Symphorien Champier who, in dedicating his commentary on Lodovico Lazzarelli's translation of the Hermetic writings (published in July 1507) to Lefèvre, addressed him as "the most erudite prince of philosophers in all France, absolutely supreme in every branch of knowledge," and saluted him as "the glory of the whole realm of scholarship."[8]

There are many other adulatory appreciations of this kind. The hyperbole of their language was characteristic of that age, but in the case of Lefèvre it should not be impatiently dismissed as empty sycophancy: the sentiment expressed is sincere and beyond doubt indicative of the very high esteem in which he was held by the learned men of his day. It is regrettably true, however, that good men never lack enemies, and Lefèvre was not without his share of these. In particular, he had to endure the animosity of many of the academics of the Sorbonne. They resented his intolerance of the unedifying quibblings and sophistries of the scholastic mind, which for so long had been dominant in the theological halls of Paris and elsewhere. The manner in which he unsettled their complacency and exposed the debility of their "establishment" aroused their hostility. Yet his aim was at all times positive and constructive, for he was firmly convinced that the declaration of what is true and genuine would not fail in due course to overcome what is false and spurious.

A man as single-minded as Lefèvre was not tempted to rest on his laurels or to let his head be turned by adulation; nor was he moved by ambition to gain for himself a position of power and prestige in the church or at the court, as he might easily have done through the influence of exalted friends. His whole life was concentrated on the more worthy objective of attaining

---

6. Heinrich Stromer, in his epistle prefacing Lefèvre's introduction to Aristotle's *De anima*, which was published together with Clichtove's commentary. Rice, p. 150.

7. Rice, p. 163.

8. Ibid., pp. 166, 168.

that truth which is both the original and the ultimate reality. With this goal before him, the arid speculations of medieval scholasticism could not but be repugnant to him. Human philosophy failed to bring him the satisfaction he sought, despite all the years of intense labor he expended on it. Mystical theology appealed strongly for a while to his naturally devout spirit, but it was no more than a station on the journey rather than its terminus. As his life unfolds, we see him being drawn, as by some centripetal force, to the biblical revelation, finding in its doctrine the truth he was seeking.

Lefèvre's life may, in fact, be divided into two parts: pre-1509 and post-1509—1509 being the year of the publication of his *Fivefold Psalter (Quincuplex Psalterium)*, in which he announced his discovery of the primacy of Scripture and the gospel. This, however, does not imply that prior to that year he did not acknowledge the authority of the Bible and the necessity of Christian faith. He had always been a sincerely religious man, but it was at this time that he crossed the line that separates, as he saw it, human wisdom from divine revelation. He described this transition in the opening paragraph of the dedicatory letter, addressed to Cardinal Guillaume Briçonnet, prefixed to the *Fivefold Psalter*. There he asserts that while virtually all studies are pleasurable and beneficial, only the study of divine verities promises not just pleasure and benefit but also the highest happiness; and he testifies that, after having long paid little more than lip service to these truths, the light he now experiences from them shows all human learning to be darkness in comparison, so that nothing on earth comes close to their sweetness. Furthermore, he is convinced that those who do not know this sweetness have never tasted the true food of the soul, since it is by every word that proceeds from the mouth of God that we live (Deut. 8:3; Matt. 4:4): "And what," he asks, "are these words but the Holy Scriptures?"[9]

It is plain, then, that Lefèvre himself was conscious that the publication of this volume on the Psalms marked a turning point in his life. Yet he did not immediately dissociate himself from all extrabiblical studies. There were certain works he had in hand that he felt obliged to complete before he could devote himself entirely to the exposition and translation of the Scriptures. His literary output continued unabated, and its impressiveness is unquestioned. Yet he was never so busy with the preparation of his own works that he did not find time to encourage and superintend the publication of numerous other scholarly projects to which he had directed the industry of his pupils and disciples. There was, moreover, a flow of works dedicated to him or commenting on his publications. He was indeed the hub, the dynamic center, from whom radiated the inspiration of the energetic and enthusiastic scholarly activity that was characteristic of his circle.

---

9. Ibid., p. 193. See pp. 53ff. below.

In 1512, three years after the appearance of the *Fivefold Psalter*, when his great commentary on the Pauline Epistles was published, the high esteem in which Lefèvre was held in the world of letters was expressed by a contemporary author who extolled him as "the most celebrated philosopher of our age." He is described as one who, "divinely endowed for the task of repairing the realm of letters in this our day, has set philosophy in all its parts free from the barbarous obscurity of certain sophists." The encomium continues:

> In speaking, indeed, he is sublime, in judgment weighty, in imagination refined, in composition diligent and penetrating. This is true not only of his own works but also of his understanding of the works of others. He seems really to have been born for this one purpose, that he might devote himself to the literary arena, reestablish standards of excellence, and recover the splendor of antiquity.

The writer also draws attention to the biblical studies that have now become supremely important for Lefèvre:

> Not content with his labors in the liberal arts, this most devout man concentrates his attention on divine matters and has dedicated himself totally to them; and he will bring great enrichment and assistance to our theologians and to students of God's word as he explains what is implicit, elucidates what is obscure, simplifies what is complicated, and everywhere restores passages that are defective and mutilated.[10]

The anonymous author of this eulogy evidently had personal knowledge of the man he was praising. There is no doubt that the admiration which Lefèvre evoked, for his humanity as well as for his scholarship, was thoroughly deserved.

---

10. These extracts are taken from the supplementary biographies published in the 1512 Paris edition of Triphemius's *Ecclesiastical Writers*. The Latin text is given in Rice, pp. 288f.

The Quest for Authenticity

THE SOURCES OF PHILOSOPHY

Lefèvre's scholarly labors were animated by a dedication to truth and a desire to purge the streams of knowledge of alien elements. This is evident in the very first of his works to be published, his paraphrases of Aristotle's *Physics*, printed in Paris in 1492. In the prologue he not only praises Aristotle as "the supreme leader of all genuine philosophers" but also assails the professors of the Sorbonne for their subservience to a tradition of medieval sophistry that he regarded as useless and unedifying. "They consider it unworthy," he complains, "and as far removed from the dignity of philosophy as possible, to attack the sophistical manner of exposition and to oppose the footling distinctions dear to the sophists." Their lack of intellectual seriousness and vitality is to be condemned, he maintains, "with the same firmness as Socrates displayed when he condemned Euthydemus and Dionysodorus as damned sophists whose studies were contemptible and those who busy themselves with such studies as ridiculous."[1] In the preface addressed to the reader Lefèvre denounces the "dreadful wranglings" of such sophists as "much more appropriate to empty jabbering than to calm and peaceful philosophy, which alone is beautiful and concentrates on the contemplation of beautiful things, without slandering anyone, and avoiding noisy altercations." It is better to shun these sophists, he says, and to overcome them by keeping silent, than to seem to associate oneself with them in their babblings.[2]

In the prologue to two dialogues on Aristotle's natural philosophy, which he included in this volume, Lefèvre observes that the terms "philosophy" and "philosopher" originate in love: "For what is philosophy," he asks, "if it is not love of wisdom? What is a philosopher if he is not a true lover of the same?" Properly understood, then, philosophers are friends. "Consequently, when they see spiteful and

---

1. Rice, pp. 5, 6; Plato, *Euthydemus* 305A.
2. Rice, pp. 11f.

1

malevolent men tearing each other to pieces they no longer regard them as philosophers.[3]

Thus we see that in the very first of his publications Lefèvre issued an open challenge to the exponents of medieval sophistry then ensconced in the theological halls of Paris. His perspective was that of the new learning which, tired of what was secondhand and second best (or worse), was determined to receive nothing uncritically, no matter how strongly entrenched it might be, and to reopen the path to the sources of wisdom. For Lefèvre, at this stage, this meant the recovery of the genuine text and teaching of the Greek philosophers and simultaneously the exposure and elimination of the corruptions that had accumulated along the way.

The next of Lefèvre's works to appear was his introduction to Aristotle's *Metaphysics*. This, together with four dialogues, was published in Paris early in 1494 (though it had in fact been completed in 1490). In the dedicatory letter to Germain de Ganay, Lefèvre explains that he had dedicated an arithmetical work to his brother Jean de Ganay, "a dispenser of French justice," because the Peripatetics had shown that all justice is related to geometrical and arithmetical principles and that "arithmetic is as it were a mirror and rule of justice"; whereas he offers the present volume, which he describes as a theological work, to Germain, "as to a priest with a profound care for the divine mysteries." He reminds Germain of the tradition that in former times "the Egyptian priests and Chaldean magi handled divine mysteries" and passed them on down to the philosophers. He asserts, further, that the Platonic and Aristotelian theology "harmonizes with and is conjoined to Christian wisdom with a wonderful accord and affinity," because these were "pious philosophers, whom in their own day God made his priests and prophets, and beacons that give light to our day." He observes that, "although the Lord (who illumines every man)[4] had not yet appeared visibly in the world, yet he, who is the measureless and infinite light enlightening all ages, enlightened them from heaven."[5] The designation of the classical philosophers as—to all intents and purposes—Christians *before* the advent of Christ, a notion that can be traced back to the Alexandrian school of the third century, appealed strongly to the Renaissance mind. Lefèvre may well have taken it over from Pico della Mirandola, who a few years previously had propounded it with enthusiasm. (Pico died in this same year, 1494.)

The "arithmetical work" dedicated to Jean de Ganay was the *Elements of Arithmetic* by the thirteenth-century mathematician Jordanus Nemorarius. (Its publication was delayed until 1496.) In the dedicatory letter to this work, Lefèvre remarks that "Pythagoras maintained that it was impossible to know

---

3. Ibid., p. 16.
4. Cf. John 1:9.
5. Rice, p. 21.

anything without the aid of numbers,'' and that Plato engraved the follow-ing epigram in the vestibule of his academy: "Let none enter here who is ignorant of mathematics." Lefèvre adds that "in almost the whole of the *Timaeus* Plato discusses the nature of things by means of numbers, and also has much to say on this subject in the eighth and ninth books of the *Republic*."[6] It is not unreasonable to discern the influence of Pico again in this emphasis on the importance of numbers.

In the middle of 1494 Lefèvre's introduction to Aristotle's *Nicomachean Ethics* was published, and in the dedication, addressed once more to Germain de Ganay, he extols Aristotle as "most subtly rational in the *Logic*, a philosopher of the universe in the *Physics*, completely prudent and practical in the *Ethics*, legally authoritative in the *Politics*, and a priest and theologian in the *Metaphysics*." He then gives us a glimpse of his own method as a teacher of philosophy:

> It follows that those who wish to philosophize in a rational manner must first be instructed in Aristotle's *Logic*; then they must turn to the *Ethics*, by which they will be introduced to the blessed life; after that, their mind now purged, they will be carried on more happily to the contemplation of both natural and divine truths as they follow the precepts of both Platonists and Aristotelians.[7]

Also in 1494 Lefèvre was responsible for the publication of Marsilio Ficino's translation of the work entitled *Pimander*, or "the book of Mer-curius Trismegistus on the power and wisdom of God," together with a commentary from his own pen. This work was part of the *Corpus Hermeticum*, which was believed to enshrine truth that was primeval. Lefèvre was moved to undertake this labor, he says, "both by his love for Marsilio, whom he venerates like a father, and also by the magnitude of the wisdom of Mercury."[8] Ficino, who was the head of the Florentine Academy founded by Cosimo de' Medici, was convinced (and his convic-tion had been shared at least for a time by his friend and compatriot Pico della Mirandola) that the Hermetic wisdom reached back through the heroic figures of Greek legend, like Prometheus and Atlas, to Moses as its unsullied source in Egypt, and that from Hermes (Mercury) the line of philosophical succession continued down through Orpheus, Aglaophemus, Pythagoras, Philolaus, and Plato. The concept of the essential harmony of all theological and philosophical truth was one on which Pico had eagerly seized. In reality, however, the Hermetic writings were a syncretistic collection dating back to about the third century *after* Christ; consequently, they were mistakenly invested with the authority of a venerable antiquity. Their ingredients

---

6. Ibid., p. 18.

7. Ibid., pp. 23f.

8. Ibid., p. 135.

included a considerable admixture of Gnostic and Neoplatonic mysticism, which Lefèvre found attractive at this stage of his intellectual journey. In 1505, as we shall see, he would bring out a complete Latin edition of the *Corpus Hermeticum.*

Early in 1495 Lefèvre returned to mathematics with the publication of the text of the *Sphere* of Sacrobosco (John of Holywood), to which he added his own commentary. In the dedication to Charles Bourré, he recounts how George Hermonymus of Sparta, in the course of a recent visit, had praised the Parisian academy, but at the same time had remarked that it was deficient in the area of mathematical studies, reminding him that "mathematics (if we believe the seventh book of Plato's *Republic*) is of the greatest importance in the realm not merely of learning but also of civil government."[9] The next year (1496) Lefèvre brought out another mathematical work, his epitome of the *Principles of Arithmetic (De institutione arithmetica)* by Boethius, written by the latter as part of his fourfold introduction to philosophy. Familiarity with this work, Lefèvre tells Gianstefano Ferrero, to whom the epitome is dedicated, "will open the door to numerical proofs by following particular methods of Pythagoras, and students will readily understand the instruction given in these books which are full of pristine wisdom." He assures Ferrero that "by a careful comparison of Severinus [Boethuis] and Jordanus [Nemorarius]" there is ready to hand "a comprehensive exposition of the study of numbers which is most elegant and beyond praise and an easily grasped introduction into whatever things require the use of numbers."[10]

In this same volume Lefèvre included two other writings that he placed in the category of arithmetical studies. One of these was "the game of *Rithmimachia* which is also called the battle of numbers," a medieval form of numerical competition. In the preface, addressed to Bernard de Le Venquière, "a lover of numbers," Lefèvre commends this game as "not illiberal, but one which adolescent students may fittingly use lest their instruction should seem to advance too tediously," and as a "leisurely pastime that is both useful and respectable, by which beginners can conserve their energy when at times they tire of study." The second writing was a treatise on the elements of music. In the first of two prefatory epistles Lefèvre lists for Nicole de Hacqueville the names of twenty-eight wise men of antiquity who have commended the virtues of music, starting from Mercury, Orpheus, and Pythagoras, including Plato and Aristotle, and ending with Boethius. He speaks of the marvelous effects produced by this art, observing that the Pythagoreans were accustomed to pacify ferocious spirits with lutes and lyres, and that the ancients knew how to cure all kinds of physical ailments and injuries by the use of melody. Music indeed is "a

---

9. Ibid., p. 27.

10. Ibid., pp. 34f.

kind of law and rule of moderation. . . . By means of lute and song Orpheus
tamed the passions of wild beasts, which means that by singing to the
accompaniment of his lyre he reduced the savage customs and practices
of men to those of temperate humanity."[11]

Another publication of Lefèvre's to appear in 1496 was called *Logical
Introductions (Introductiones logicales)*. He dedicated it to Thibault Petit
and Gilles de Lille, whom he described as his "fellow soldiers in the study
of philosophy."[12] Some six months later, in April 1497, two more
Aristotelian works came off the press as a single volume, namely, Lefèvre's
edition of the *Nicomachean Ethics*—using the translations of Argyropoulos,
Bruni, and Grosseteste, but including Lefèvre's own commentary on the
text—and his edition of Giorgio Valla's translation of the *Great Ethics
(Magna Moralia)*. Prefaced to the former is a letter addressed to Jean de
Rély, in which Lefèvre states that in his comments on the text he has tried
to be as brief as possible, "since Aristotle is like the most expert master-
builder who prepares his edifice in such a way that nothing remains to be
added and nothing can be removed without harm." His method, he continues, is "not that of questioning and argumentation, excepting where
doctrinal matters occur in the text, because morality does not arise from
lengthy disputation about words but from sound understanding and correct
education (as Plato insists, and likewise Aristotle), and because it is generally
the case that to think up contentious problems as opposed to practical propositions hinders rather than benefits the hearers." In the letter to Guillaume
Budé that introduces the *Magna Moralia*, Lefèvre relates how Gianstefano
Ferrero had recently lent him Giorgio Valla's translation of this work and
how he had studied it with the greatest eagerness. He adds that the revision
and correction of the text had involved him in much labor. Lefèvre also
included in this same volume, as a virtual equivalent of Aristotle's *Eudemian
Ethics*, Bruni's *Introduction to Ethics (Isagogicon moralis disciplinae)* and
his own introduction to the *Nicomachean Ethics* (first published in 1494).[13]

All the Aristotelian editions were carefully and critically prepared for
the press, in accordance with Lefèvre's design to make available to his
generation the authentic teaching of Aristotle, together with a sound commentary for the assistance of students. He seems, as we have already noticed,
to have followed a definite sequence of instruction as a teacher of philosophy,
introducing his pupils first of all to the study of logic and, simultaneously,
mathematics (made more palatable by the occasional resort to an entertaining competitive game), and then moving them on in turn to ethics, physics,
and metaphysics. The admiring tributes paid to him as a teacher, and the
young men of outstanding ability who attended his classes with such

---

11. Ibid., pp. 30f., 32, 36f.

12. Ibid., p. 38.

13. Ibid., pp. 41ff.

eagerness provide ample evidence of his prowess as an instructor who was content with nothing but the highest standards. Though uncompromising in the thoroughness of the demands he made on his students, he was nonetheless compassionate and sincere in his attachment to them, which was an attachment not merely of master to pupil but also of friend to friend.

DIONYSIUS THE AREOPAGITE

Near the beginning of 1499 Lefèvre published the works of Dionysius the Areopagite under the title *Life-giving Theology, Solid Food (Theologia vivificans: Cibus solidus)*—a title that indicates the high value he placed on these writings at this time. Mystical and Neoplatonic in character, there were distinct affinities between these writings and the Hermetic composition *Pimander* that he had brought out some five years previously. Certain preconceptions seem, however, to have inhibited Lefèvre from forming a critical assessment of the genuineness of these writings, purported to come from the pen of St. Paul's Athenian convert (Acts 17:34). For one thing, he was unprepared to abandon the conviction, so long held in the church, that they emanated from one instructed by St. Paul himself and were virtually a fount of apostolic and canonical truth. If this seems somewhat out of character, there was another factor that undoubtedly swayed his judgment. This was a national or patriotic consideration the significance of which he wished all Frenchmen to appreciate, for, according to a tradition enthusiastically accepted by Lefèvre, Dionysius had been the original apostle to France and the first bishop of Paris, and therefore one whom the French should venerate as their own father in the faith.

Although the genuineness of the Dionysian writings was then still generally unquestioned and remained to all intents and purposes an article of ecclesiastical orthodoxy, Lefèvre could hardly have been unaware of the criticism by which, earlier in the fifteenth century, Lorenzo Valla and Bessarion had exposed their spuriousness; and he certainly was familiar (as will soon be shown) with the opinion of another scholar, Valla's contemporary, Nicholas of Cusa, that Dionysius was a Platonist. Though he held Nicholas of Cusa in the highest esteem, Lefèvre was not prepared, at this juncture, to approve the soundness of this judgment and to abandon his view of the Dionysian works as all but apostolic. Not only did Thomas Aquinas by his frequent quotations seem to place them on a par with the canonical writings but he also was one of a number of leading theologians of the medieval church, such as Hugh of St. Victor, Albert the Great, and Bonaventure, who composed commentaries on them. Soon, indeed, Erasmus and the early Reformers would reject their authenticity, and the day was approaching when Lefèvre himself would turn away from them and devote all his attention to the canonical books. Today it is not disputed that the Dionysian writings are the work of a pseudonymous author who lived some 500 years after Christ (and Paul!).

For the present, however, Lefèvre classifies Dionysius as one of the "hearers of the apostles," who was therefore "close to the source."

> The nearer a luminary is to the sun [he says in his preface] the more resplendent is its brilliance, surpassing the power of human vision; and the closer anything approaches to its source so much the more does it hold and preserve the purity of its nature; nor is it to be imagined that divine things differ from human in this respect. Hence of all Scripture the sacred Gospels are recognized as attaining the supreme peak of dignity, the highest distinction, and as being especially venerable and authoritative, since they flowed most nearly from God and were transfused into prepared minds. They are closely followed by those holy and arcane revelations of Jesus, the Acts and the Epistles of the apostles, and by the monuments of the prophets contained in the system of the old law. And all these writings which constitute the twofold Old and New Testament are called oracles. Moreover, those hagiographa and sacred writings which the hearers of the apostles left as a future heritage for the building up of the faithful church follow these oracles most closely in dignity and authority. Among these are the most sacred works of Dionysius the Areopagite, so outstanding in their excellence that one could never find words to praise them adequately.

Lefèvre explains that it was through the goodness and the will of God that "these riches of divine wisdom, this heavenly ambrosia," derived from the high noon of the apostolic age, had become available again, now, however, in the more readily understood Latin language. In his view, it was obvious that literary monuments that have come down to us from apostolic times differ from other works "as much as living things differ from dead, heavenly things from earthly, and immortal from mortal things, preserving in themselves as they do something life-giving and marvelously enlightening beyond other compositions." Lefèvre assures his readers that Dionysius was one of those concerning whom the apostle Paul said, "We speak wisdom among those who are perfect" and "Solid food is for those who are perfect,"[14] and that the understanding of the writings of Dionysius is indeed solid food.

There follows a notion that is reminiscent of what Pico della Mirandola had propounded some ten or twelve years previously: the oracles of Scripture, says Lefèvre, "are like a chest in which the treasures of wisdom lie hidden in darkness impenetrable to our eyes, unless someone should unlock it and train upon it a sacred light." This, he affirms, is precisely what Dionysius has done, for he not only opens the divine chest but also provides a sacred light "by which we are enabled to contemplate the marvelous beauty of the unlocked oracles"; and he modestly adds that this will everywhere be more plainly revealed by their reading Dionysius for themselves than by any explanation or instruction he may offer. He pro-

---

14. 1 Corinthians 2:6; Hebrews 5:14. The Pauline authorship of the Epistle to the Hebrews, though disputed in the early church, was universally accepted when Lefèvre wrote this.

ceeds, however, to propose certain admonitions. He urges, first, that "the sacrosanct oracles[15] and these other divine works similar to them (which uncover the mysteries of the oracles)[16] should be handled with all reverence and read attentively, in the manner of one who is praying to God with a mind that is humble, submissive, and obedient." Second, he insists that Dionysius, "this most holy author who unlocks divine wisdom, is neither a Platonist nor an Aristotelian nor a Stoic nor an Epicurean, but a philosopher of Jesus, the author of life, and of the Holy Spirit, a man who had Paul and Hierotheus for his most divine instructors."[17]

Yet at the same time Lefèvre was not willing to concede that Dionysius could have been ignorant of the things that were known to Plato and Aristotle; indeed, he asserts that either of these philosophers, had they lived in the time of Dionysius, would have counted it a blessing to be among his disciples. He warns his readers in particular not to listen to any who dismiss Dionysius as a Platonist. His thought, Lefèvre contends, is far more sublime than that of Plato, and it would be just as preposterous to call John the Evangelist a Pythagorean or a Platonist, "as some persons have done," rather than "a heavenly supramundane scribe or the divinely sounding trumpet of Jesus Christ and the Holy Spirit." Lefèvre warns, still more specifically, against being influenced by Nicholas of Cusa who, "though a student of the supreme wisdom of this most blessed father, was deluded by a common error and called him a Platonist."[18] Nicholas, an edition of whose works Lefèvre would bring out in 1514, had in fact said that Dionysius imitated Plato to such an extent that he is frequently found using the same words as Plato and in the same order;[19] and his contemporary, Cardinal Bessarion, whom Lefèvre also respected highly and whose version of Aristotle's *Metaphysics* he would publish in 1515, had likewise stated that Dionysius made use not only of the sentiments but also of the very language of Plato in all his works.[20] Similarly, Thomas Aquinas had admitted as a difficulty the fact that Dionysius "uses the mode of expression which the Platonists used."[21] It was not, however, the intention of Aquinas, Bessarion, or Nicholas of Cusa to depreciate Dionysius by their judgment that so much of his thought and terminology was Platonic. Indeed, the characteristic theories of Nicholas of Cusa's own theological system—his doctrine of "learned ignorance," with its insistence on the necessity of speaking about

---

15. That is, the canonical Scriptures.

16. Specifically here the writings of Dionysius.

17. Rice, pp. 60ff. Hierotheus, who is mentioned in the work on the Divine Names (ii.9), seems to have been an invention of Pseudo-Dionysius or of some earlier author.

18. Rice, p. 64.

19. Nicholas of Cusa, *Apologia doctae ignorantiae* 10.

20. John Bessarion, *In Calumniatorem Platonis* I.vii.2.

21. Thomas Aquinas, *In Dionysii de divinis nominibus expositio*, Preface.

God by way of negation, and his postulation of the coincidence of opposites—can be said to have been derived or developed from the teaching of Pseudo-Dionysius.

The translation of the *Corpus Dionysiacum* that Lefèvre used was that of Ambrogio Traversari, which dated back to 1436, though he actually worked with a later edition of 1480. A more recent version was that of the *Mystical Theology* and *Divine Names* by Marsilio Ficino. In introducing his translation Ficino, too, had described Dionysius as a Platonist, praising him as "the crown of Platonic learning and pillar of Christian theology"[22] and "easily the first of Platonists"; yet even so devout a Platonist as Ficino, who, at least in earlier years, had burned candles before Plato's bust and adored him as a saint, was prepared to give Dionysius pride of place over Plato while still applauding him as a Platonist. "Though at times we speak of Dionysius as though he were a follower of the pious Plato," he wrote, "yet we judge that he should be given pre-eminence not only over other Platonists, as being the crown of Platonic doctrine, but even over Plato himself, as being the new light of Christian truth."[23] Ficino, like Pico and other scholars of that age, was persuaded of the essential harmony of Platonism and Christianity, and in fact of all philosophical and religious knowledge (this was the basic concept behind the 900 Theses published by Pico in 1487); and it was a view that was not at all foreign to Lefèvre's own thinking at this period. Convinced, as he then was, that Dionysius was a genuinely apostolic man, just one step removed from an apostle, and the first to bring the Christian faith to France, he appeals to his fellow countrymen in the final part of his prefatory letter to salute him as their own apostle:

> Not without the divine overruling and the highest providence did it come about that this man, the most holy and by far the most illustrious of the fathers by reason of his divine wisdom, was the first to rule the Attic church as bishop of Athens and displayed his light in the foremost, indeed the parent civilization of all literature, and then, despatched as an apostle to France by the most blessed Clement, chose for his see-city the distinguished city of the Parisians—known as Paris or Lutetia, but which might more appropriately have been called "Dionysia" after Dionysius, its first bishop and apostle, its first patron and regenerator.

"Therefore," he urges his fellow Parisians,

> you, the Dionysiac academy of all good learning, the Parisian academy, which one father has made the companion and sister of Athens, applaud your apostle, your first bishop, your parent who first brought you life

22. Bessarion had called Dionysius a "prince of Christian theology," loc. cit.
23. Rice, pp. 68f.

and light, receive with honor his sacred teachings, and study them to your profit day and night.[24]

The sturdy element of patriotism in Lefèvre's perspective should not be overlooked. He was mistaken, however, in his belief that St. Paul's convert became the first bishop of Paris, an honor that belongs to a personage of the same name, commonly known in France as St. Denys, who lived in the third century. Lefèvre was not alone in confusing the two. And, as we have said, he was also mistaken in attributing to St. Paul's convert the writings he was now commending. By fostering national pride in Dionysius he hoped to turn his fellow countrymen to studies that he considered intellectually profitable and conducive to personal sanctity.

Bound in together with this edition of the Dionysian works were eleven epistles of Ignatius, bishop of Antioch, who was martyred c. A.D. 107, and the epistle of Polycarp, bishop of Smyrna, who was martyred c. A.D. 155. The Latin version Lefèvre used dated back to the sixth or seventh century. The Ignatian correspondence includes what are now acknowledged to be the seven genuine letters of Ignatius; the rest are later forgeries. In his preface to this correspondence Lefèvre describes Ignatius as a disciple of John the Evangelist, but in doing so seems to have confused Ignatius and Polycarp, for it is the latter that Irenaeus and other early Fathers say had been instructed by the apostle John. With these letters (although he did not realize it) Lefèvre was much closer to the time and the teaching of the apostles than he was with the mystical writings of Pseudo-Dionysius. He was filled with admiration, as so many others have been, for the joyful and indomitable spirit of Ignatius as he was being hustled on to martyrdom: "exulting in his chains because he was counted worthy to suffer shame for the name of Jesus, sent to Rome in order to fight with savage beasts and as the ardent soldier of God to provide a spectacle in the arena in the midst of raging lions that have been let loose." His letters, Lefèvre writes, are "full of the fervor of the Holy Spirit." Accordingly, they should be read with pious attention, "not negligently, not languidly, not with a wandering and enervated mind, but with fervor; for it was thus that this most holy martyr wrote them, totally inflamed, totally dedicated, totally enthused, desiring to depart this life and to be with Christ, intoxicated with the love of God."[25]

Turning to Polycarp's letter to the Philippians (the only one of his letters now extant), Lefèvre remarks that both Irenaeus and Eusebius make mention of Polycarp[26] and that his letter bears witness to those of Ignatius,[27] as do also the writings of other patristic authors, and he tells how this

---

24. Ibid., pp. 65f.

25. Ibid., p. 71.

26. Irenaeus, *Adv. Haer.* III.4; Eusebius, *Hist. Eccl.* IV.xivf.

27. Polycarp, *Ad Phil.* 13.

venerable martyr expressed an earnest longing to be offered up. He explains that he very willingly added these letters of Ignatius and Polycarp to the writings of Dionysius, "because Dionysius cited testimony taken from these epistles when he was discussing love in a spiritual and transcendental manner"[28] (an anachronistic impossibility if the author was really St. Paul's convert!), and also because in his comments on the text of Dionysius he refers to "the holy teaching contained in these epistles."[29]

RAMON LULL

Two months later, on 6 April 1499, Lefèvre published a volume containing four works by the Spanish monk, mystic, and missionary Ramon Lull (c. 1235—1315). A stern opponent of Averroism, Lull labored in the course of his travels for the conversion of the Muhammadans, by whom at last he was stoned to death in North Africa. Lefèvre had been an admirer of Lull's writings for a number of years prior to the appearance of this volume, for in the preface to the November 1505 edition of two more of Lull's works he recounts how more than fourteen years previously—that is, in 1491—he had received a visit from a friend from Narbonne who brought with him a book he wished to sell since he was struggling with ill health and pressed by poverty. Noticing that the subject of the book was the contemplation of God, Lefèvre was seized with a longing to read it; and since he happened to have a golden obol for which he had no need at the time, he offered it to his friend, not to purchase the book, but to be allowed to read it. His friend, however, insisted that he should keep the volume. "So the book remained with me," says Lefèvre, "and brought me the greatest consolation; indeed, it all but caused me to leave the world behind and to seek God in solitude." His wish to embrace the monastic life (he explains) was frustrated by the onset of illness, itself a consequence of the unremitting labor in which he engaged with a view to completing the tasks he had in hand preparatory to his withdrawal from the world. Afflicted by chronic sleeplessness, he lapsed into a state of weakness that persisted for several years. Under these circumstances, he yielded to the counsel of others and put aside his desire for the contemplative existence of monastic solitude.[30]

It was thus, in 1491, that Lefèvre first became acquainted with Lull's thought. During his journeyings Lull had visited Paris and manuscripts of his works were accessible to Lefèvre not only in the library of the Sorbonne but also in the Carthusian monastery at Vauvert and the monastery of St. Victor. It was probably from one of these places that Lefèvre borrowed

---

28. *De divinis nominibus* IV.12.

29. Rice, p. 72.

30. Ibid., pp. 141f.

the manuscripts of the works he edited in 1499. Lefèvre himself informs us that the monks of Vauvert provided the manuscript of Lull's *Tree of the Philosophy of Love,* which he edited in 1516, together with the *Book of Proverbs,* the text of which had been sent to him by Marguerite of Angoulême's physician, Jean Chapelain, "than whom none is a greater lover of Ramon." Lull's *Book of Lover and the Beloved,* which Lefèvre published in 1505 in association with the *Book on the Contemplation of God* (acquired as described above), he copied from a manuscript at the Benedictine monastery of Santa Giustina in Padua, when he was traveling in Italy in 1500.[31]

Lefèvre's attraction to Lull was threefold. First and foremost, he was drawn to the mystic's pursuit of inner, contemplative union with God, which found outward expression in a life of practical holiness. Second, he thoroughly approved Lull's denunciation of the Moslems ("Turks") and their religion as devilish and anti-Christian, and he shared Lull's conviction, widely and obsessively held in Christendom, that their overthrow would usher in a golden age for the true faith. (In 1509, as we shall see, Lefèvre would bring out an edition of two anti-Muslim works.) Third, Lefèvre concurred with Lull's antipathy for the twelfth-century Arab philosopher Averroes as one guilty not only of corrupting the doctrine of Aristotle but also of apostatizing from the Christian faith, which he had professed to embrace.

Of the four works of Ramon Lull contained in the volume published by Lefèvre in 1499, the first was a book of praises of the Virgin Mary,[32] the second a treatise on the nativity of the infant Jesus,[33] the third a catechism for ignorant clerics,[34] and the fourth, called the *Phantasticus,* a dialogue between a priest and a layman (the latter representing the viewpoint of Lull himself) *en route* to the Council of Vienne. The layman's hope was to persuade the council to introduce into the schools the teaching of oriental languages in preparation for a campaign to convert the Saracens and to drive the doctrines of Averroes from the universities. "These books," Lefèvre says in his preface, "which usefully set forth things that are rare and necessary, ought to be deemed precious." He urges, further, in terms similar to those previously used of the Dionysian writings,[35] that these compositions should be read "with devotion and singleness of mind in the manner of one who is praying, coming as they do from a saintly man devoted to God."

The readers of these works are advised not to be put off by the fact that Lull lacked an academic education. The Latin terminology Lefèvre used

---

31. This information is found in the prefaces of the editions mentioned.

32. *Liber de laudibus beatissimae virginis Mariae.*

33. *Liber de natali pueri parvuli Christi Jesu.*

34. *Liber Clericorum.*

35. See p. 8 above.

here, *"idiota et illiteratus,"* implies no more than that Lull was a lay as distinct from a professional scholar who had received formal training in theology and philosophy. The concept of the *idiota* gathered much importance in Lefèvre's thinking, in that it symbolized for him the ideal of the unsophisticated man whose mind is unencumbered by academic elaborations, and who therefore is naturally able to come close to God with a directness that is scarcely open to the man who has been conditioned by the artificialities of a scholastic upbringing. For Lefèvre, the simple, even rustic style of expression characteristic of the *idiota* was no hindrance to the communication of divine truth; quite the contrary. Lull, whose unaffected simplicity was shown in his choice of "a rough cave and vast solitude" for his dwelling-place, was deemed worthy, says Lefèvre, of "a certain heavenly infusion, thanks to which he excels by far the wise men of this age." In line with his way of looking at things at this stage, Lefèvre conceived that Lull enjoyed the benefit of divine inspiration, not, however, as though he were on a level with the biblical authors, but rather as an elucidator of the truth mediated through them. Even so, his application of 2 Timothy 3:16 to Lull's teaching must be judged extravagant: "Be instructed by Paul," he urges the readers of Lull's works, "that all divinely inspired doctrine is profitable for teaching, for reproof, for correction, for training." Nor should the plainness of his language turn them away, for, Lefèvre warns, again citing the apostle, "it is those whose hearing is too fastidious who should fear, lest they be of the number of those concerning whom St. Paul prophesied, 'The time is coming when people will not endure sound teaching, but having itching ears will accumulate for themselves teachers to suit their own likings, and will turn away from listening to the truth and wander into myths'" (2 Tim. 4:3-4). But "he who is able to penetrate below the surface sees nothing barbarous and nothing which does not contain a significance most worthy of knowing." It seems somewhat inconsistent, then, for Lefèvre to mention that in places he has improved Lull's style, "without in any way altering the sense," even though in doing so he has only acquiesced in what Lull, conscious of his literary shortcomings, "has graciously requested everywhere in his books."[36]

Pico della Mirandola's influence may well be reflected in the defense that Lefèvre makes of Lull's unpolished literary style. In June 1485, soon after returning from his first visit to Paris, Pico had written a lengthy letter to his friend Ermolao Barbaro. The letter was a good-humored rejoinder to one in which Ermolao had spoken slightingly of the barbarisms of the Teutons and praised the polish and elegance of the classical style as a means to the achievement of immortal fame. Pico identified himself with the "barbarians" for whom Ermolao had expressed contempt (thus, with Ermolao's second name in mind, introducing a note of amiable irony). "You will find,"

---

36. Rice, pp. 76f.

he wrote, "that the barbarians, if lacking in eloquence, were not destitute of wisdom"; and he drew attention to the fact that "sacred matters are written in a rustic manner rather than with studied eloquence, since there is nothing more unbecoming or harmful than this elaborate method of expression whenever the investigation of truth is involved."[37] The latter statement is consonant with Pico's conviction, at that time, that the crude exterior wording of the Old Testament Scriptures covered over a kernel of profound esoteric truth that was revealed only to the enlightened few. He had, indeed, been persuaded that the secret Jewish tradition of wisdom known as the cabala was none other than an esoteric exposition of the law communicated by God to Moses at Sinai but not committed to writing, of which the five books of Moses were but the outer shell intended for the general populace. "To set openly before the people the esoteric mysteries and secrets of the highest divinity which lie hidden beneath the shell of the law and the rough covering of words, what would that be except to give what is sacred to dogs and to scatter pearls among swine?" Pico asks.[38] So also Lefèvre was disposed to regard rough and ready language as a suitable covering for deeply hidden truth, and compared Scripture, as we have seen, to a chest containing hidden treasures imperceptible to our understanding apart from a key such as that provided by Dionysius.[39]

As we come to the beginning of the sixteenth century, we find Lefèvre occupied with a variety of intellectual activities that were, for the most part, the continuation of projects set in motion in the preceding years. The first three years of the century saw the completion of his work on the logical writings of Aristotle. Divided into three sections, they were published in a single volume in October 1503. The first section, however, had been finished and published separately in 1501. It contained Porphyry's *Isagoge* or Introduction to Aristotle's *Categories* (a work which for many years had been treated as standard in the philosophical schools) as well as the text of the *Categories* and the work on *Interpretation*. The second section is undated and without a preface, but presumably was completed during the following year. Its contents were the *Prior* and *Posterior Analytics*. The third section comprised the *Topics* and *Sophistici Elenchi* or "Sophistical Refutations" designed to counteract the specious and deceptive type of argumentation employed by the sophists, as Lefèvre explains in the prefatory letter addressed to Germain de Ganay. We shall easily avoid the snare of this sophistry, he asserts, if, already prepared by the instruction of the *Topics,* we are well versed in the correct method of logical disputation.

37. Pico della Mirandola, *Opera* I: 351ff. The reference is to the 1572 (Basel) edition of the *Opera Pici*, of which Volume I contains the works of Pico, and Volume II works by his nephew Giovanni Francesco Pico della Mirandola.

38. *Opera Pici* I: 328. The passage is from the *De Hominis Dignitate*. The biblical allusion is to Matthew 7:6.

39. See p. 7 above.

These works, which together constitute Aristotle's *Organon*, are provided by Lefèvre with annotations and paraphrases (except for the third section, which lacks paraphrases because, as he explains in the preface, he considered that an accurate translation and the addition only of elucidatory comments where the meaning might be obscure would suffice for the student).[40]

Another publication in 1503 was a volume of mathematical works containing Lefèvre's epitome of the arithmetical books of Boethius (previously published in 1496), a commentary by Josse Clichtove on this work, Clichtove's own arithmetical treatise entitled *Praxis numerandi*, an *Introduction to Geometry* composed by Charles de Bovelles, and Lefèvre's *Astronomicon*, which, as the name suggests, was a disquisition of the science of the stars.

THE STARS AND MAGIC

In dedicating his *Astronomicon* to Germain de Ganay, Lefèvre observes that not only the ancient Assyrians and Egyptians but also many famous Greeks and Romans were diligent students of the stars and their movements, and that he does not understand how the science of the stars, when approved by so many great men, should be judged as anything other than highly important. He points out that he is referring to that part of "astrology" (used synonymously for astronomy, as had long been the practice) which is a subject of "genuine and liberal contemplation" and a not ignoble division of philosophy. To study the heavens, he maintained, was to find that they are full of potent imagery; and this was only to be expected, for the movements of the celestial bodies are the reflections or "images of the true movements of the divine mind." Lefèvre is careful to distance himself from the astrological superstition and credulousness that were prevalent in his day, mentioning in particular the readings of horoscopes and calculations made from birth dates as a futile waste of time.[41]

Closely connected with the superstitions of astrology were those of magic, and in February of the following year (1504) Lefèvre availed himself of the opportunity afforded by the publication of his edition of the *Lausiac History* of Palladius,[42] the fifth-century chronicler of monasticism, and certain other works to dissociate himself from the distinction postulated by some between good or natural magic and evil or demonic magic. The other writings bound in with the *Lausiac History* were a letter attributed to Clement of Rome, the (pseudo-Clementine) *Recognitions of the Apostle Peter,* and two other letters (both pseudo-Isidorian) attributed to Clement and Anacletus,

---

40. Rice, pp. 87ff.

41. Ibid., pp. 112ff.

42. Lefèvre titled the work *Paradysus Heraclidis*, following a mistaken tradition that attributed it to "Heraclides the Alexandrian."

reputedly Clement's predecessor as bishop of Rome, though Lefèvre, following the text of the letter before him, presents Anacletus as Clement's suc-
cessor. He cites, moreover, the judgment of Pico ("Mirandola of most
renowned memory") that the book of *Recognitions* "contains apostolic
teachings."[43] Although the *Recognitions* and the accompanying letters were
spurious compositions of later centuries, with the consequence that Lefèvre's
confidence in them was misplaced, the publication of this edition of the
Recognitions served the purpose of supporting his opposition to the practice of magical arts. This work, he says, "refutes the absurdities of magic,
so that no one may now seek justification for his errors under the veil of
some kind of magic; for the fact is that no magic is good, and it is a delu-
sion to imagine that there is any kind of magic that is natural or good."
Magic, on the contrary, is a device of those "who seek to veil their ini-
quities under an honest name to the perversion of many persons." Much
space is devoted in the *Recognitions* to the denunciation of the blasphemous
pretensions to magical and supernatural powers of Simon Magus,[44] whom
St. Peter had confronted in Samaria (Acts 8:9ff.).

Lefèvre declares that the same work also refutes astrological sooth-
saying, "an insidious evil now approved by many," by means of which
"fortune-tellers, necromancers, and impure sorcerers disguise all their
impieties under the name of the science of the stars,"[45] claiming that it
"completely overthrows the cult of the gentile gods and the stupidities of
the rites connected with them,"[46] while at the same time "it plants in human
minds teaching containing the highest truth concerning all piety and
knowledge of God."[47]

In the development of his attitude toward astrology and magic, Lefèvre,
as we shall see, was following the path previously trodden by Pico della
Mirandola. Pico had at first been indulgent toward astrological claims and
in his *Nine Hundred Theses* of 1486 found room for a group of magical
conclusions, the most notorious of which was the one affirming that "there
is no science which makes us more certain of the divinity of Christ than
magic and cabala."[48] Lefèvre no doubt was somewhat familiar with the

---

43. The reference is to the section of Pico's *Apologia* in which the question of the salva-
tion of Origen is discussed, though Pico is actually in this place *disputing* the claim that St.
Peter was the apostolic source of the teaching of the *Recognitions*—something that escaped
Lefèvre's notice!

44. See, e.g., *Clementine Recognitions* ii.5ff.

45. See *Clementine Recognitions* ix.12ff.

46. Ibid., x.15ff.

47. Rice, p. 118.

48. The most recent edition of the *Nine Hundred Theses (Conclusiones sive theses DCCCC)*
is that edited by Bohdan Kieszkowski, "avec introduction et annotations critiques" (Geneva,
1973). The one cited is number nine of twenty-six conclusions on magic (p. 79); also *Opera
Pici* I (ut supra), p. 104.

views of Pico prior to his first visit to Italy, which took place in 1492 (one would like to know whether the two scholars met when Pico visited Paris in 1485), but it was after meeting Pico in Florence that he wrote a treatise on the subject of natural magic[49]—that is to say, the good as distinguished by Pico from the evil form of magic. However, the work, divided into six books, was never published.[50]

Pico previously had been careful to make a distinction between the two kinds of magic. Thus, for example, in his *Oration on the Dignity of Man,* with which he had intended to introduce the *Nine Hundred Theses,* he explained, with reference to his theses on magic, that "the term magic has a double significance, the one kind consisting entirely in the work and authority of demons, something altogether execrable and unnatural, whereas the other, when it is carefully investigated, is nothing else than the absolute consummation of natural philosophy."[51] In his unpublished work, Lefèvre points out, in a manner strongly reminiscent of Pico, that there is a virtual identification of those whom the Chaldeans call *magi* with those whom the Greeks call philosophers, except that philosophers concern themselves more with contemplation and *magi* more with the demonstration of the secret effects of philosophy. Where, then, natural philosophy is conceptual, the science of magic is practical, teaching us to discern those forces and practices both that are harmful and also that are beneficial. The foundation of natural magic is a knowledge of the affinities or antipathies that things have for each other, particularly with reference to the relationships existing between heavenly and earthly entities.

The active celestial influence is attributed to the potencies of the constellations above. Together these compose the zodiac, and its signs are viewed as "the great animal" (*magnum animal*) that acts on the passive and "lower animal" (*inferius animal*) of the human body by virtue of the correspondences that exist between them. These are the correspondences that the practitioner of magic knows how to control and manipulate for our well-being, because he is skilled in the immensely complicated art of relating the influences of the heavenly bodies to the various needs and tempers of men. The effects produced by different plants or herbs, or by different animals and their parts, are attributable to the planets with which they are associated. Substances that cause stupefaction or death, for example, come under the planet Saturn; those that make us bold to meet danger come under

---

49. *De magia naturali.*

50. Three manuscript copies are known to exist: the Olomouc *MS* in Czechoslovakia (Universitni Knihovna), which is a complete copy; a *MS* in the Vatican Library containing the first four books, parts of which are not easily legible; and a fragment in the Bibliothèque Royale in Brussels.

51. The Latin text, with an Italian translation, is given in *Edizione Nazionale dei Classici del Pensiero Italiano*, vol. I, *G. Pico della Mirandola*, ed. Eugenio Garin (Florence, 1942), p. 148.

Mars; and those that induce living that is lustful and luxurious come under Venus. The practice of natural magic, which is in no way connected with demons or the forces of evil, leads to results that to the ordinary person appear to be miraculous; but the *magus* knows them to be natural rather than supernatural, and as such they may be described as "miracles of nature."

The second book of Lefèvre's *Natural Magic* discloses the mystical significance of numbers. In his treatment of this subject Lefèvre seems, again, to be following the lead given a few years earlier by Pico, who had postulated that "the way to the investigation and intellection of all that is knowable is found through numbers."[52] Pico certainly did not regard himself as an innovator but rather as the restorer of a once honorable science, which was in fact "ancient, since it was used by the pristine theologians, by Pythagoras in particular, by Aglaophemus, by Philolaus, by Plato, and by the earlier Platonists"; and he recalled the saying of Plato that man is the wisest animal precisely because he has knowledge of numbers.[53]

Lefèvre similarly presented his doctrine of the mystical significance of numbers as having been derived from the secret philosophy of Pythagoras. He, too, saw the doctrines of the ancient sages of the East, the philosophers of Greece, the *magi* of Egypt, and the Hebrew cabalists as tributaries flowing together into the single river of pristine wisdom, and numbers as a key to the understanding of the mysteries of the universe; and he believed that to comprehend the profound symbolism of numbers was to be able to ascend from the multiplicity and diversity of our world to the simplicity and unity

---

52. This was number eleven of "85 conclusions concerning mathematics following his own opinion"; *Conclusiones*, ed. Kieszkowski (ut supra), p. 74.

53. Pico, *Oratio de hom. dign,* ed. Garin (ut supra), p. 146. Plato, *Epinomis* 977; *Republ.* VII.522C; cf. Aristotle, *Probl.* XX.6.955. The following passage from Aristotle, *Metaphys.* 985ᵇ24–986ᵃ4, is of interest:

> The Pythagoreans applied themselves to mathematics and were the first to develop this science and through studying it they came to believe that its principles are the principles of everything. And since numbers are by nature first among these principles, they fancied that they could detect in numbers, to a greater extent than in fire and earth and water, many analogues of what is and what comes into being—such and such a property of number being *justice*, and such and such *soul* or *mind*, another *opportunity*, and similarly, more or less, with all the rest—and since they saw further that the properties and ratios of the musical scales are based on numbers, and that numbers are the ultimate things in the whole physical universe, they assumed the elements of numbers to be the elements of everything, and the whole universe to be a proportion of number. (Loeb edn., trans. Hugh Tredennick)

Cf. also Aristotle, *De coelo* 300ᵃ15–19. Among the Neoplatonists, see Plotinus, *Enneads* VI.6, and Porphyry, *Vita Pythag.* 48, who says, citing Moderatus, that the Pythagoreans, being unable to express clearly in words the primary forms and principles because of their abstruse nature, resorted to numbers in the interests of precise teaching. An application of the Pythagorean theory is discernible in Plato's view of number as the principle underlying our understanding of time, which, according to him, is the sensible image of the eternity that belongs to the intelligible universe (*Timaeus* 37D–38A).

of the celestial reality and of God himself. As Eugene Rice has said regarding the opening section of the second book of Lefèvre's *Natural Magic:*

> This numerical ascension was for Lefèvre the most ancient teaching of the *magi,* and from it he derived the most profound lesson of natural magic: the correspondence of the planets and fixed stars with the first nine numbers, the association of the hierarchies of angels with the planets, and the harmony of natural magic, understood now as a form of *prisca theologia,* with Christianity.[54]

Still more remarkable in its potencies and significances than natural magic, however, is the secret tradition of the Hebrews known as the cabala, in which the power of numbers, particularly those of divine import, is combined with the power of letters, particularly those that form the divine names; this system is amazingly effective for promoting the secret work of magic. The technique involved is that of *gematria,* in which each letter of the alphabet has its own numerical equivalent. Thus the most sacred of all the divine names, the tetragrammaton,[55] is composed of the letters YHWH whose numerical values are ten, five, six, and five; these add up to a total of twenty-six, which accordingly is regarded as a number of the deepest mystery. The aim of the Hebrew sages, Lefèvre tells us, was "to translate the cabala of letters into the secret and magical philosophy of numbers"; and this was the derivation of "the secret philosophy of Pythagoras," who thus owed a debt to Hebrew wisdom.

Lefèvre, in fact, is preparing the ground for the disclosure of the greatest mystery of all, which involves the secret significance of the number 300, the numerical equivalent of the Hebrew letter *shin;* for this is the middle letter of the name "Joshua," which in turn is identical in Hebrew with the name "Jesus." Moreover, this name is composed of the four letters of the tetragrammaton plus the letter *shin,* as follows: *yodh, he, shin, waw, he.* The new letter *shin* effects the conversion of the ineffable name of the invisible God into an "audible name" and a "visible word." Thus that name becomes known which is "the name of the Mediator derived from the name of the Father's mind, the name which is above every name . . . and in which the ineffable name of the Father resides." It is, consequently, "a holy, blessed, and most powerful name, by which spirits are commanded, diseases driven out, the dead raised, and all miracles performed," and it is "the name of him whom all the *magi* and prophets foretold and whom David had in mind in his psalms." Three hundred, therefore, is "the number of redemption and restoration." Lefèvre says that this discovery filled him

54. Eugene F. Rice, Jr., "The *De Magia Naturali* of Jacques Lefèvre d'Etaples," in *Philosophy and Humanism: Renaissance Essays in Honor of Paul Otto Kristeller,* ed. Edward J. Mahoney (New York, 1976), pp. 27f.

55. Yahweh or Jehovah, which is compounded of the four Hebrew letters *yodh, he, waw,* and *he.*

with such joy that he was scarcely able to contain it, portending as it did the reformation of the world and the restoration of man. He sees the letter *shin*=300 as the symbol, the mystical portent, of life.[56]

In the Midrashic and Talmudic lore of Jewish tradition, names, and the changes of names, were seen as deeply significant, and associations also were made with the planets and their influence. The symbolic import of the identity of the names Joshua and Jesus was affirmed from the earliest times in Christian circles,[57] as also was the powerful efficacy of the names of the Hebrew patriarchs when united with the name of God, and of Jesus.[58] Jerome was one who had a great interest in the significance of names and their numerical equivalents. When drawing attention to the sacred mystery of the name Jesus as incorporating the letters of the tetragrammaton and the letter *shin,* he quaintly observed that as in Hebrew *shin* means "tooth," and as the sound of speech is reproduced through the teeth, this letter pointed us to the mystery of Christ, who is the Word spoken by God.[59] To the same effect, Nicholas of Cusa explained *shin* as meaning "utterance" and the name Jesus as signifying "the Word of God spoken."[60] Nicholas belonged to the line of those who were convinced that the arcane truth concealed in the very structure of the name Jesus, in its Hebrew form, provided marvelous confirmation of the apostolic assertion that Jesus is "the name which is above every name."[61] Beside the ineffable tetragrammaton, which he held to be "above the intellectual realm," Nicholas admitted the existence of other significant divine names that might be learned from the Chaldean, Greek, Egyptian, and other pagan sages of antiquity, but that belong to the intellectual realm and owe the power they possess to God and not to any other source.[62]

Pico had answered his critics by claiming the support of the patristic authors. He cited Hilary as having held that the Psalms were arranged in their present order by the scholars who produced the Septuagint because they understood the spiritual and celestial science of the virtue of the Psalms and assigned to each a number in accordance with its effiency and potency. He invoked the testimony of Jerome who affirmed that twenty was an unlucky number and two a bad number, with the consequence that it was

---

56. The remaining books of Lefèvre's work expound more fully the importance of astrological knowledge for the understanding of the interrelationship between the images of this inferior world and the celestial realities, and the magical significances of the gods and heroes of classical mythology in conjunction with the signs of the zodiac.

57. Cf., e.g., Justin Martyr, *Dialogue with Trypho* 113.

58. Cf., e.g., Origen, *Contra Celsum* i.24; v.45.

59. Jerome, *Tractate on Ps. 10*; Letter 30, to Paula.

60. *Nicolai Cusae Opera Omnia*, ed. Lefèvre (Paris, 1514), II, fol.lv.

61. Philippians 2:9; though St. Paul does not actually specify what this supreme name is.

62. *Nicolai Cusae Opera Omnia* (ut supra), fols. xiff., xxix, lii.

not said on the second day of creation "And God saw that it was good" (Gen. 1:6–8); and, further, that the unclean animals went into the ark by twos, but the clean by sevens.[63] "You will find similar things a hundred times over," Pico declared, with much justification, "in Basil, Gregory of Nazianzus, Ambrose, Origen, Augustine, and others. Moreover, Rabanus, an illustrious doctor of the church, composed a special book concerning the virtue of numbers;[64] and you will always find that the ecclesiastical doctors everywhere observe the properties of numbers, even when, if one may say so, it is only for the sake of curiosity."[65]

The primary stimulus of Lefèvre's interest in the mysteries of magical and cabalistic wisdom as concealing and confirming the doctrines central to the Christian faith came, without doubt, from Pico della Mirandola, who devoted much time and toil to the study of this esoteric tradition. Pico's enthusiasm for the cabala as a secret repository of Christian truth proved to be highly contagious, and many other scholars absorbed themselves in the studies he had initiated. The claims he made had at least one good and positive effect, namely, the reflorescence of interest in the Hebrew language.

A study of the *Nine Hundred Theses* shows that Pico takes the *shin* in the Hebrew form of the name Jesus as signifying both *man* (for which the Hebrew is *ish*), thus indicating the human nature assumed in the incarnation, and also *fire* (for which the Hebrew is *esh*), symbolizing the Holy Spirit.[66] In his book on *The Wonder-Working Word*,[67] which was written at the same time at Lefèvre's work on natural magic, Johann Reuchlin, another one of those who were enthused by Pico, disclosed to his readers the climactic revelation that "the wonder-working word" was none other than the name Jesus written in Hebrew characters, which show it to be a sacred pentagrammaton compounded of the tetragrammaton and the letter

---

63. Genesis 7:1–2. Jerome, Letter XLVIII.19, to Pammachius; cf. Letter CXXIII.12, to Ageruchia.

64. Rabanus Maurus, *Liber de Computo*, Migne PL, CVII.669ff.

65. Pico, *Apologia*. Jerome (Letter XLVIII) in fact held that odd numbers were good and even numbers bad, claiming the support of Clement, Hippolytus, Origen, Dionysius, Eusebius, and Didymus among the Greek authors, and of Tertullian, Cyprian, Victorinus, Lactantius, and Hilary among the Latin authors, as well as some of the classical writers. Of the number two he said: "We are meant to understand," i.e., from the creation account, "that there is something not good in the number two, separating us as it does from unity, and prefiguring the marriage-tie"(!). He was repeating what he had previously written in his work *Against Jovinianus* I.16.

66. See esp. the following theses: No. 80 of "80 philosophical conclusions following his own opinion"; Nos. 19, 20, and 25 of "26 magical conclusions following his own opinion"; No. 15 of "47 cabalistic conclusions following the secret doctrine of the wise Hebrew cabalists"; and Nos. 7, 8, and 14 of "71 cabalistic conclusions following his own opinion entirely confirming the Christian religion from the very fundamentals of the Hebrew sages" (actually there are 72 theses in this group); *Conclusiones*, ed. Kieszkowski, pp. 60, 79, 80, 51, 84.

67. J. Reuchlin, *De verbo mirifico* (1494).

shin, the letter symbolical of fire assigned by Jerome to the Logos in his mystical exposition of the alphabet, and the letter that, in the incarnation, made the unspeakable name of God speakable.[68] Fire was also regarded as the symbol of the presence and power of God and as the mode of the divine self-manifestation to Moses in the wilderness (Exod. 3:2). Reuchlin, who had taken up the study of Hebrew when he was nearing the age of forty in order that he might study the cabalistic mysteries, went on to become the leading Hebraist of his day. The essential unanimity between him and Lefèvre in their exposition of the mystical significance of the name Jesus may be taken to all intents and purposes as of a piece with the proof that Pico would have offered of his theses on the same subject if his expectation of their public disputation had not been disappointed.

The concept of the mystical significance of the divine names continued to fascinate Lefèvre for at least another fifteen years, for it recurs in his *Fivefold Psalter* of 1509. Thus in his comments on Psalm 71 and also in his introduction to the second part of the work he gave attention to this theme and spoke with approval of the manner in which Reuchlin had expounded the import of the name Jesus in his *Wonder-Working Word*. Lefèvre, however, as we have seen,[69] had by 1504 abandoned his earlier approval of a form of magic that was supposedly beneficial and legitimate as distinct from a form that was diabolical and harmful. At the same time he repudiated the astrological superstitions of his day. Even though his change of mind about the worth of the esoteric studies that had at first attracted him took place gradually rather than instantaneously, his with-holding from publication the treatise *Natural Magic* would indicate that soon after completing it in 1494 he had lost confidence in the validity of its contents. Pico, by the time of his death in that same year, had discarded his enthusiasm for the science of magic, and his last major work was a lengthy exposure of the falsity of the pretensions of astrology[70] (the first part of a projected refutation of all heresies). Lefèvre, who held Pico in such high esteem, must have known of this, and such knowledge would have provided adequate reason for his own reconsideration of the issue. Pico's attack on astrology was published posthumously in 1495 and his collected works in

---

68. *De verb. mir.* II.ix. On Lefèvre's *De magia naturali* see B. P. Copenhaver, "Lefèvre d'Etaples, Symphorien Champier, and the Secret Names of God," *Journal of the Warburg and Courtald Institutes* (1977):189ff.; Eugene F. Rice, "The *De Magia Naturali* . . ."; Lynn Thorndike, *A History of Magic and Experimental Science* (New York, 1934), 4:513ff.; Renaudet, pp. 150ff.

69. Pp. 14ff. above.

70. *Disputationes adversus astrologos.* As W. G. Craven points out: "Given Pico's general rejection of astrology, it is very probable that he also abandoned magic. . . . Pico listed magic as one of the superstitions dependent on astrology, and as one of the adversaries in his programme in defense of the faith: 'magic, which is nothing but an amalgam of idolatry, astrology and superstitious medicine' " (*Giovanni Pico della Mirandola: Symbol of his Age* [1981], p. 153).

1498, and Lefèvre, if he had not already acquired or had access to copies, would have taken the opportunity to study Pico's polemic when he paid another visit to Italy in 1500. Whatever the sequence of events, his 1494 treatise was not put into print and the 1504 introduction to his edition of the *Lausiac History* of Palladius announced to the world his repudiation of belief in the influence of magic and the stars.

Further conclusive evidence of this *volte-face* is present in his comments, found in the *Fivefold Psalter* (1509), on Psalm 131:1f., where the psalmist says: "I do not exercise myself in great matters or in things too high for me. Surely I have behaved and quieted myself as a child that is weaned of his mother: my soul is even as a weaned child." Warning his readers against being "deceived by too much curiosity and vainly occupying themselves with matters too high for them, he denounces those "who insanely pursue magical ravings and assemblies of demons," and gives a list, which includes the names of Zoroaster and Simon Magus, of those who have done so in past centuries—"monstrous names of all who are branded with this infamy." He then goes on to observe that in his own day, "which is all the more deplorable, there are those whose minds are so darkened that they dare to call themselves magicians [*magi*]" and claim the most fantastic powers, even going so far as to pretend that they are "able to reveal and investigate with precision the secrets of the supreme mind."

The brazenness of these impostors is such that they boast that by their art it is possible within the space of a single hour to master the knowledge of any and every language. Lefèvre expresses his opinion that any who had given credence to them should be rendered ignorant of all their indoctrination within the space of a single hour—something much more desirable than to be rendered ignorant of all learning by following them. Lefèvre has every excuse for adopting a strongly sarcastic tone:

> There are others who promise copious rivers of gold, while they themselves miserably beg for a cent. They promise perfect health, while they themselves groan from the pains of ophthalmia and gout. Indeed, it seems too small a thing for them to promise health unless in addition they stupidly boast that they are able to make men immortal, far removed from the necessities of warming and cooling, drinking and eating, and to purify them in such a way that they become omniscient and by their own power omnipresent, claiming that they provide all these things by certain distillations and by propitious dispositions of the stars, and, to heap up their infamy, that they can create new angels. All such persons occupy themselves with things too great and marvelous for them. Cutting themselves off from God and his grace, they are weaned as a child is weaned away from his mother. It is in them that the oracle of the psalm is fulfilled.

These charlatans, with their divinations and sacrilegious astrological pretensions, "wish to occupy themselves with things too great and wonderful for them and are weaned away from the grace of God."

But what [Lefèvre continues] are we to say about those who administer magic potions in order that the stigmata of Christ's hands, feet, and side may appear as new lying portents of miracles, and who give people sleep-inducing draughts to drink, potions by which the mind is poisoned and thus more readily subjected to illusory visions, and made to believe the illusions are divine, whereas in reality they are diabolical? It is not difficult to see that they are weaned away and delivered to death and hell with which they have made a fatal covenant.[71]

Lefèvre includes in his denunciations "those who pray and fast and perform other biblical observances in order that they may experience revelations and obtain knowledge of future events," declaring that they, too, wish to occupy themselves in matters too great and wonderful for them and that any visions seen by them are delusions. He urges that popes, remembering that they will be "summoned to render a reckoning before the tribunal of Almighty God," should give special care to the eradication of all such practices. They ought to be watchful, he says, "lest magicians, sorcerers, charlatans, diviners, senders of dreams, familiar spirits, and suchlike from the school of demons, should, like false and poisonous plants, spring up among the healthy plants"; and they ought with the utmost diligence to commit the whole stock-in-trade of such persons—sorceries, poison, incantations, necromancies, exorcisms, mirrors, symbols, images, rings, dice, etc.—to the flames as absolutely vain and useless rubbish. Lefèvre, however, is not hopeful that it is a tide that can soon be turned back: "If this seems an evil of which our age is incurable," he writes, "yet it is to be hoped and prayed and longed for that future ages may be rid of this disease."[72]

Lefèvre's interest in the symbolical properties of numbers continued at least for a few years longer and was communicated by him to his pupils. Early in 1510, for example, Charles de Bovelles, one of his most loyal disciples, published a work entitled *The Perfect Numbers,* which he dedicated to his master;[73] a few months later he brought out another book, *The Twelve Numbers.* At that time Lefèvre was also preparing an edition of the writings of Nicholas of Cusa, which was published later (1514). In June 1508, in the course of a correspondence with Germain de Ganay on the significance of numbers, Bovelles, then in Picardy, wrote excitedly about the contents of Nicholas of Cusa's treatise, *The Divine Numbers,* which Michael Hummelberg was transcribing for Lefèvre. Another of Lefèvre's disciples, Josse Clichtove, published *The Mystical Significance of Numbers* in

---

71. Cf. Isaiah 28:15, 18: "We have made a covenant with death, and with hell [sheol] are we at agreement; when the overflowing scourge shall pass through, it shall not come unto us: for we have made lies our refuge, and under falsehood have we hid ourselves. . . . Your covenant with death shall be disannulled, and your agreement with hell [sheol] shall not stand; when the overflowing scourge shall pass through, then ye shall be trodden down by it."

72. *Quincuplex Psalterium,* ad loc.

73. *De perfectis numeris ad Iacobum Fabrum Stapulensem philosophum clarissimum.*

December 1513. Thorndike laconically remarks that "Erasmus regarded the works of Bovelles as unreadable, and, at least so far as those about mystical numbers are concerned, was quite right."[74]

HERMETIC AND MYSTICAL WRITINGS

The flow of works from Lefèvre to the printer continued unabated. The *Lausiac History* of Palladius was followed, early in 1505, by an edition of a treatise on the military general and his duty that was written in the middle of the first century A.D. by a Greek author named Onosander (or, more accurately, Onesander).[75] Lefèvre made use of a Latin translation done by Niccolo Sagundino nearly fifty years previously. It is a work of ethical counsel, not a handbook of tactics and strategy, for the author had no competence in the art of warfare. In the spring of the same year Lefèvre completed his labors on the hermetic writings with the publication of a volume containing the full *Corpus Hermeticum* and also Lodovico Lazzarelli's *Cup of Hermes*,[76] a work in dialogue form that had been composed some dozen years earlier, about the same time as the appearance of Lefèvre's edition of the hermetic work *Pimander*, which came out in 1494. To the *Pimander* Lefèvre now added the *Asclepius*, a work on the divine will ascribed to Mercury Trismegistus, thus bringing together the whole hermetic collection.[77] As before, he gave his own commentary on the text. With Ficino, whose translation he adopted, Lefèvre believed at this time that Mercury Trismegistus was the most ancient of theologians, next in succession from Moses by a line, as we have seen, that proceeded not through the sages of the Old Testament but through the early philosophers of Greece to Plato. In his prefatory epistle, addressed to Bishop Briçonnet, Lefèvre further indicated that the aim of his studies was not merely the intellectual but also the moral and spiritual improvement of himself and others. Observing that "the chief end of our life is to know God and to hasten to him under full sail, as the saying goes, and with complete devotion," he believed he would be "doing something not unwelcome to the piety of [Briçonnet's] spirit" by bringing to his attention these "two small works of Mercury Trismegistus, the most ancient theologian, one concerning the wisdom and power of God known as *Pimander,* and the other concerning the divine will known as *Asclepius.*" Lefèvre expressed the hope that by reading these compositions Briçonnet would "gather the nourishment of divine meditation for a short while by turning to tranquil contemplation."[78]

---

74. Thorndike, op. cit., VI:442; see Renaudet, p. 610.

75. *De optimo imperatore.*

76. *Crater Hermetis.*

77. Three chapters were in fact omitted. For the explanation of this omission see Rice, pp. 134f.

78. Ibid., p. 134.

In the winter of 1505 Lefèvre published two more works by the Spanish mystic Ramon Lull, four of whose treatises he had brought out in 1499. Of the two works that now issued from the press, the first comprised books I and II of Lull's *Art of Contemplation,* which had come into Lefèvre's possession in 1491, and the second was the *Book of the Lover and the Beloved* from the *Blanquerna* that he had copied from a manuscript when he was in Padua in 1500.[79] In dedicating this new publication to a Carthusian novice of the monastery at Vauvert (Paris) named Gabriel, he wrote of the labor he was expending in the production of books "which shape minds in piety." Lull, he said, deserved first place among the devout worshipers of God; hence his desire, he tells Gabriel, that Lull's work, "multiplied from a single copy, should pass on to very many other persons, and first of all to you who are a novice and as yet a tender plant of religion." He added that he was sending copies to friends in Switzerland, Pannonia (the Balkans), and Poland; and he explained that he had chosen to address the prefatory letter to Gabriel rather than others he had mentioned because the first volume of Lull's *Art of Contemplation* was missing from the library at Vauvert: "thus those who seek the complete work will find it with you (to whom the contemplative life is appropriate)." The little treatise from the *Blanquerna* on divine love he described as "a sort of lover's seal" with which he had closed the volume of contemplations.[80] In this writing the Lover is the Christian and the Beloved is God. It is not surprising that Lefèvre was moved by the poetic intensity of its outpourings.

Resuming his labor on the collection of Aristotle's works, Lefèvre published the *Politics* and *Economics* in the spring of 1506, using the Latin translation made by Leonardo Bruni some seventy years previously, and adding his own commentaries on the text. The *Economics* is not in fact a genuine work of Aristotle's but a composition of mixed origin from the late fourth century B.C. Furthermore, as Lefèvre was aware, Bruni had translated books I and III of the work (believing them to be books I and II), and in restoring book II, of whose authenticity he entertained some doubt, Lefèvre made use of an older translation.[81] In this same publication Lefèvre included a collection of seven hundred propositions culled from the *Republic* and the *Laws* of Plato, which he entitled *Hecatonomia,* because, as he states in the dedication to Jean de Ganay, each of the seven sections into which the collection was divided contained one hundred laws. He explained, further, that he had decided to add these to the present volume because Aristotle in his *Politics* frequently cites Socrates and Plato in a critical manner, and the arrangement would serve to indicate the justice of Aristotle's criticisms in a manner less tedious for him as well as more useful for the readers.

---

79. See pp. 11ff. above.

80. Rice, pp. 141f.

81. For a fuller account see Rice, pp. 153f.

There was a certain ambivalence in Lefèvre's attitude toward the Pythagoreans and Platonists. He could speak highly and with reverence of Pythagoras and Plato as important links in the chain of arcane truth and wisdom; but at this stage Aristotle was still for him the supreme philosopher.[82] In his comments on the *Politics* in this volume he dismisses the thoughts of the Pythagoreans as "vain and empty," calling in Irenaeus as witness that the Pythagoreans were "the most vicious opponents of the Christian religion," and citing Origen, Epiphanius, and Augustine as witnesses that second only to the Pythagoreans were those "blasphemers of the word of God," the Platonists. He also added contemptuous marginal comments on many of the Platonic propositions in the *Hecatonomia,* in effect calling them stupid and absurd.[83] This helps to throw some light on his unwillingness in 1499 to believe that (Pseudo-)Dionysius the Areopagite, whom he contended was purely Christian, could have been a Platonist.

Lefèvre's commentary on Aristotle's *Politics* provides some interesting information regarding his methods of education and his insistence on going back to the authentic source of the original text of any author being studied. For example, "grammarians who teach Virgil," he says, "should never say that they have understood Virgil if they have not studied the actual text and the poems as the author composed them." It is only as the authors themselves are known at first hand that interpretations and commentaries should be recommended for the fuller comprehension and clarification of the text. A thorough grounding in grammar was requisite. For poesy, "Virgil and his fellow Mantuan" (the contemporary Italian poet Baptista Spagnuoli of Mantua) and also "the chaste and celibate Prudentius" (the Christian poet and hymn writer who died early in the fifth century) should be read; for prose, the letters of Cicero, the younger Pliny, and Francisco Filelfo (the Florentine humanist who died in 1481); for rhetoric, the precepts of Cicero; for history, after that recorded in the sacred text, Josephus and Hegesippus, as being "more reliable," and Heraclides and the hagiographers, as being "more religious";[84] for dialectic, the *Logic* of Aristotle, with an accurate text and the help of Boethius and other faithful exponents as interpreters; for arithmetic, the *Nicomachus* of Boethius; for music, the

---

82. In 1492 he had described Aristotle as "the supreme leader of all genuine philosophers," and in 1494 he had extolled him as, *inter alia*, priest and theologian and philosopher of the universe. See p. 2 above.

83. See Rice, "Humanist Aristotelianism in France: Jacques Lefèvre d'Etaples and his circle," in *Humanism in France at the end of the Middle Ages and in the early Renaissance*, ed. A. H. T. Levi (Manchester and New York, 1970), pp. 132ff.

84. Lefèvre would bring out (in 1510) a christianizing fourth-century translation (which he attributed to Ambrose) of *The Jewish War* by "Hegesippus"—actually a corruption of the name Josephus, which led to the work being attributed to the second-century author Hegesippus and thus treated as a Christian composition. Lefèvre had already, in 1504, published a recension of Palladius's *Lausiac History* that he erroneously assigned to Heraclides. See p. 15 above.

work by the same author; for geometry, Euclid; for astronomy,[85] the theory of Ptolemy; for the natural sciences, ethics, politics, and economics, the "waters from the pure source" of Aristotle on these subjects, and then on to his *Laws*—not, however, for the sake of self-aggrandizement but in order to be "a faithful and uncorrupted minister of justice"; for higher and happier objectives, the metaphysical writings of Aristotle that treat transcendental or supramundane matters; and beyond all these there must be the study of holy Scripture "with veneration," in which Cyprian, Hilary, Origen, Jerome, Augustine, Athanasius, Gregory of Nazianzus, John of Damascus, and such like will be found helpful companions. With the mind purged, the perceptions sharpened, one's activities in harmony with right living, and one's conduct morally honorable, one is equipped to trample down vices. Lefèvre adds that any who aspire to "loftier contemplations" will find instruction in the books of Nicholas of Cusa and (Pseudo-)Dionysius.[86] This, then, is a summary or conspectus of Lefèvre's educational program at this juncture of his life.

THE ORTHODOX FAITH

Evidence of a developing transition in Lefèvre's intellectual orientation from the systematics of philosophy seen through Christian spectacles to those of a more strictly biblical theology is afforded by the publication, in 1507, when he was resident at the royal court in Bourges, of his own translation of the treatise *The Orthodox Faith*[87] (which is actually the third part of a major work entitled *The Source of Knowledge*) by the eighth-century author John of Damascus. The treatise is a digest of the teaching of the Greek fathers on the principal doctrines of the Christian faith and, as such, is a model of catholic orthodoxy. There are indications that it helped to form Lefèvre's thinking on some subjects and to confirm it on others. For this reason the following positions defined by John of Damascus deserve attention:

that the knowledge of God's existence has been implanted by him in all people by nature;

that we can know God only through his own self-revelation;

that this revelation has taken place through the Holy Scriptures and in the person of "his only-begotten Son, our Lord and God and Saviour Jesus Christ";

that "all things, therefore, which have been delivered to us by Law and Proph-

---

85. Called, as was then customary, astrology.

86. Guy Bedouelle, *Lefèvre d'Etaples et l'Intelligence des Ecritures* (Geneva, 1976), pp. 50f.

87. *De orthodoxa fide*.

ets and Apostles and Evangelists we receive and know and honor, seeking for nothing beyond these'';

that what God is in his essence and nature is absolutely unknowable to man, and consequently that we can say what the being of God is not rather than what it is;

that ''it must not be supposed that the heavens and the luminaries are endowed with life, for they are inanimate and insensible'';

that there are seven planets and twelve (zodiacal) signs in the stars, but ''we have been created with free wills by our Creator and are masters over our own actions,'' and, accordingly, ''the stars are not the causes of the things that occur, nor of the origin of things that come into being, nor of the destruction of those things that perish'';

that ''it behoved the Redeemer to be without sin and not be made liable through sin to death'';

that ''he in his fulness took upon himself me in my fulness, and was united whole to whole that he might in his grace bestow salvation on the whole man'';

that ''all Christ's actions and miracles are most great and divine and marvelous, but the most marvelous of all is his precious cross'';

that in the adoration of the cross and images the adoration passes beyond them to God, and that the honor shown to Mary and the saints ''is a proof of good feeling toward the common Master'' and the honor ''is referred to him who of Mary was made incarnate'';

that since all Scripture is given by inspiration of God it possesses ''inexhaustible grace,'' and we should constantly rejoice and revel in it as from this fountain we draw ''perennial and purest waters springing into life eternal.''

In such teachings Lefèvre found support for his critique of astrological superstition, the rationalization he would adopt for the next twelve years to justify the practice of invoking saints and worshiping before images, and the emphasis on the cardinal significance of the incarnate Son and his cross and on the authoritative sufficiency of Holy Scripture, which would soon become central in his own perspective.

November 1508 saw the publication of Lefèvre's edition of George of Trebizond's *Dialectics*, which was written about 1440 but first printed some thirty years afterward in Venice. In dedicating his edition to Robert Fortuné, Lefèvre describes how, when he was in Rome sixteen years previously—that is, in 1492, when Ermolao Barbaro was still alive and living in the Italian capital—he had been introduced to two very intelligent and well-educated young men who had a remarkable comprehension of logic and philosophy, and whose accomplishments were attributed largely to their study of this work by George of Trebizond. One of the young men had presented him with a copy of the *Dialectics*. When it was suggested that he had been slow to encourage other young men to pursue studies of this kind (which in comparison with the type of scholasticism then dominant at the Sorbonne were more cultured and more authentic), Lefèvre retorted:

"The fact is that I have never ceased and never shall cease by word and writing to do so." He then hinted at the hostility with which he had been meeting because of his attempts to restore sound methods of learning:

> If there should be some who hate me for this reason, I do not hate them; for I know that persons who are afflicted, even through they may hate the physician who gives them correct advice, will when they are well again love him all the more intensely whom formerly they hated.

Should the question be asked: "Why have you not published this work before now?", he would answer: "Because now more than previously I see that in the case of a great many, our university is better disposed to accept my medicine"[88]—a remark indicating that Lefèvre felt he was at last making some headway with his purpose of reforming the methods and standards of academic training.

This treatise, thanks to Lefèvre now made available in France, was an exposition of the Aristotelian dialectic. Its author, George of Trebizond, had incurred the wrath of Cardinal Bessarion because of an ill-considered attack on Plato and his philosophy.[89] Beatus Rhenanus alludes to this controversy in a letter to Johannes Kierher prefixed to Lefèvre's edition of George's *Dialectics,* which Rhenanus, another of Lefèvre's loyal disciples, published the following year (1509) in Strasbourg, in response to a request from Michael Hummelberg to make the work available in Germany. "Moved by the impiety of certain Platonists," Beatus wrote, "George of Trebizond published a notable work comparing the philosophers,[90] in which he showed by compelling arguments that the Aristotelian method of philosophizing is far more compatible with the Christian religion than that of Plato; and this caused Cardinal Bessarion of Nicea to attack him with four books"—that is, the four books of his work entitled *Against Plato's Calumniator* (1469).[91]

Apart from the debate over the relative merits of Plato and Aristotle, the question of the affinity, if any, of Greek philosophy to the Christian religion was one that demanded attention in the early church because of the frequent contention of opponents of Christianity that the noblest Christian sentiments had been more ably and clearly expressed by the pagan philosophers, especially Plato. The heathen scholar Celsus, for example, charged that Christ and his apostles had borrowed much of their teaching from Plato, whose writings they understood imperfectly and even perverted. To this calumny Origen retorted (in the next century) that the alleged

---

88. Rice, pp. 190f.

89. Lefèvre would publish an edition of Bessarion's translation of Aristotle's *Metaphysics* in 1515.

90. *Comparatio Platonis et Aristotelis.*

91. *In calumniatorem Platonis.*

borrowing from Plato could without difficulty be matched by passages from the Old Testament Scriptures, which were much older than the works of Plato.[92] Even in the concluding years of the fourth century Augustine expressed a desire to see certain books composed by Ambrose "with much care and at great length against some most ignorant and pretentious men who affirm that our Lord was instructed by the writings of Plato."[93]

The Christian countercharge, that Plato had been enlightened by an acquaintance with the Old Testament writings, was pressed by the church apologists. It is found, for instance, in Justin Martyr in the middle of the second century,[94] and is well illustrated by the following passage from Clement of Alexandria:

> Whence, O Plato, is that hint of the truth that you give? . . . You have learned geometry from the Egyptians, astronomy from the Babylonians; the charms of healing you have acquired from the Thracians; the Assyrians also have taught you many things; but for the laws which are consistent with truth and your sentiments respecting God you are indebted to the Hebrews.[95]

Clement affirmed, further, that Plato "fanned the spark of Hebrew philosophy" and "was not unacquainted with David," and he quoted the saying of his contemporary, the philosopher Numenius: "What is Plato but Moses speaking in Attic Greek?"[96] Clement also cited the Jewish author Aristobulus of Alexandria, who lived in the second century B.C., as saying that Plato had followed the Mosaic laws and had "manifestly studied all that is said in them,"[97] and he declared (later in the same work) that Aristobulus composed "numerous books to show that the Peripatetic philosophy was derived from the law of Moses and from the other prophets."[98] Indeed, Clement saw two streams meeting in the advent of Christ, that of the Jewish law and that of Greek philosophy, though he believed that the truth of the latter was derived from the former.

PICO DELLA MIRANDOLA

When he compiled his *Nine Hundred Theses,* this perspective was also thoroughly congenial to Pico, whose ruling concept was that of universal

---

92. Origen, *Contra Celsum* V.65; VI.12-19; VII.27-35.

93. Augustine, Letter 31, to Paulinus and Therasia (A.D. 396).

94. Justin Martyr, *First Apology* 59f.

95. Clement of Alexandria, *Exhortation to the Heathen* 6; cf. *The Pedagogue* II.1, 10 and *Stromata* I.15, 19, 25, 29; V.14.

96. *Stromata* I.22. Pico alluded approvingly to this dictum in the dedication of his *Heptaplus* to Lorenzo de' Medici.

97. *Stromata* I.22.

98. Ibid., V.14.

intellectual concord. As he then saw things, Hebrew was the original language and the Mosaic law the pristine science, and in particular the esoteric interpretation of it supposedly entrusted to Moses at Sinai—or, according to another strand of cabalistic lore, an essentially identical communication to Adam in Eden—and handed down by a secret tradition as the pure fount of all religious truth and philosophical wisdom. If this was true of Pico in 1486, it was true also of Lefèvre just a few years later; for, as we have noticed,[99] in 1494 he regarded the Egyptian priests and Chaldean *magi* as dispensers of divine mysteries which were passed on to the great philosophers, and believed there was a "wonderful accord and affinity" between the Christian faith and the wisdom of Plato and Aristotle. Pico, however, moved away from this position; and so did Lefèvre. As early as 1487, an interesting passage in the *Apologia* seems to adumbrate an incipient change of orientation in Pico's thinking as he insists that the options of the ecclesiastical authors are to be approved only if they are consonant with the teaching of Scripture.

> Although the writings of the holy doctors, placed outside the biblical canon, should be handed down and read and received with proper reverence [he says], yet their sayings are not of such firm authority and unassailability that it is not permitted to contradict them or to have doubts concerning them, unless they are evidently and expressly proved by Holy Scripture, or by the authority and decree of the Church they are to be held as fixed and indubitable truth. Therefore by the extra-canonical sayings of the saints an opinion cannot be precisely demonstrated as manifestly heretical, for certain and indubitable faith does not exist where infallible truth is not found.[100]

By 1492 it was plain that Pico's face was indeed set in a new direction. On 15 May of that year he sent a revealing letter to his nephew that was full of spiritual counsel supported by frequent reference to biblical texts. Its tone is one of evangelical earnestness. Thus, among many other things, he writes:

> What madness it is not to believe the Gospel, whose truth the blood of martyrs proclaims, apostolic voices announce, miracles prove, reason confirms, the world attests, the elements utter, and the demons confess. But it is far greater madness if, while not doubting the truth of the Gospel, one should live as though not doubting its falsity.

Pico appealed to his nephew to devote himself wholly to the study of Scripture: "I entreat you to set aside the fables and triflings of poets and ever to have Holy Scripture in your hands. There is nothing that you can do more pleasing to God and more profitable to yourself than to study the

---

99. See p. 3 above.

100. *Opera Pici*, pp. 143f.

sacred text day and night without ceasing.'' And he concluded the letter
with this admonition:

> Finally, I wish to advise you—as I did frequently when you were here
> with me—that there are two things which you should never forget: firstly,
> that the Son of God died for you, and, secondly, that you too, however
> long you live, shall surely die. With these, as with two spurs, the one
> of fear and the other of love, urge forward your horse through the brief
> course of this fleeting life to the prize of eternal blessedness.[101]

This letter indicates plainly that Pico, in his thirtieth year, had reached
a point where biblical doctrine and the gospel of Christ were at the center
of his attention. The "fables and triflings of poets" and most of his other
intellectual fantasies and fascinations were being left behind, and a grand
new purpose was beginning to take shape within his heart. His nephew
describes how one day shortly before his death, when they were walking
together in an orchard at Ferrara and conversing on the love of Christ, Pico
revealed to him that he had formed a secret purpose, namely, after dis-
pensing his remaining wealth to the poor and completing certain books on
which he was working, to travel barefoot through the world preaching
Christ.[102] It was a project that would not be realized. Within two weeks
Pico was dead, struck down at the age of 31 by a malignant fever that resisted
all medicines. The funeral sermon was preached by Pico's friend and
spiritual mentor, Girolamo Savonarola. The preacher spoke of the
phenomenal brilliance of Pico's intellect, and he told the congregation of
Pico's private purpose of devoting his life to the cause of the gospel, declaring his conviction that Pico's early death was an unexpectedly severe punishment from God because he had delayed to put this purpose into effect.
Savonarola symbolically invested Pico's body with the habit of the Preaching
Friars, however, before it was interred in the church of San Marco.

It is certainly worthy of remark that the intellectual and spiritual journey
of Pico della Mirandola was virtually recapitulated in the experience of
Lefèvre, who also turned away from the preoccupations of his earlier years.
Like Pico, Lefèvre wished to complete the literary and philosophical projects to which he had set his hand, so that he might be free to give himself
to the task of making the Bible and its message available to all. His massive
enterprise of providing the works of Aristotle in reliable Latin translation
with commentaries was completed in 1515. Between the years 1512 and
1519 he published a number of mystical writings by various authors, the
works of Nicholas of Cusa (1514), as well as a treatise of Euclid on geometry
(1517). These were the last of his extrabiblical labors. Meanwhile, however,

---

101. Ibid., pp. 340ff.

102. This account is given in the life of Pico written by his nephew Giovanni Francesco
Pico della Mirandola. The *Vita* is included in the *Opera Pici*, but its pages are not numbered.
Pico died, age 31, in 1494.

he had started the biblical task, commencing, as Pico had done, with the book of Psalms (the *Fivefold Psalter* appeared in 1509) and continuing with the great commentary on St. Paul's Epistles (1512). The final part of his life was occupied wholly with the translation and interpretation of the Scriptures and the preaching of the gospel for the benefit of his fellow countrymen. What early death prevented Pico from doing in Italy length of days enabled Lefèvre to do in France. There is much to justify Guy Bedouelle's suggestion that Pico was Lefèvre's model.[103]

---

103. G. Bedouelle, op. cit., p. 232.

The Attractions of Mystical Theology

THE BRETHREN OF THE COMMON LIFE

The fascination that the writings of the mystical authors had for Lefèvre during the middle years of his life belonged to the period of his transition from classical philosophy to biblical theology. In terms of dates, this period cannot be neatly isolated, since his interest in the mystics started while he was still occupied with the production of Latin translations and commentaries on the works of Aristotle and other ancient philosophers, and it continued for some time after he had discovered and affirmed the primacy of the Bible as the source of authentic wisdom. Moreover, as we should not leave out of account the probability that Lefèvre's youthful years were to some degree influenced by the mystical piety associated with the Brethren of the Common Life, it seems appropriate to make this the starting point of the present discussion.

The founder of the movement known as the Brethren of the Common Life was Geert (or Gerard) de Groote of Deventer (1340–84). He actually studied in Paris, where he acquitted himself with the highest distinction. A man of means, he lived a life of luxury and selfishness until his conversion in 1374, after which he devoted himself to spirituality and sought to reform the abuses of the church by preaching, by the establishment of community houses for the practice of piety and the service of society, and by the founding of schools to provide an education of excellence for the young. In an attempt to dispel the spiritual ignorance of the common people he also translated parts of the Bible into the vernacular. The most famous adherent of the movement he began was Thomas à Kempis (c. 1380–1471), whose writings included a life of the founder as well as the spiritual classic entitled *The Imitation of Christ*.

Students at the University of Paris were divided into four "nations"; Lefèvre, coming from Etaples in Picardy, belonged to the second. In the days of his youth, in fact, Picardy together with the Flemish and Dutch territories was governed by the Duke of Burgundy; consequently, students

from the Netherlands were among those assigned to the Picard "nation."
This being so, it is not unreasonable to suppose that Lefèvre may first have
encountered the influence of the Brethren of the Common Life when he
arrived in Paris as a student, presumably in his teens.[1] We do, in any case,
know that Wessel Gansfort (c. 1420–89), a native of Groningen who had
been both pupil and instructor in the Brethren's school in Zwolle for some
seventeen years from 1432 to 1449, and who then went to Cologne and
obtained his master's degree in 1452, moved to Paris in 1454 and spent
most of the next twenty years there, acquiring a reputation not only as an
outstanding teacher but also as an outspoken critic of ecclesiastical corruption and superstition.

John Standonck of Mechlin (Malines) in Brabant, Lefèvre's contemporary (he was born in the 1450s), was another disciple of the Brethren
of the Common Life who settled in Paris. He had been a scholar at the
Brethren's school in Gouda, Holland, and had matriculated at Louvain
(1469) before coming on to Paris, where as an impecunious student he obtained board and lodging in return for the performance of menial duties.
On obtaining his master's degree (1475) he enrolled as a student of theology
in the Collège de Montaigu. His association with this institution was to be
a long one, as student, as teacher, and, after the death of Amâtre Chétart
in 1483, as principal. Ascetic in his way of life and a rigorous disciplinarian,
he won a reputation as a powerful preacher and an outspoken advocate of
church reform.

The most famous of the young men who came to the Collège de
Montaigu to pursue their studies was Desiderius Erasmus, whose boyhood
had been passed in the schools of the Brethren of the Common Life in his
native Holland, and who prior to his arrival in Paris in 1495 had endured
eight years as a member of the monastic (Common Life) community of Sion
in Steyn, where the general ignorance and intellectual laziness of the brothers
was altogether uncongenial to him. The harsh discomforts of the life at Montaigu he found no more easy to tolerate. Renaudet, however, suggests that
"the need for a personal and inward religion, which would inspire the whole
of his theological work, perhaps came to him, without his realizing it, from
the Brethren of the Common Life and from the tradition of Gerard de Groote
and Ruysbroek."[2]

That Lefèvre was influenced by those who had brought the ideals of
the Brethren of the Common Life to Paris is beyond question. As early
as 1496 he dedicated his *Elements of Music* to the politician and church-
man Nicole de Hacqueville who was an ardent patron of this reforming

---

1. See C. Louise Salley, "Jacques Lefèvre d'Etaples: Heir of the Dutch Reformers of
the Fifteenth Century," in *The Dawn of Modern Civilization*, ed. Kenneth A. Strand (1962),
pp. 75ff.

2. Renaudet, p. 263.

movement and an admirer of its mystical doctrines, particularly as set forth in John Mombaer's *Rosetum* ("a rosary of spiritual exercises and sacred meditations"). By the end of the century de Hacqueville had acquired, in exchange for benefices under his disposal, the abbey of Livry, and he took steps to reform it by bringing in monks of the Windesheim persuasion from the Netherlands. Before his death at the beginning of 1501, he transferred the title of the abbey to John Mombaer, with a view to preserving and advancing the cause he had enthusiastically supported. Mombaer had been the leader of a mission of half-a-dozen monks sent out, in 1496, by the Windesheim community to minister on French soil. This enterprise was the result of negotiations conducted through Standonck, and the missionaries were placed in the monastery of Château-Landon, where at first they were received with the harshest hostility.

The following year, in response to a pressing request from the Parisian authorities, another small contingent of missionaries was sent from Windesheim, this time to revive and reform the once-celebrated monastery of Saint Victor. Here, too, they met with antipathy from those who were already in residence and, despite valiant attempts to fulfill their mission, were forced to abandon the project. This was a severe disappointment for the promoters of this venture, and not least for Mombaer who, envisaging the spiritual renewal of France, had written to Reynier Koetken of Windesheim: "The reform of the whole French church is in your hands." It was at this stage that Mombaer was appointed abbot of the Augustinian monastery of Livry. Death removed him from the scene less than a year after the decease of his patron Nicole de Hacqueville.

Of Lefèvre's contact with Mombaer we know little apart from the information given in the epistle prefixed to his edition of Lull's *Art of Contemplation* and *Blanquerna* (1505). There he mentions Mombaer as one of "the restorers of almost innumerable community houses to holier living" and also praises Standonck for his sanctity and austerity of life.[3] In 1510 an edition of Mombaer's *Rosetum*, which had originally appeared in 1494, was published by Josse Bade at Lefèvre's instigation.[4] Bade, who had himself been a pupil of the Brethren of the Common Life at Ghent, and whose press was used for the printing of many important works, had previously, in 1500, brought out the works of Thomas à Kempis. He would also print Lefèvre's 1514 edition of Nicholas of Cusa.

Mombaer's *Rosetum*, a book of instruction on the ascetic and contemplative life, drew on the moral teachings not only of the exponents of the so-called *Devotio Moderna* but also of less recent authors such as Augustine, Bernard, Aquinas, and the Victorines, while at the same time it provided a detailed method of mystical meditation. Concerned primarily

---

3. Rice, pp. 141f.

4. Renaudet, p. 547.

with the cultivation of the inner life and the reform of monastic communities, Mombaer and his colleagues made no pretensions to academic superiority. They held to the customary fourfold method of biblical interpretation, with a predilection for the tropological (or moral) and allegorical explanation of Scripture. In this, though themselves Augustinian Canons Regular, they showed a cast of mind that was more medieval than Augustinian. They were aware, however, of the importance of determining the scriptural text that conformed as closely as possible to that of the original. Thus Mombaer diligently followed the tradition of his movement in collating available manuscripts of the Vulgate for the purpose of correcting errors and purifying the Latin version.

This, as we shall see, is precisely what Lefèvre did in his first biblical work, the *Fivefold Psalter* (1509). It is one respect in which the influence of Mombaer and the movement he belonged to may be detected, or at least suspected. Equally, one may suggest, Lefèvre must have been impressed by Mombaer's emphasis on the supreme importance of the study of Holy Scripture over against the scholastic preoccupations of the Parisian and other professors. Lefèvre, however, would insist that the only sense proper to Scripture is its "literal" sense.[5]

THE THREEFOLD ASCENT

Another contributor to Lefèvre's interest in mystical theology was Richard of Saint Victor who, Scottish by birth, had been abbot of the Augustinian abbey of St. Victor in Paris in the twelfth century. Richard taught the threefold ascent to the mystical summit, namely, purification from sensuality, illumination of rationality, and union through intellectuality. It was teaching with roots in Neoplatonic soil. In 1510 Lefèvre published Richard's work on the Trinity[6] together with his own commentary on the text. In his prefatory letter addressed to Louis Pinelle, who at the time was chancellor of Notre Dame and the University of Paris, Lefèvre describes "the three ways in which men are accustomed to inquire after God" as "imagination, reason, and intellect." By "imagination" he means the non-rational sense perception registered in the form of images that is characteristic of animals and is displayed by humans in the worship of images and idols. By "reason" he means the rational faculty that distinguishes man from the animals. By "intellect" he means that perfect suprarational apprehension that angels enjoy. "Reason," accordingly, has an intermediate position between "imagination" and "intellect." That is why we fall into error when inquiring after God we depend too much on "reason," much more

---

5. See below, pp. 55ff. On Mombaer see Renaudet, pp. 219ff., and Pierre Debongnie, *Jean Mombaer de Bruxelles, abbé de Livry* (1928).

6. *De Trinitate*. This was the first printed edition.

so when we limit ourselves to "imagination," but less so when we aspire to the heights of "intellect." Man is in a middle position between angels and brute beasts.[7]

There is a close affinity between the position described by Lefèvre and the mystical doctrine of Nicholas of Cusa,[8] and it is also apparent that Lefèvre was indebted to the thought of Ficino and Pico, while all had felt the influence of Pseudo-Dionysius and his formulations. Pico had affirmed that so long as we speak of God in an affirmative manner "we are in the light, whereas God has appointed darkness as his hiding-place"—an allusion to Psalm 18:11. "This being so," Pico continues, "we have not yet arrived at God." It remains for us to ascend into "the light of ignorance" and there to be "blinded by the darkness of the divine splendor."[9]

Another doctrine characteristic of mystical theology is that God is absolutely one, or simple, and all that is less or other than God is multiple and particular. Implicit in the distinction between the "rational" and the "intellectual" spheres is this distinction between multiplicity and simplicity. Lefèvre propounded this distinction in the preface, addressed to the physician Leonard Pomar, that he wrote for Charles de Bovelles' *Introduction to the Art of Opposites*.[10] Even though in the paradoxical realm of mysticism silence is more eloquent than utterance, just as intellect is superior to reason, nonetheless the philosophy of reason is a necessary, albeit a lower, stage in the ascent to the philosophy of intellect.

> Those who are busy trying to attain to the intellectual manner of philosophizing without prior instruction in the rational seem to me like a blind man wishing to learn to paint and a deaf man deciding to study music. . . . This being so, Aristotle is the life of studies, but Pythagoras the death of studies, superior to life; hence the latter appropriately taught by keeping silent, but the former by speaking; yet silence is action and voice deprivation. To benefit you and many, then, let me explain that in Paul and Dionysius there is much silence, also in Cusa and in Victorinus on *Homoousios*; but in Aristotle very little silence and many words: for silence speaks and words are silent.[11]

Lefèvre's association of Pythagoras with silence is reminiscent of Pico's assertion that Pythagoras, "had he been able to convey his thoughts by looks, or by some other method not involving speech, would not have spoken at all, so much did he shun the embellishment and adornment of language."[12]

---

7. Rice, pp. 224f.

8. See p. 44 below.

9. Chapter 5 of Pico's *De ente et uno; Opera Pici* I:246ff.

10. *In artem oppositorum introductio.*

11. Rice, pp. 94ff. The Victorinus reference is to the *De homoousio recipiendo* by Victorinus Afer (fourth century).

12. In the letter to Ermolao Barbaro cited on pp. 13f. above.

The theme recurs in the letter addressed to Denis Briçonnet, bishop of Saint-Malo and brother of Bishop Guillaume Briçonnet, which introduced Lefèvre's edition of the works of Nicholas of Cusa, published in 1514. Here again Lefèvre postulates three theological levels: the first and highest, intellectual; the second and intermediate, rational; and the third and lowest, sensuous and dependent on images. The first, he explains, investigates the truth in peace; the second is polemical as by the use of reason it sets truth free from error; while the third insidiously attempts to overthrow the truth with all sorts of errors.

> In the first, the greater light absorbs the lesser; in the second, light is opposed to darkness; in the third, darkness is opposed to light. The first teaches in silence; the second with words in moderation; the third uses a strident multiplicity of words.

Lefèvre explains, further, that Nicholas of Cusa's theology belongs to that intellectual theology of the first level which more than any other assists us to approach the sacred shrine of Dionysius the Areopagite and of others who have excelled in philosophizing sublimely about God.[13]

GERMAN MYSTICISM

Lefèvre was traveling in Germany when his edition of Richard of Saint Victor's treatise on the Trinity was published. In Cologne he sought out the Brethren of the Common Life who welcomed him as an honored guest and introduced him to the writings of Jan van Ruysbroeck. The sincerity of their piety and the simplicity of their way of life were entirely congenial to him. In Rupertsburg, near Bingen, he spent some time at the Benedictine convent where Adelheid von Ottenstein was abbess, and while there he read a book, entitled *Scivias*, by Hildegard of Bingen who had founded the convent in the twelfth century. In this work Hildegard gave an account of the visions she had received, denounced the corruption of the clergy, popes included, and predicted that the church would be punished and purified. Among the manuscripts he collected or copied there were some further compositions by Hildegard; the writings of Elizabeth of Schönau, another visionary of the twelfth century; a treatise on special grace by Mechthild of Hackeborn, a thirteenth-century Cistercian nun of Helfta near Eisleben; two works by the mystic and prophet Robert of Uzés, who died in Metz in 1296 after traveling through Europe preaching repentance to the church and in particular the clergy; and the book of the vision of the monk Uguetinus—actually the *Visio Wettini* as told by Hatto when he was abbot of Reichenau at the beginning of the ninth century. In Mainz Lefèvre came across the manuscript of a treatise on the office of the mass by Berno

---

13. Rice, pp. 345f.

(d. 1048), who had been abbot of Reichenau in the eleventh century. At his request a copy of this was made and sent to him in Paris.

Such writings fueled his desire to advance beyond reason to intellection, as the mystics claimed to have done in their experience of visions and revelations. The intensity of his own devotion urged him in this direction. But at the same time these writings nourished in him the ardent spirit of the reformer who not only sees and deplores the corruption and materialism that stifle the church's spirituality but also sets his hand to the task of purging out evil and restoring authentic Christian piety. He published Berno's treatise on the mass in Paris in November 1510, and in the dedicatory letter, addressed to the priests of the church, he expressed his confidence that the work would be of benefit to all priests. He warned, moreover, that God would send a curse upon them if they performed the duties of their sacred office in a negligent and ignorant manner.[14] This publication, accordingly, was intended as a contribution to the campaign for the reform of ecclesiastical abuses.

The appearance of the other writings acquired as a result of his German excursion was delayed because certain omissions made by the copyists had to be restored. However, the works mentioned above by Hatto, Robert of Uzés, Hildegard of Bingen, Elizabeth of Schönau, and Mechthild of Hackeborn were published in that order in one volume in May 1513, together with the so-called vulgate version of *The Shepherd of Hermas*, which was placed at the beginning (Lefèvre's edition was the first to appear in print). The volume was given the general title *The Book of Three Men and Three Spiritual Virgins*.[15] Lefèvre dedicated it to Adelheid of Ottenstein. Persons of pious mind would undoubtedly approve the writings now brought together, he told her, and especially the works of Hermas and Elizabeth, "because they show more energy of spirit and more fully represent angelic speech in the simplicity and sincerity of their sacred visions."

Lefèvre believed that the author of *The Shepherd* was the Hermas mentioned by St. Paul in Romans 16:14 and, along with Dionysius, a disciple of that apostle. He was aware that the work was spoken of as apocryphal, but he explained to Adelheid that the term "apocryphal" was used with two significances, the one good, the other bad:

Writings are called apocryphal in the favorable sense which are closest to and virtually indistinguishable from the sacred oracles to which the first and highest authority belongs. But all superstitious, heretical, exotic, profitless, and fanciful writings are called apocryphal in the unfavorable sense. The latter writings holy men command us not only to avoid but also to abhor; they should never be read and never encouraged, since they are

---

14. Ibid., pp. 234f.

15. *Liber trium virorum et trium spiritualium virginum.*

in no way edifying, but rather are contrary to and totally destructive of edification and all piety.[16]

Lefèvre, of course, placed *The Shepherd* in the former category, citing patristic testimony in support of this evaluation. Attributed to the earlier part of the second century, the esteem in which it was held by some now seems somewhat surprising. In the Codex Sinaiticus (fourth century) it is accorded a position, in company with the Epistle of Barnabas, at the end, after the canonical books. The Muratorian Fragment, which originated late in the second century, indicates that it was permissible to read *The Shepherd* in church but not to treat it as part of the canon; a few decades later, however, Origen states that readings from it were not customary. Lefèvre apparently was attracted to Hermas, for a while at least, as supposedly a near-apostolic exponent of visionary experience, and, as such, an early type of the other writers represented in this volume.

In the preceding summer (August 1512) Lefèvre had published an edition of Jan van Ruysbroeck's composition entitled *The Spiritual Marriage*,[17] a work written in the middle of the fourteenth century and translated into Latin shortly after by Willem Jordaens, whose translation Lefèvre now used.[18] Lefèvre intended this edition, another of the fruits of his Rhine journey, to serve the cause of religious spirituality. Ruysbroeck's mysticism had its own special appeal to him personally. In the prefatory letter, addressed to Raemundus, identified only as a young monastic friend of Lefèvre's, he speaks of the sweetest fruit of the contemplative life as consisting of the experience of true oneness with God, and of the spiritual state as being perfectly known by "the blessed souls that have already put off the garment of mortality," while those who are still wearing this garment can know that state but imperfectly. Those who have sought the solitary life for the purpose of giving themselves to the practice of contemplation "have a great love for the books of contemplative men," he says, "not just because they make those already experienced in contemplation more perfect, but because they prepare and stimulate those who are only beginning."

Lefèvre goes on to mention that Jean Gerson, the distinguished chancellor of the Cathedral of Notre Dame and the University of Paris a hundred years previously, had criticized Ruysbroeck for being deficient in education and in certain respects in error. Actually, Gerson had argued that *The Spiritual Marriage* was a work of human art rather than divine enlightenment, and that it was erroneous to teach that in the state of perfect contemplation the human soul experienced identification with or absorption into

---

16. Rice, pp. 309ff.

17. *Die Gheestelike Brulocht.*

18. *De ornatu spiritualium nuptiarum.*

the divine essence. Rice judges that Lefèvre "knew Gerson's criticisms in a tradition which deformed them." In any case, Lefèvre supposed that Gerson regarded Ruysbroeck as unlearned because he wrote in his native Dutch instead of in Latin, the language of scholars. Lefèvre contended that this fact afforded no proof that the author must have been a man of little education; "for even the most highly educated of men is able to publish books in the vernacular perhaps far better than an uneducated man." He concluded that Gerson must have read a corrupt or inaccurate copy of the work.[19]

But even if Lefèvre misconceived Gerson's attitude toward Ruysbroeck, the controversy, though slight in itself, may well have marked a new stage in the development of his intellectual perspective, especially as he was now becoming increasingly concerned with the cause of spiritual renewal in his native land; for he had now come to see that Latin was not necessarily the sacrosanct language of scholarship, though it had for long been regarded as such, and that a serious scholar might well use the vernacular as a vehicle of expression. The next stage was the conviction that a scholar who has truth to communicate to the populace *must* use the vernacular. If ordinary men and women were to be reached and instructed, it must be in the language they themselves commonly use, and that language was no longer Latin. It is ironic that the Latin version of the Bible known as the *Vulgate* precisely because it was in the "vulgar" tongue commonly used in the western church of the fourth century had now come to be regarded as to all intents and purposes sacrosanct, even though Latin was no longer commonly spoken or understood. After a few more years the seed that was germinating in Lefèvre's mind would spring up and flourish as he devoted himself and his scholarship to the task of providing his compatriots with the Bible and with clear expositions of its teaching in the French language.

The emphasis in Ruysbroeck's thought that seems to have impressed the mind of Lefèvre most strongly was that on the blessedness belonging to the conformity of our human nature, as bride, to Christ, the Bridegroom. *The Spiritual Marriage* is built around the theme of Matthew 25:6: "See, the Bridegroom comes: go out to meet him." In the concluding section Ruysbroeck discusses the nature of "superessential contemplation, which is the foundation of all holiness and of all the life that man can live"; to it, however, few can attain, and it can be understood only as it is experienced. To achieve this summit or climax of spiritual contemplation a person must not only be virtuous outwardly as well as inwardly but also divested of all means or methods, thus ensuring that he is in no way distracted by this-worldly images. The goal is, in effect, the shedding of the creaturely finitude of his being and his reason to the act of contemplation so that he may be enfolded in the divine light that is at the same time darkness because it is the negation of creaturely competence. The "seeing" of this con-

---

19. Rice, pp. 276ff.

templative enlightenment involves also a "going forth" to meet the
Bridegroom and the "loving meeting" itself with him, in which there is
the enfolding of the essential unity of the divine Persons "in the abyss of
God's namelessness," and "a delectable passing-over and a flowing-away
and a sinking-down into the essential nakedness"; and this, Ruysbroeck
declares, is to attain "the unfathomable joy of simplicity." It is "the dark
silence in which all lovers are lost."[20]

There is something to be said for Gerson's criticism of Ruysbroeck's
theological position. Contemplation by way of negation and nakedness and
the renunciation of reason has more in common with Neoplatonism than
with Christianity. The genuineness of Ruysbroeck's faith need not be denied,
nor the reality of his devotion, nor the blessedness of the loving union that
bound him as believer to Christ as Bridegroom; but the way of this kind
of mysticism is virtually that of self-isolation and esoteric escape from one's
humanity. Christlikeness or Christiformity would become a dominant
emphasis in Lefèvre's conception of Christian spirituality, as we shall see,
but in a manner much more closely attuned to the teaching of the New Testament. In this respect he would come to have more in common with Thomas
à Kempis's *Imitation of Christ* than with Ruysbroeck's *Spiritual Marriage*.[21]

NICHOLAS OF CUSA

In Nicholas of Cusa (c. 1400–64), whose writings Lefèvre sought out
and studied with enthusiasm and then published in a three-volume edition
in 1514, as has previously been mentioned, another bond with both German mysticism and the Brethren of the Common Life becomes apparent.
A native of the German village of Cues on the Mosel, Nicholas is reputed
to have run away from home as a boy to escape the harsh treatment of an
unsympathetic father and to have been placed in the Brethren's school at
Deventer by Count Theodoric von Manderscheid, in whom he found a pro-
tector. Lefèvre admired Nicholas for his religious devoutness, moral integrity, and intellectual profundity. In the letter that introduced his edition
of Cusa's works,[22] Lefèvre quoted from the panegyric of Nicholas by his

---

20. For an English version see *The Spiritual Espousals*, translated from the Dutch by
Eric Colledge (London, 1952).

21. Interestingly, Lefèvre, in his letter to Raemundus, cites Thomas à Kempis as a witness
on the side of Ruysbroeck, maintaining that Gerson "is the only one who accuses him, while
a multitude of holy men defend him." This, he tells his young friend, "will be perfectly obvious if you read the devout little works of John à Kempis, a man of blameless life." As
Rice observes, Lefèvre seems to have mistakenly named John as the author instead of Thomas.
John, the elder brother, was the first prior of Agnietenberg (1399–1408). Rice, p. 277. So
also Renaudet, p. 600. In his life of Gerard de Groote, Thomas à Kempis had praised Ruysbroeck
and spoken of the high esteem in which he was held by de Groote and others.

22. See p. 40 above.

friend and secretary Giovanni Andrea dei Bussi, who, in effusively praising his master, described him as "a most penetrating exponent of Aristotle's
philosophy, a consummate interpreter of Christian theology, and the wisest
master of the secrets of heaven."[23] It is with the mystical thought of Nicholas
of Cusa, his doctrine of "the secrets of heaven," that we are at present
concerned. Though the extent to which he was influenced by the teaching
of the Brethren of the Common Life is debatable, affinities between him
and them in both moral and spiritual doctrine are readily discernible.

We have already noticed[24] that the postulation of three levels of apprehension, namely, sensual, rational, and intellectual, was adopted and
expounded by Nicholas of Cusa. He held that sensual perception understands
reality only in a confused and disconnected manner, and that rational perception operates by the formulation of abstract concepts in accordance with
the principle of contradiction, whereas intellection rises above this to the
resolution of rational incompatibilities and the coincidence of opposites in
God, from whom all things come and in whom they find their unity. The
mystical ascent, then, is from sense to reason, and from reason to intellection, whereby the absolute simplicity of all things in the divine mind is
grasped. Because of his complete transcendence, God is unknowable to his
finite creature, man, and can more appropriately be spoken of by the use
of negative rather than positive terms—hence the affirmation of "learned
ignorance." This pattern of mystical theology is rooted in the soil of the
"negative method" *(via negativa)* of Pseudo-Dionysius and the
Neoplatonism of still earlier centuries.

In *Learned Ignorance*[25] Nicholas of Cusa drew attention to the incompetence of human reason, which could not comprehend the connections
and combinations of the varieties of things that go to make up the reality
of our world. He reminded his readers of the wisdom of Socrates who
"thought he knew nothing save his own ignorance." We are, he suggested,
comparable to "owls trying to look at the sun," and the natural desire for
knowledge that is implanted in us should lead us to the acquisition of learned ignorance. The distinction between positive and negative theology that
was maintained by Nicholas rests on the premise of the inability of the finite
to comprehend the infinite. The former proceeds by way of positive affirmations about God, which, though not untrue, are yet unsuitable, since a
positive affirmation also suggests the existence of its opposite, whereas
negative definition specifically rules out what is contrary (to call God infinite, for example, is to deny anything of finiteness in him). Accordingly,
"it is by the process of elimination and the use of negative propositions
that we come nearer the truth about God." And so, "in a way we cannot

23. Rice, p. 344.
24. See pp. 39f.
25. *De docta ignorantia.*

comprehend, absolute truth enlightens the darkness of our ignorance''; and this, Nicholas explains, is ''the learned ignorance for which we have been searching.''[26]

The connection between Christology and Christian holiness conceived as the imitation of Christ or Christlikeness is clearly stressed by Nicholas. In Christ, he says, ''human nature by its union with God is raised to the highest power and escapes the weight of temporal and downward-dragging desires.'' Christ himself is the perfect exemplar of absolute love: ''All that is possible to human nature in the way of love of one's neighbor stands out as most generously achieved in the perfect charity of Christ, who gave himself to death even for his enemies.'' It is only in Christ, on the basis of that sacrificial death, and not at all in ourselves that we can stand justified before God: ''Our justification is not from ourselves but from Christ. He is all fulness and therefore if we possess him we possess all things.'' For the person who is justified the ambition of all his living should be growth in likeness to Christ, who himself is the personification of all virtues, such as constancy, courage, charity, and humility. ''The higher, then, a man rises in these immortal virtues, the closer the resemblance he bears to Christ.'' In the perfection of Christ, moreover, there is the bringing together and the reconciliation of opposites: ''Here the maximal and minimal coincide: maximal humiliation with exaltation, the most shameful death of the virtuous man with the most glorious life; and so with the rest, all of which are manifested to us in the life, passion, and crucifixion of Christ.''[27]

Nicholas affirms that it is solely by faith that we are able to follow Christ in suffering, to be conformed increasingly to his likeness, and to enjoy the blessedness of union with him.

> Great indeed is the power of faith which makes a man *Christlike*,[28] so that he forsakes sensible things, denudes himself of the contagions of the flesh, walks in fear in the way of the Lord, follows in the footsteps of Christ with joy, and willingly and even exultantly takes up the cross. . . . What is that amazing gift of God which by faith raises us, poor pilgrims in frail flesh though we be, to such power above all that is not Christ by union with him. Let us brace ourselves that each one may aspire by daily mortification to rise by steps to union with Christ, even, as far as may be, to the deep union of absorption in him. Such a one, leaping above all visible and mundane things, reaches the complete perfection of his nature. Here is the perfected nature which, the flesh and sin being destroyed, we may attain in a transformation into the image of Christ.

The word ''Christlike'' has been italicized in the quotation above because in the Latin it is the term ''Christiform'' *(christiformis)*, and *Christiformity*,

---

26. Ibid., I.i; xxiv–xxvi.

27. Ibid., III.vi.

28. The Latin reads: ''Magna est profecto fidei vis, quae hominem *christiformem* efficit.''

as we shall in due course see, will become a central theme of Lefèvre's spirituality in his later years.[29] The concept is not novel, but the term, which is rare, may have been derived, at least in part, from Nicholas of Cusa.

The consummating perfection of this Christiformity is not now but hereafter. Christians who are separated from the church militant at death will afterward be raised by the power of Christ to experience the completeness of eternal union in him.[30] Nicholas strongly denied that the system of his thought was pantheistic. His mysticism, indeed, ends up being positive rather than negative; and this is because his theology, far from being nebulously theosophic, is emphatically redemptive and christocentric, and its goal is not some kind of bodiless absorption but the fulfillment of the potential of total humanity in Christ. The church in its union with Christ is "the gathering together of many into one," in such a way, however, that "one member is not another, but each with the others is one body which unifies them all."[31]

THE INFLUENCE OF LULL

We have already given some indication of Lefèvre's interest in the writings of the Spanish philosopher and mystic Ramon Lull, whose vigorous thought continued to stimulate the minds of scholars at this time—two hundred years after his death.[32] Pico della Mirandola was somewhat familiar with his doctrines,[33] and so also, a generation before Pico, was Nicholas of Cusa whose library contained manuscript copies of works by Lull. It may fairly be asserted that Lull's literary activity was prolific and the scope of his thought encyclopedic, and that the extent of his influence on European philosophy has not yet received the recognition it deserves. In Nicholas of Cusa we find the distinctively Lullian emphasis not only on the principle that all things created by God were made in his likeness and thus are symbolical of his attributes, but also on the competence of man to ascend to a knowledge of God by contemplating the created order as a mirror of the divine perfection. Man, himself created in the image of God, is seen as being in a unique sense a microcosm able by reason of his constitution to survey the universe and to transcend the limitations of his environment. This concept played a prominent part in Pico's philosophy of man and his

---

29. See pp. 192ff. below.

30. Op. cit., III.xif.

31. Ibid. The translation followed, with one or two exceptions, is that of Germain Heron, *Of Learned Ignorance* (New Haven, 1954).

32. See pp. 11ff. above.

33. There is a reference to Lull's *Ars combinatoria* in the *Apologia* where Pico defends his thesis that "there is no science which makes us more certain of the divinity of Christ than magic and cabala": *Opera Pici*, p. 181.

place in the created order.[34] Another postulation that recurs in Pico and in the earlier, philosophical period of Lefèvre's thinking, which was central in Lull's system, was that of the unity and harmony of all knowledge, itself correlative to the unity and harmony of the cosmos.[35]

We would be mistaken to imagine that the extent of Lefèvre's acquaintance with Lull's writings was limited to those works that he published. One of his most dedicated disciples, Charles de Bovelles (1479–1553), devoted much time to the study and exposition of Lull's philosophy. The origin of his interest in Lull may be attributed to Lefèvre, whom he revered as his intellectual father. "You alone are the one to whom I owe everything, as a son to a learned father," he wrote to Lefèvre in 1505, reminding him that in 1495, on leaving Paris because of an outbreak of the plague, he had had the good fortune to come across Lefèvre in the country. Bovelles, then a stripling of sixteen years, was initiated by Lefèvre into the profundities of philosophy: in this same letter Bovelles acclaimed him as "the cause of all my philosophical progress and academic research."[36] After studying under Lefèvre at the Collège du Cardinal Lemoine, he became his colleague as a teacher there when he was twenty years of age. Like Lefèvre, Bovelles was a Picard.

The line of Bovelles' intellectual development was soon apparent. In 1501 he published an *Introduction to the Art of Opposites*,[37] and an enlarged revision of the same work followed eight years later, now with the addition of an explanatory commentary. He gave the reason for the latter in the dedicatory epistle addressed to François de Melun: "My little *Introduction to the Art of Opposites*, most worthy Sir, no one has hitherto been able to understand, for when our friend Lefèvre d'Étaples, the most renowned man of our age, arranged for its publication it lacked the light of a commentary."[38] Also included were disquisitions on such subjects as the intellect, sense, nothing, generation, wisdom, and the perfect numbers that attest the justness of his claim that Ramon Lull and Nicholas of Cusa were his intellectual ancestors. In 1511 Bovelles published a biography of Lull,[39] describing Lull's acts rather than his thought and containing a catalogue of his numerous writings; two years later Bovelles published a treatise on the divine attributes,[40] in which he combined the logical system of Lull and

---

34. See, e.g., the opening section of the *Oratio de hominis dignitate*.

35. This is the governing principle behind the *Nine Hundred Theses*. Cf. also the *De ente et uno*, which is professedly a reconciliation of Plato and Aristotle, and thus an essay on the theme of harmony.

36. Rice, p. 78

37. *In artem oppositorum introductio.*

38. Rice, p. 209.

39. *Vita Raemundi Eremitae.*

40. *Libellus de praedicamentis divinis.*

the mystical theology of Nicholas. The latter's doctrine of "learned ignorance" Bovelles developed more fully in a work entitled *The Divine Darkness*[41] (1526). There are unmistakable Augustinian and Dionysian strains that come down through Lull and Nicholas to Bovelles; but the most distinctively Lullian element in his thought is that of the concord or reconciliation of opposites through the agency of the medium between the two extremes, which Lull elaborated particularly in the *Art of Opposites*. In this respect, some have seen a line reaching from Ramon Lull through Nicholas of Cusa, Charles de Bovelles, and others to Hegel and his dialectical theory of the resolution in the course of history of thesis and antithesis by the mediation of synthesis. Be that as it may, what is of primary interest here is that it was Lefèvre who set Bovelles off on his study of Lull's works.

Mention should also be made of the Spanish scholar Bernardo de Lavinheta, the leading exponent at that time of Lull's encyclopedic philosophy. Lavinheta traveled widely in Europe as a teacher of Lullist doctrine and in the year 1515 spent some time in Paris debating and lecturing on his special subject. Subsequently, in 1523, while a resident at the Franciscan convent of St. Bonaventure in Lyon, Lavinheta completed and published his main work, which he called an "explanation and compendious application of the 'art' of the *Doctor Illuminatus*, Ramon Lull." In the letter addressed to Alfonso of Aragon, archbishop of Saragossa, on Christmas Day 1516, which introduced his edition of Lull's *Book of Proverbs* and *Tree of the Philosophy of Love*, Lefèvre mentions the favorable manner in which the lectures given the previous year in Paris by "the distinguished doctor of theology" Bernardo de Lavinheta had been received, and informs the Spanish prelate of the presence of writings by Lull in some of the Parisian libraries. He speaks also of papal statements issued from Rome against "malevolent calumniators" of Lull. At the same time, he is not unaware that there was reputedly a time when Lull did not enjoy the pontifical approval, but if this was so, he says, it is attributable to the hostile influence of the Averroists. The allusion is to the condemnation of one hundred propositions from the works of Lull in a bull issued by Pope Gregory XI in 1376, mainly at the instigation of Nicholas Eymeric, the Dominican inquisitor for Aragon, according to whom Lull was "a merchant, a layman,[42] a fantasist,[43] unskilled, the author of numerous books in the Catalan vernacular,[44] totally ignorant of grammar, one whose teaching, now widespread, was attributable to the devil, since it was derived not from

---

41. *Divinae caliginis liber.*

42. As a young man Lull had had a position at the court of King James I of Aragon. After his conversion at the age of thirty he became a Franciscan tertiary.

43. *Phantasticus* was a designation under which Lull presented his own opinions in a work of 1311. See p. 12 above.

44. A derogatory observation implying that not to write in Latin was unscholarly.

man or from human study or from God, because God is not a teacher of heresies and errors."[45] In the past there had also been determined opposition to Lullism in Paris. In 1419, however, Gregory's bull was cancelled as a forgery by Pope Martin V.

In this same letter Lefèvre scornfully dismisses Averroes as first an Arab, then a Christian, and finally an apostate. "Against him and his followers Ramon fought vigorously and spiritedly by both the spoken and the written word at a time when the truth gave rise to hatred," Lefèvre asserts; but now justice has been done, for "the impious Arab has been laid low and the pious Ramon is acclaimed the victor." The former was a soldier of the devil, the latter a soldier of Christ, "by whose light, *idiota* though he was, he won over the wise of this world and for love of whom he did not shrink even in the least degree from martyrdom." "What possible reason or justification can there be," Lefèvre asks, "for us to reject the writings of this most godly man and martyr of Christ—writings which uplift the minds of those who read them only to divine things?"[46]

Here we encounter again Lefèvre's idealistic conception of Ramon Lull as an *idiota* whose rough and unsophisticated simplicity is admirable because it surpasses the wisdom of the schoolmen and ensures his unencumbered closeness to God.[47] Although strictly speaking not a mystic, Lefèvre because of the intensity of his own religious aspirations, found Lull's devout spirituality powerfully attractive. Some three years later, in August 1519, he would be responsible for the publication of one more composition within this classification, namely, the *Contemplations of an Idiota*.[48] It is the work of an author at that time unidentified but who is now known to have been Raymundus Jordanus, a French Augustinian of the fourteenth century. In dedicating the work to Michel Briçonnet, bishop of Nîmes and cousin of Guillaume Briçonnet, Lefèvre explains how he had come across this "small volume of a certain contemplative, a pious and holy man, who designates himself with no other name than that of *Idiota*." The book, he says, teaches the reader three things: "to arouse himself, to accuse himself, and to look not to self but to God, which are the same as to enlighten, to purge, and to make perfect. "The style," he adds, "is humble, but pure and sincere and thoroughly Christian."[49] The sincerity of Lefèvre's own spirituality is clearly revealed in his enthusiasm for the spirituality of others.

Lefèvre has been described as "perhaps the single most important figure in the history of sixteenth-century Lullism," in that, with the collaboration

---

45. Rice, p. 377. For other adverse criticisms of Lull's literary and scholarly ability in the next century see Mark D. Johnston, "The Reception of the Lullian Art," *The Sixteenth Century Journal* 12 (1981):35-37.

46. Rice, pp. 373ff.

47. See p. 13 above, p. 127 below.

48. *Contemplationes Idiotae*.

49. Rice, p. 412.

of Bovelles, he "was responsible for the resurgence of Lullist studies at Paris between 1499 and 1516," though his interest was "almost exclusively in Lull's mystical and contemplative programs." It was left to Lavinheta and Heinrich Cornelius Agrippa von Nettesheim to expound and refine the dialectical pansophism of the Lullian "Art" in works that were published in 1523 and 1531 respectively.[50]

Renaudet, confirming the opinion of others before him, writes that there were two men, Lefèvre and Erasmus, who made a profound impression on their world in the early part of the sixteenth century. The contribution of Lefèvre up to the time when Martin Luther first appeared on the public scene, in 1517, he sums up admirably as follows:

> Desiring above all to restore the teaching of philosophy and prepared for this work by the counsels of Ficino, Pico della Mirandola, Poliziano, and Ermolao, [Lefèvre] attempted, with a patient and indefatigable tenacity, to lead the tired mentality of nominalism back to the discipline of Greek wisdom. Now, thanks to him, the Parisians possess an almost complete encyclopedia of Aristotle, faithfully translated and commented on. They have learnt again the art of discussion, the rules of reasoning, the methods of scientific research: the *Physics*, the *Metaphysics*, the *Ethics*, and the *Politics* offer them a precise theory of the universe, of man, and of society. But Lefèvre wishes his pupils to pass beyond Aristotelianism and the prudent exploration of the world of appearances. He anxiously interrogates the mystics, inquiring from them to what supreme realities their gaze has penetrated. He has savored the Neoplatonism of Ficino and Pico and has published in turn Ramon Lull, Dionysius, the Hermetic books, Richard of Saint Victor, Ruysbroeck, Hildegard, and Mechthild. Nicholas of Cusa, whose complete works he has just published, has taught him, since 1501, in speculation to distinguish the rational order and has passed on to him his theory of knowledge, his methods of reasoning, and his metaphysical hypotheses. And it is not only the humanists with their interest in elegant learning and Greek philosophy who find satisfaction in the books of Lefèvre. A great number of those who, toward the end of the fifteenth century, tired of the scholastics and their empty battles over words, were seeking refuge with the contemplatives and the ascetics, became indebted to him for new texts and new consolations. . . . The students shaped by his lectures on Aristotle found themselves prepared to read the Bible in a more precise and diligent manner. Clerics, likewise, whom he introduced to the ecstasies of Lull or Richard could no longer be content with the verbal disputations of the nominalists. But having himself become, since 1509, a commentator on the Bible, the master contributed still further to the founding of this new theology, of which his own publications had created the need.[51]

---

50. Mark D. Johnston, loc. cit., pp. 39ff. and passim. Lavinheta's work, published in Lyon in 1523, was entitled *Explanatio compendiosaque applicatio artis Raymundi Lulli*, and Agrippa's, published in Cologne in 1531, *In artem brevem Raymundi Lulli commentaria*.

51. Renaudet, pp. 698-700.

The Assertion of Biblical Authority

THE FIVEFOLD PSALTER

The publication in July 1509 of his *Fivefold Psalter* was unquestionably a significant milestone in Lefèvre's spiritual and intellectual career; for, even though he had not yet said farewell to the ancient philosophers and the medieval mystics, the appearance of this work gave notice that from now on the Bible and the propagation of its teaching would occupy the central position in his life. The *Fivefold Psalter* was so named because in this work Lefèvre gave five different Latin versions of the text of the Psalms in separate columns. These may be briefly described, in chronological order, as follows: 1) the Old Latin version *(Psalterium Vetus)*, which was in use up to the time of Pope Damasus and the revision of the Latin Bible undertaken by Jerome late in the fourth century at the request of that pope; 2) the Roman version *(Psalterium Romanum)*, which corresponds with Jerome's first revision of the Psalter and has continued to be the version used in St. Peter's, Rome, and in some other places in Italy (though there is now some question as to whether this is not in fact an Old Latin psalter wrongly regarded as a revision of Jerome's); 3) the Gallic version *(Psalterium Gallicanum)*, which is the product of Jerome's second revision of the Psalter completed in Bethlehem in or about A.D. 392 by collating the Old Latin and the Septuagint version contained in Origen's *Hexapla*, so called because the churches of France (Gaul) were the first to adopt it, and which is also the version of the Psalms found in the Vulgate Bible and the Roman breviary; 4) the Hebraic version *(Psalterium Hebraicum)*, which is Jerome's third version, made after he had acquired a knowledge of Hebrew, and, not surprisingly, since it was based on the Hebrew text, more accurate than the preceding versions; and, 5) a harmonized version *(Psalterium Conciliatum)*, which is Lefèvre's own revision of the Vulgate, corrected by comparison with the Hebrew original.

Lefèvre himself was well aware that the *Fivefold Psalter* marked a turning-point in his career. The introductory letter clearly indicated the direction he was now taking. Addressed to Cardinal Briçonnet, he writes in the concluding sentence: "We must pray our Lord Christ, who is the beginning and the end of the whole of this psalmody, that our work may not only be acceptable to him but may also be used to bring many to happiness."[1]

Though always an intensely devout person, Lefèvre's transition from the widely ranging study of philosophy and religion to the concentration of his energies on the text and teaching of the canonical Scriptures was dramatically announced in the opening section of this same letter:

> While virtually all studies may be expected to bring some degree of pleasure and usefulness [he says], the study of divine truth alone promises not just pleasure and usefulness but the highest happiness: "Blessed are they who search thy testimonies," the psalmist declares [Ps. 119:2]. What study, then, should we pursue more eagerly or embrace more willingly?

There follows Lefèvre's description of the crisis in his own personal experience:

> For a long time I pursued human studies and paid little more than lip service to the study of divine things (for they are majestic and not to be approached rashly); but once I had tasted them as it were from a distance so much light shone forth that all human learning seemed to me to be darkness in comparison, and so wonderful was the fragrance they breathed that nothing can be found on earth to compare with its sweetness. . . . I am accustomed to the cloistered life, but those who do not know this sweetness in my judgment have never tasted the true food of the soul; for our spirits live by every word which proceeds from the mouth of God [Deut. 8:3; Matt. 4:4], and what are these words but sacred utterances?[2] Such persons, therefore, have dead spirits. And whenever these pious studies cease, monasteries decay, devotion dies out, worship is extinguished, spiritual blessings are exchanged for earthly things, heaven is abandoned and earth welcomed—truly the most disastrous of transactions.

Lefèvre informs Cardinal Briçonnet that he had on many occasions asked monks who sought nourishment from the Holy Scriptures what sweetness they had derived from them, and that for the most part they had replied that they had found nothing but some kind of "literal" sense, with the result that their reading had left them sad and dejected. It is interesting that a few years earlier Erasmus had reached the same conclusion. "In my judgment," he wrote in the *Enchiridion* (1503), "there is no other reason for the evident fact that monastic piety is everywhere cold and sluggish, indeed vanishing, than that the monks are spending their years in the letter and fail to discover the spiritual understanding of the Scriptures."[3] It was

---

1. Rice, p. 197.

2. The reference is to the Scriptures.

3. *Desiderii Erasmi Opera Omnia* (London, 1962), V.2.9

this failure to advance beyond a merely superficial reading of the Psalms that caused Lefèvre to consider whether the monks had in fact missed the true literal sense and allowed a false understanding to take its place. "Thereupon," he continues, "I betook myself to our first leaders, namely, the apostles, evangelists, and prophets, who were the first to entrust the divine seed to the furrows of our souls and to open the door to the literal understanding of Holy Scripture." What Lefèvre discerned was "another sense, which was the sense intended by the prophet and by the Holy Spirit speaking in him." This sense, "which coincides with the Spirit," he calls *the literal sense.* And this, he insists, is the only proper sense: there can be no question of one sense being intended for the prophets and another for the readers of their writings. He adds that it is not his wish to deny allegorical, tropological, and anagogical senses where one or other of them is required by the context, since the literal sense is always the appropriate sense.

Yet Lefèvre also recognizes an inadequate literal sense, wherein, for example, David is regarded "not as a prophet but just as one who in the Psalms is narrating things he has seen and done, as though he were composing an autobiographical account." This, Lefèvre objects, is to disregard what David said about himself: "The Spirit of the Lord has spoken through me, and his word is on my tongue," and to ignore the fact that the sacred text calls him a man "who was appointed the illustrious singer of Israel to sing of the the Christ of the God of Jacob."[4]

THE TWOFOLD LITERAL SENSE

These considerations led Lefèvre to postulate a twofold literal sense (*duplex sensus literalis*) of the biblical text. There is, on the one hand, "the improper sense of those who are blind and fail to see, and who therefore understand divine things only in a carnal manner," and, on the other hand, "the proper sense of those who see and are enlightened." Of these two senses, "the former is fabricated by human reason, the latter is imparted by the divine Spirit; the former is degrading to the mind, the latter raises it on high." This explains the dejection of the monks mentioned earlier: they had advanced no further than the improper literal sense of the Psalms. It was with the purpose, then, of displaying their proper literal sense that

---

4. Lefèvre is citing 2 Samuel 23:1-2. His Latin coincides with that of the Vulgate, the grammar and sense of which are obscure in this place. Evidently he interprets *cui constitutum est de Christo Dei Iacob* as referring to Christ, the Messiah, for he adds the rhetorical question, *et ubi illi constitutum est de Christo Dei Iacob et vero Mesiah nisi in psalmis?* And at the end of the next paragraph he designates the Holy Spirit as the agent by whom he was appointed: *de quo* [sc. Christo] *illi per spiritum sanctum . . . constitutum erat.* The Hebrew original, however, is not speaking here of Christ (= Anointed) but of David himself as "the anointed of the God of Jacob."

Lefèvre prepared this "short exposition of the Psalms, with Christ, who is the key of David [Rev. 3:7], as helper."

Lefèvre presses home his point by showing how the apostolic authors of the New Testament, under the inspiration of God's Spirit, take passages from the Psalms and proclaim their literal fulfillment in the person and work of Christ.[5] This, he contends, is in contrast to the rabbinical interpreters who allow a literal fulfillment only with reference to David and his experience, thus making David a historian rather than a prophet. His argument leads him to the important conclusion that "the literal sense and the spiritual sense coincide," so that the true sense is "not what is called allegorical or tropological, but the sense which the Holy Spirit speaking through the prophet intends." "And this," he assures Cardinal Briçonnet, "is the sense I have striven to bring out, to the extent that the Spirit of God has enabled me."

In the concluding section of this dedicatory letter, Lefèvre disclaims any wish to argue with persons who may say that what he has done has been done imperfectly; indeed, he readily grants it, since he is not a prophet to whom divine inspiration has been granted. His guiding principle in the exposition of the Psalms has been that of "the harmony of the Scriptures" (concordia scripturarum). Anticipating the objection that his labor in expounding the Psalms is a waste of time because commentaries written by famous patristic authors are available, he responds by acknowledging the distinction of these writings, but at the same time points out that there are particular respects in which his work differs from theirs: to be specific, their treatment was diffuse, his is succinct; they propounded more than one sense, he has sought primarily "that one sense which is the intention of the Holy Spirit and of the mind of the prophet"; they had to make do with a single text of the Psalter (Augustine, for example, used an Old Latin Psalter whose accuracy left much to be desired), he has consulted a variety of texts in order to recover the original sense of the Psalms.

Lefèvre denies, moreover, that there is ground for complaint that he has given no less than five different texts, all of them in Latin, observing that such a procedure is not at all novel, since he can claim the excellent company of Origen, who produced a Greek "pentaplus" (the equivalent of his Latin "quincuplex") of the Psalms in Alexandria, together with an epitome; a work for which, far from being blamed, Origen has constantly been praised. Actually, Origen's was a sixfold work, covering not just the Psalms but the whole of the Old Testament; hence the title *Hexapla* by which it is known. Its six columns comprised the Hebrew original, a transcription of the Hebrew in Greek letters, the Greek translations of Aquila and Sym-

---

5. The following references fit the examples he gives: Psalm 2:1–2 in Acts 4:25–28; Psalm 2:8–11 in Acts 2:22–28 and 13:32–37; Psalm 19:4 in Romans 10:18; Psalm 22:1, 6–8, 14–18, 22 in Matthew 27:46, 39, 42–43, 35, John 19:24, and Hebrews 2:12.

machus, a corrected version of the Septuagint, and the Greek translation of Theodotion. Thus five of the columns were in Greek characters, leading Lefèvre to designate it as a "pentaplus."

Lefèvre mentions, further, that he had added "a very brief exposition and a few other things, such as harmonies, annotations, arguments, and cross-references."[6] The actual format of his *Fivefold Psalter* is as follows: 1) the text of each psalm in three columns, giving the Gallic, Roman, and Hebraic versions; 2) the theme of the psalm *(titulus)*; 3) an expository expansion of the text *(expositio continua)*; 4) a harmonizing comparison with other passages of Scripture *(concordia)*—discontinued, however, after the first two dozen or so psalms; 5) annotations *(adverte)* on matters of vocabulary, linguistics, interpretation, and patristic opinions; and 6) the Old Latin text and his own harmonized version in two further columns at the end. It is worth remarking that Lefèvre's *Fivefold Psalter* was the first edition of any portion of the biblical text to follow the Massoretic division into verses.

While it must be granted that Lefèvre's competence as a Hebrew scholar and textual critic was less than distinguished, his *Fivefold Psalter* has nonetheless been justly described as "a turning-point in the domain of hermeneutics."[7] His principles of biblical exposition both anticipated and also influenced the method of interpretation that the Reformers would follow in their exegesis of Scripture. He consciously abandoned (at least in intention if not altogether in practice) the fanciful allegorical manner of interpretation that for so long had been esteemed as the most profound of the commonly accepted senses of the scriptural text.

Perhaps some credit for this hermeneutical transition should go to the habits of Aristotelian thought, of which Lefèvre had made himself a master. The dualistic perspective of Platonism had postulated matter and spirit as two irreconcilable opposites and had depreciated the body as an encumbrance and a prison-house from which the spirit needed to be set free. In the case of many minds this led to a dichotomy of word and meaning, the word in its natural sense being treated as a superficial entity under whose cover a hidden meaning was waiting to be liberated. It is hardly surprising that this mentality has proved itself readily susceptible to the temptation to allegorize, spiritualize, and mysticize the text of the Bible, or that Alexandra, where in former times Plato was to all intents and purposes beatified as a Christian saint, should have been renowned as a breeding-ground of allegorists. The Aristotelian philosophy, however, whatever else may be said for or against it, stressed the dignity of the physical and refused to sunder it from the spiritual.

---

6. Rice, pp. 193ff.

7. Richard Stauffer, "Lefèvre d'Etaples artisan ou spectateur du la Réforme?", *Bulletin de la Société de l'Histoire du Protestantisme francais* (1967):407.

The bizarre consequences and virtually unlimited possibilities of an interpretation that is unconcerned with the natural sense of language have been apparent in every period of the church's history. In the subapostolic age, for example, the author of the *Epistle of Barnabas* explained that the number of men in Abraham's band that rescued his nephew Lot, namely, 318, signified that our redemption is by the cross of Jesus, since the Greek letter corresponding to three hundred is T (tau), whose form makes it a symbol of the cross, while that corresponding to ten is I (iota) and to eight is H (eta), which are the first two letters of the Greek form of the name Jesus. The author regarded this as a piece of knowledge of the highest excellence, suitable for communication only to those who were worthy to receive it.[8] And later in the second century no less a champion of orthodoxy than Irenaeus proposed that the three persons of the Trinity are found in the parable of the Good Samaritan: the inn-keeper to whom the Samaritan brought the man on whom he had taken pity signified the Holy Spirit, and the two denarii paid for his lodging signified the Father and the Son; thus, he explains, "by the Spirit we receive the image and superscription of the Father and the Son."[9] The Christian Platonists of Alexandria in the third century and the medieval schoolmen in general have a reputation for their allegorizing propensities; and the cabalistic interpretation of the Bible so enthusiastically welcomed by Pico della Mirandola is a further illustration of the extremes to which fine but misguided minds can be induced to go. Such aberrations of judgment become easily possible when the plain, natural sense of language is passed by as little better than a crude cortex, beneath which, however, supposedly lies hidden a boundless treasure of esoteric truth to be enjoyed by a few who are ingenious and imaginative enough to discover it. To posit this as the way to the understanding of Scripture is to remove it from the competence of ordinary men and women.

The fourfold method of interpreting the Bible was an artificial stereotype of scholastic traditionalism with which Lefèvre had little sympathy. As we have already seen, he did not wish to deny that the rich diversity of Scripture provided scope for a variety of meanings and applications. But the expounder of the Bible was not intended to be a sort of religious conjuror producing rabbits out of a hat to the stupefaction rather than the edification of his audience, and Lefèvre was concerned that the biblical text should be handled with the sober respect due to the Word of God. For him, the vitality of Scripture derived from the fact that the human author had written under the inspiration of the Holy Spirit, with the result that the product, though completed in the past, possessed an inherent quality of dynamic presentness. Furthermore, as Christ was "the beginning and the need of the whole psalmody," so also was he the focus of all Scripture. Hence Lefèvre's emphasis, which would increase as his biblical work progressed,

---

8. *Epistle of Barnabas* 9. See also Clement of Alexandria, *Stromata* VI.11.
9. Luke 10:35. Irenaeus, *Adv. Haer.* iii. 17.

on an essentially *christological* understanding as the right and proper understanding of the written word.

Yet while Lefèvre became dissatisfied with the extravagant interpretations that were much in vogue and, insisting on the close bond between words and meaning, affirmed the fundametal importance of the literal or natural sense of Scripture, we would be mistaken to imagine that he had no intellectual ancestry in arriving at this position. Not every scholastic mind was beguiled by the fanciful pretensions of the allegorical method. Ever since the early centuries there had been a tradition of literal as well as a tradition of symbolical exegesis, an Antiochene as well as an Alexandrian school, a Clement of Rome as well as a Clement of Alexandria, a Theodore as well as an Origen—though it would be an oversimplification to assert that the two traditions never touched or overlapped each other, or to deny that even the most determined literalist was capable of lapsing into far-fetched allegorical interpretations of the text.

The line of those who stressed the importance of adhering to the natural sense of the text included such names as Augustine (354–430), who warned that "anyone who takes a meaning out of Scripture other than the writer intended goes astray"; Rabanus Maurus (784–856); Herveus of Bourg-Dieu (d. 1150); 11 Hugh of St. Victor (d. 1141); Thomas Aquinas (c. 1125-74), who insisted that the spiritual sense "is based on and presupposes the literal sense"; Nicholas of Lyra (c. 1270–1340), who complained that "the literal sense has been practically obliterated because of the method of exegesis commonly passed on by others"; and John Wycliffe (c. 1329–84), who objected to those who "rashly overturn the whole sense of Scripture by denying the literal sense and inventing a figurative sense at will."[10] The hermeneutical doctrine propounded by Lefèvre in the preface to his *Fivefold Psalter* was essentially a recovery and development of a principle of interpretation that, though widely disregarded and even despised, had through the centuries been kept alive by scholars of note.

The postulation of the fourfold sense of Scripture is first found in the writings of Augustine's contemporary, John Cassian (c. 360–435);[11] but two centuries earlier Origen had posited a threefold understanding of the sacred text. Cassian's indebtedness to Origen (perhaps indirectly) is indicated by his citation of the same text from the book of Proverbs[12] as justifying and indeed enjoining the interpretation of Scripture in a threefold sense.

---

10. See esp. Augustine, *De doctrina christiana* (I. 26)—a work concerning principles of biblical hermeneutics; Rabanus Maurus, *De clericorum institutione;* Herveus of Bourg-Dieu's valuable Latin commentaries (Migne, PL, 181); Hugh of St. Victor, *Didascalicon;* Thomas Aquinas, *Summa theologiae,* la. 1. 9f.; Nicholas of Lyra, *De intentione auctoris et modo procedendi,* prolog. secund., *De commendatione Scripturae sacrae in generali* (Migne PL, 113. 28); and John Wycliffe, *De veritate Scripturae sanctae,* 12.

11. John Cassian, *Collationes,* xiv, 8

12. Proverbs 22:20–21. The interpretation is based on the questionable rendering of the Septuagint.

Cassian applied this passage to his three spiritual or figurative senses—allegorical, tropological, and anagogical—as distinct from the fourth, which is the literal sense; whereas Origen (c. 185–c. 254) had taught a total of three senses, namely, the obvious or historical sense, suitable for simple persons, derived from the "flesh" of Scripture; a more profound sense, suitable for those who have made some spiritual progress, derived from the "soul" of Scripture; and the most profound sense, suitable for those who are perfect, derived from the "spirit" of Scripture. Thus he saw these three senses as corresponding neatly to the tripartite constitution of man as body, soul, and spirit.[13]

LEFÈVRE'S HERMENEUTICAL INFLUENCE

The very considerable interest aroused by the publication of the *Fivefold Psalter* extended far beyond the boundaries of France. Lefèvre's literal-spiritual-christological method of interpretation challenged the scholars of his day to turn to a more sober and sensible manner of expounding the biblical text in place of the fanciful and academically disreputable inventions that were commonly accepted without question. His work marked the turning of the tide that would come in to the full in the following decades, by way of his own masterly commentary on the Pauline Epistles, with the sanity and wealth of the exegesis of the Reformation theologians.

One of the first to discover and appropriate Lefèvre's hermeneutical principles was Martin Luther (1483–1546), while he was still an unknown monk. In 1885 a copy of the first edition of the *Fivefold Psalter* was found in the library of Dresden with its margins profusely annotated in the handwriting of Luther. Obviously the young German scholar had studied it with great care. Luther's expository writings give abundant evidence of the influence exerted by Lefèvre on his method of scriptural interpretation. In his subsequent labors as preacher and commentator Luther would assign a place of central importance to the christological significance of the text. Like Lefèvre, he devoted his first endeavors in biblical exegesis to the book of Psalms; and from Lefèvre he learned the primary importance of the literal sense and the twofold distinction within that sense. In expounding the Psalter he, too, sought to bring out the native sense—that, namely, intended by both divine and human authors, which he described as the "prophetic" literal sense, and which, as distinguished from the bare "historic" literal sense, pointed to and was fulfilled in the person and work of Christ. For Luther, as for Lefèvre, Christ was the key to the Psalter and to the Scriptures in their entirety.

The preeminence of the prophetic sense for Luther is clear, for exam-

---

13. Origen, *De principiis* IV.i.11.

ple, together with his association of the prophetic with the literal sense, in the following observations on Psalm 119:

> I have not yet seen this psalm expounded by anyone in the prophetic sense, nor is there anyone who has attempted a systematic exposition without distorting and doing violence to the verses and words. This, I think, is because they have not first sought the prophetic, that is to say the literal, sense, which is the foundation of the others—the master and light and author and fount and origin.[14]

Referring to the opening verse of the fourth psalm he explains that, as Christ is the head of all the saints and the fount of all things, so the principal sense of all Scripture and not least the Psalms relates to Christ. In all essential respects Luther's hermeneutical theory coincides with that of Lefèvre.[15]

Lefèvre's influence as an interpreter crossed the Channel into England through the writings of William Tyndale (c. 1494-1536) by way of Martin Luther, with whom Tyndale had fruitful contact. It is well known that Luther's principles of biblical exposition made a decisive impression on Tyndale. In terminology reminiscent of Luther's, Tyndale affirmed that the literal sense is the only true sense of Scripture:

> Thou shalt understand, therefore, that the Scripture hath but one sense, which is the literal sense. And that literal sense is the root and ground of all, and the anchor that never faileth, whereunto if thou cleave, thou canst never err or go out of the way. And if thou leave the literal sense, thou canst not but go out of the way.[16]

It was Tyndale's conviction that "the greatest cause of (the) captivity and decay of the faith, and this blindness wherein we now are, sprang first from allegories";[17] yet he did not frown on the use of similitudes and allegories provided the following rule was respected: "I must keep me within the compass of the faith and ever apply mine allegory to Christ, and unto

---

14. Martin Luther, *Dictata super Psalterium, 1513-1516, D. Martin Luthers Werke: Kritische Gesamtausgabe* (Weimar, 1883ff.), 4, 305, 3ff.

15. Ibid., 3, 46, 16ff. Gerhard Ebeling, while acknowledging the "important hermeneutical stimulus" provided by Lefèvre's work and Luther's agreement with Lefèvre in maintaining the unity of the literal and the spiritual or prophetic sense of Scripture, is, in our judgment, mistaken in asserting a "profound difference," based on the assumption that Lefèvre completely abandoned the fourfold sense, whereas for Luther the fourfold sense remained "indispensable," so that "he combined Lefèvre's literal christological exegesis with the traditional scheme of the fourfold sense of Scripture." Lefèvre in fact admitted the legitimacy of the other senses where they were appropriate to the context—in which case they coincided with the intended sense of the passage, which is the literal-spiritual sense. See G. Ebeling, "Die Anfänge von Luthers Hermeneutik," *Zeitschrift für Theologie und Kirche* 48 (1951):172ff.

16. William Tyndale, *The Obedience of a Christian Man*, in *Doctrinal Treatises*, Parker Society edn. (Cambridge, 1848), p. 304.

17. Ibid., p. 307.

the faith.''[18] Like Lefèvre, Tyndale insisted that the divinely intended literal sense is spiritual, indeed that ''all God's words are spiritual, if thou have eyes of God to see the right meaning of the text, and whereunto the Scripture pertaineth, and the final end and cause thereof.''[19] This ''final end and cause'' he affirmed to be essentially salvific, and therefore christological, directing the reader to Christ as the focal point and true goal:

> The Scripture is that wherewith God draweth us unto him, and not wherewith we should be led from him. The Scriptures spring out of God, and flow unto Christ, and were given to lead us to Christ. Thou must therefore go along by Scripture as by a line, until thou come at Christ, which is the way's end and resting-place.[20]

The emphasis on the primacy of the literal or natural sense of the biblical text became a distinguishing characteristic of Reformed exegesis as a whole. John Calvin, for example, deprecated the manner in which St. Paul's use of allegory in the Epistle to the Galatians had been misconceived as providing an excuse for the immoderate practice of allegorization:

> As the apostle declares that these things are *allegorized,* Origen, and many others with him, have seized the occasion of torturing Scripture, in every possible manner, away from the true sense. They concluded that the literal sense is too mean and poor, and that, under the outer bark of the letter, there lurk deep mysteries, which cannot be extracted but by beating out allegories.[21]

Calvin denounced this practice as ''undoubtedly a contrivance of Satan to undermine the authority of Scripture, and to take away from the reading of it the true advantage.''[22] In his commentary on the book of Daniel he spoke of ''the plausible nature of allegories,'' but pointed out that ''when we reverently weigh the teachings of the Holy Spirit those speculations which at first sight pleased us exceedingly vanish from our view,'' adding that ''nothing can be better than a sober treatment of Scripture.''[23] His own expositions, which cover nearly the whole of both Old and New Testaments, exemplify to a remarkable degree the sobriety that he advocated in the interpretation of the text.

The pattern of exegesis that was common to Lefèvre and the Reformers

---

18. Ibid., p. 305.

19. Ibid., p. 310.

20. Ibid., p. 317.

21. John Calvin, on Galatians 4:22; *Commentaries on the Epistles of Paul to the Galatians and Ephesians,* tr. William Pringle (Grand Rapids, 1948), p. 135.

22. Ibid.

23. On Daniel 10:6; *A Commentary on Daniel,* tr. Thomas Myers (London, 1852), 2:242.

of the sixteenth century, and for which the latter were much indebted to
the former, may be summarized under the following heads:

(1) The primary author of Scripture is God.

(2) The proper sense of Scripture is that intended by God through the inspired
human author.

(3) This sense is at once the literal and the spiritual sense.

(4) This literal-spiritual sense may be historical, allegorical, tropological, or
anagogical—or, more simply, historical or figurative—in accordance with the meaning proper to the text.

(5) Christ is the true key to the understanding of Scripture, and saving faith
in Christ is the true purpose and end of Scripture.

(6) In interpreting the text the analogy of faith must be observed, Scripture
being interpreted by Scripture, so that the harmony and integrity of the whole are
maintained.

The appearance of the *Fivefold Psalter* was welcomed as an event of
unusual importance by many of the leading scholars of the day who perceived
that Lefèvre was ploughing fallow ground in the field of biblical interpretation. "You will find a new kind of exposition," Lefèvre's pupil Wolfgang
Pratensis wrote enthusiastically in July 1509 to Johann Amerbach, the Basel
printer;[24] and in January of that year the latter's son, who had studied under
Lefèvre, had received a letter from Michael Hummelberg, another of
Lefèvre's pupils, who informed him that the *Fivefold Psalter* had gone off
to the printer (Henri Estienne), and said, "I know of nothing that is being
produced greater than this Psalter."[25] At the end of July Lefèvre's disciple
Beatus Rhenanus wrote from his native Alsace to Hummelberg (both were
then young men in their twenties): "The purpose of his [Lefèvre's] studies
is to restore not only those disciplines which are called liberal but also
theology itself, the supreme discipline, to its own pure brilliance." Beatus
could not praise too highly "the superb instruction of a man who, recogniz-
ing that inferior things have been ordained to lead us to the pursuit of higher
things, first duly arranged the steps themselves by which one may mount
to the summit."[26] The extent to which the progression from the exposition
of ancient philosophy to that of Holy Scripture was the result of a conscious
policy on Lefèvre's part is certainly questionable; but we have seen that
in turning to the close study of the biblical text he believed he had passed
from darkness into light and was approaching the true height of Christian
scholarship.

Approbation of the *Fivefold Psalter* was not slow in coming from Spain,

24. Renaudet, p. 516.

25. Ibid., p. 513.

26. Ibid., p. 516.

where Lefèvre had a not inconsiderable reputation, and from no less a personage than Cardinal Ximenes de Cisneros, archbishop of Toledo, Primate of Spain, and founder of the University of Alcala, where he assembled a team of scholars to collaborate in the preparation of the famous Complutensian Polyglot Bible. In a letter written from Alcala on 16 November 1509 to Charles de Bovelles he declared his inability to refrain from praising the new volume: "It is a work so learnedly conceived and composed that nothing could be more serviceable for the understanding of the Psalms. I am immensely grateful to him." And Alain de Varennes, yet another of those who, like Bovelles, had profited from studying under Lefèvre, wrote to Bovelles from Grenoble: "All learned persons welcome our friend Lefèvre's illustrious commentary on the Psalms and eagerly await more good things from him by which the Christian religion may daily be enriched."[27]

THE ANTI-MUSLIM POLEMIC

The fear of the Turks or Muhammadans and the antipathy to their religion that Lefèvre shared with his contemporaries in Christian Europe caused him to undertake as his next literary enterprise the publication, late in 1509, of a volume containing two anti-Muslim works, namely, the *Refutation of the Quran*[28] by Ricoldo da Monte-Croce and the *Treatise on the Customs, Conditions, and Wickedness of the Turks*[29] by George of Hungary. The former of these, which Lefèvre brought out with the title *Against the Muhammadan Sect*,[30] was written in Baghdad at the beginning of the fourteenth century by an Italian Dominican monk, Ricoldo Pennino (d. 1320) who, after visiting the Holy Land in 1288—the appellation "Monte Croce" is attributed to his devotion to Calvary—spent some ten years in Arabia studying the Quran and attempting to convert the Muhammadan inhabitants to the Christian faith by preaching to them in Arabic. Lefèvre may have been indebted to Nicholas of Cusa's writings for his discovery of this work, for Nicholas mentions that he had seen it in Rome.[31] The latter work, originally published anonymously in Rome in 1480, was composed by another member of the Dominican order who had died quite recently (in 1502) and who as a youth had been captured and kept for twenty years by the Turks as a slave before finally managing to escape. As we have noticed, Ricoldo da Monte Croce's contemporary, the Spanish mystic Ramon Lull,

---

27. Ibid., p. 517.

28. *Confutatio Alcorani.*

29. *Tractatus de moribus, conditionibus, et nequicia Turcorum.*

30. *Contra sectam Muhameticam.*

31. G. Bedouelle, op. cit., p. 77.

was one with whose abhorrence of Muslim beliefs Lefèvre was fully sympathetic. The atmosphere of Europe was still charged with anti-Muhammadan sentiment. At the end of the previous year (1508) the signatories to the League of Cambray had solemnly committed themselves to the defense of the Christian faith and the ejection of the Turks from Constantinople—though in actuality the league's immediate objective was the discomfiture of Venice. It is likely, however, as Renaudet suggests, that "Lefèvre was one of the rare idealists who continued to believe that the European sovereigns were genuinely thinking of the crusade."[32] His expectations were strengthened by the knowledge that the remarkable Spanish prelate Francisco Ximenes de Cisneros had, as cardinal-regent, been the leader of military excursions against Muslim strongholds in North Africa in 1505 and 1508, and, most recently in May 1509, had conducted another attack, this time on the city of Oran, which was laid waste by his troops.

In Italy, Giles of Viterbo (1469–1532), the prior-general of the Augustinian order and Lefèvre's contemporary and correspondent (who, like Lefèvre and so many others, had been strongly influenced by Pico della Mirandola), had acclaimed Lefèvre as "the most brilliant man of our time in every branch of learning, thanks to whom the Psalms have become clearly understood."[33] Giles's historical perspective was governed by the belief that all history was running its course in a sequence of twenty ages, and it was his conviction that the final and consummating age, which would witness the restoration of the golden era that had been the beginning of everything, was already dawning.[34] Signs of this fulfillment were seen by many in the magnificent new St. Peter's taking shape in Rome; in the reflorescence of the Hebrew and Greek languages; in the unveiling of the arcane mysteries of the cabala; in the discovery by Christian navigators of new and distant lands; in the anticipated overthrow of the Turk, regarded as the embodiment of anti-Christianity, and liberation of the city of Jerusalem; and even, a few years later, in 1513, in the ascent of Leo X to the papal throne—hardly an inspired choice for what was to be the age of purity and godliness!

Whether or not Lefèvre viewed things exactly in this way, there is no question that he was eagerly hoping for the triumph of the gospel throughout the world. In 1527, when his commentary on the Catholic Epistles appeared, he would recognize, more biblically and realistically, only three ages in the course of human history: "This mystery [of our redemption in Christ] was known and determined from eternity," he then wrote, "and revealed

---

32. Renaudet, p. 519.

33. See G. Bedouelle, op. cit., p. 86.

34. Giles of Viterbo's views were propounded in his *History of the Twenty Ages (Historia XX saeculorum)*, published between 1513 and 1518. See John W. O'Malley, *Giles of Viterbo on Church and Reform* (Leiden, 1968).

in the latest stage of the world's history, in the final age which began with the coming of Christ and extends to the consummation of the world. This world has three successive times: the time before the law, the time of the law, and the time after the law which is the time of grace."[35] Now (1509) in his prefatory letter, addressed to Guillaume Parvy, Lefèvre explains that his purpose in publishing these two anti-Muhammadan works is that "the men of our age may not be unaware how deceitful, crafty, impious, and cruel is this bestial sect, how those who attempt to oppose it seem to oppose not so much men as monstrous and inhuman wild beasts, as indeed evil itself, and how it is hostile most of all to Christ and God." He warns that "this most savage pestilence is spreading far and wide thanks to our shameful idleness," so much so that "it has taken over the east, is establishing itself in the south, is flowing over into the west, and is attempting to engulf the north." There are, however, some reasons for encouragement, some portents of a bright future: a new world is being opened up by God through the voyages of the Portuguese explorers; there have been successful assaults on Turkish strongholds in North Africa; flakes in the form of the cross, "the victorious symbol of our redemption," and other remarkable tokens of Christ's life-giving passion have rained down on the people of Germany; and in Italy Louis XII has been granted notable victories.

> What do these worldwide events show [Lefèvre asks] if not that Christ intends to seek his lost sheep and to rescue it from the jaws of the venomous and bloodthirsty serpent, to bring the unknown world to the light of the truth, to cause the victorious sign of the cross to shine forth everywhere, and to subdue not only the Moors but anything whatever that opposes the prince who will bear the names of Christ and bring his wars to a conclusion? Happy is that prince who shall be chosen for these things and who, once an innumerable multitude has been set free from the dreadful tyranny of this brutal and barbarous sect, will hear these words of illustrious praise: "Blessed is he who comes in the name of the Lord";[36] and fortunate and precious is the blood of soldiers which shall be shed in this warfare.[37]

The sack of Rome in 1527 would be a rude setback to the expectations of many eager persons. But well before 1527 Lefèvre would be looking and working for the spread of the gospel not by force of arms but by the quiet victory of divine grace in the lives of individuals and communities. In those belligerent times one of the first lessons it was necessary to relearn was that of the dominical admonition that those who take the sword will perish by the sword (Matt. 26:52).

Within the scheme of biblical prophecy Lefèvre regarded Muhammad

---

35. CE, on 1 Peter 1:18ff.

36. Psalm 118:26. In the Gospel (Matt. 21:9) these words are applied only to Christ.

37. Rice, p. 206.

as the first of two anti-Christs whose coming was foretold in the Revelations of St. John (chap. 13), where they are described as two beasts:

> The first beast has already come [he explains in 1512], and he was Muhammad who appeared in the time of Heraclius[38] and whose sect continues to the present, though in the mercy of God it will soon be destroyed. The second beast has not yet appeared, about whom the apostle seems to be speaking more particularly; and no wonder, for apostasy has not yet reached its fulness with the coming of the first beast.[39]

Meanwhile, he warned that "those who worship the god of Muhammad worship the prince of darkness."

The church, however, was threatened not only from without by the Turks but also from within by the corruption and unspirituality of the clergy, and Lefèvre was intent on doing everything in his power to redress this situation. He was not one to waste time, and in 1510 published his editions of Richard of Saint Victor's work on the Trinity (in July)[40] and Berno's treatise on the mass (in November),[41] designed as contributions to the promotion of spiritual enlightenment and clerical responsibility.[42]

Another significant publication that came out in September of that year was a volume of the works of Hilary of Poitiers,[43] the fourth-century Gallic bishop and champion of orthodoxy who had gained a reputation as "the Athanasius of the West." Robert Fortuné, professor of grammar, rhetoric, and philosophy at the Collège du Plessis, had undertaken the preparation of this edition at the instigation of Lefèvre, who wished his fellow countrymen to find in Hilary an authentic example of French piety and theological orthodoxy. In his prefatory letter Fortuné eulogized Yves de Mayeuc, bishop of Rennes, to whom it was addressed, as "an imitator of ancient morals, because they are chaste and holy, and a devoted lover of the old doctrine, because it is firm and irrefragible," thus showing himself to be in the true line of spiritual succession from Hilary. It was true, Fortuné wrote, that "all who are renowned for their sanctity and their teaching in the ancient church are deserving of the highest veneration"; but Hilary was worthy of the most outstanding honor as "the most ancient and learned and holy bishop not merely of Poitiers but of the whole of France." He was specially to be praised, moreover, "because he fought so strongly against the heretical corruptions which at that time were savagely rampant within the catholic flock that he could justly be called the shield of the catholic faith and the

---

38. Heraclius was the Byzantine emperor (610-642).

39. PE, on 2 Thessalonians 2:1ff.

40. *De Trinitate*, a twelfth-century work.

41. *De officio missae*, an eleventh-century work.

42. See pp. 38, 41 above.

43. *Opera complura Sancti Hylarii Episcopi.*

sword and hammer against heresy.'' So dedicated a defender of the pure truth was Hilary that ''he did not turn away from prolonged and far distant exiles, nor from hunger, thirst, heat, cold, the contempt of princes, the ferocity of heretics, the mockery of the world, and the derision of those whom this world counts wise.'' Because he was ''on fire with zeal for the house of God and the catholic faith, he refused to hide his light under a bushel measure or to dig into the ground the talents given him by God for profitable use [Matt. 5:15; 25:18, 24ff.], but by his watchfulness, study, writing, teaching, discussion, admonition, and his whole hearted commitment to the conflict he drove away the poison of heresy from the souls of the faithful.''[44] This was yet another clarion call from the circle of Lefèvre, challenging the French church to rouse and reform itself.

In November 1512 another patristic volume was edited and seen through the press by Robert Fortuné, this time the works of the third-century North Africa bishop and martyr Cyprian. In the same volume he included the commentary of Rufinus (c. 345-410) on the Apostles' Creed (which Fortuné, as was common at that time, believed to be one of Cyprian's compositions). Meanwhile Lefèvre had produced, in April 1511, an edition of the letters of Pope Leo I (Leo the Great, d. 461) and, in August 1512, his edition of Jan van Ruysbroeck's work *The Spiritual Marriage* had appeared.[45] He was now nearly ready to give to the world another composition of his own of major importance, namely, his commentary on the Pauline Epistles.

---

44. Rice, pp. 238ff.
45. See pp. 42ff. above.

Faith and Works

THE COMMENTARY ON ST. PAUL'S EPISTLES

The magnitude of this work is apparent not merely from its size (it runs to some 530 folio pages) but also from the grandeur of its conception and the worth of its content. Issuing on 15 December 1512 from the press of Henri Estienne in Paris, it marks a very considerable advance along the road of biblical exposition in the three years since the completion of the *Fivefold Psalter* in 1509. We now find Lefèvre crossing over the boundary and occupying the territory of scripturally controlled theology in advance of the Reformers themselves. This masterly production, the fruit of close and devout study of the Pauline writings, is in itself proof that Lefèvre has now, like an advance climber, pioneered the ascent to theological comprehension ahead of the dogmaticians of the Reformation. In 1512, Luther's nailing of his Ninety-five Theses to the door of the cathedral in Wittenberg was still five years off, as also was Zwingli's campaign for reform in Zürich; and Calvin was a three-year-old. The doctrines these men would proclaim as belonging to the very heart of the gospel Lefèvre had already proclaimed with assurance in his commentary on St. Paul's Epistles. The work is Lefèvre's own; it is not a rehash of the notions of earlier writers, nor a chain of quotations from others, but the result of his own penetration into the mind and heart of the great apostle. Patristic citations are noticeably infrequent. As with the *Fivefold Psalter*, Lefèvre is intent on bringing out as clearly as he possibly can the genuine sense of Scripture by deriving spiritual teaching from the plain literal meaning of the text. Renaudet has described the character of the work as follows:

> This doctrinal commentary maintains the qualities to which the paraphrases of Aristotle owed their success and their liveliness. Without employing the abstract and barbarous vocabulary of the theologians, without posing sterile questions in connection with each verse, without creating confusion by the apparatus of scholastic division and subdivision which introduced a factitious precision into the discussion and did not assist in the

clarification of any idea, Lefèvre contents himself with explaining in simple terms, closely related to the text, the thought of St. Paul, and with expounding in easily comprehended language the connection and principles of his system.[1]

The prefatory letter is addressed to Guillaume Briçonnet, bishop of Lodève and abbot of Saint-Germain-des-Prés, where Lefèvre had joined him in 1508. In it he insists on the futility of human reason apart from the illumination of divine grace. "If human minds which do not experience divine enlightenment produce anything," he writes, "it usually does more harm than good and provides no vital nourishment for our minds." Only those whose impulse to write comes not from themselves but from the action of God are competent to set down sublime and lucid truths. "But of themselves human minds are sterile; if they believe in their own ability they are presumptuous, and anything they bring forth is barren, gross, and obscure." Nor are human commentators on the sacred text to be lauded, for any benefit gained from their expository writings should evoke gratitude to God and stimulate the faithful following of God's will: "The ability which we have from the second birth is not ours but comes from the blessing of God."

That the human author even of Scripture is not to be praised is made plain by St. Paul himself when he says: "Neither he who plants nor he who waters is anything, but only God who gives the increase" (1 Cor. 3:7).

> Those who understand that these epistles are a gift of God and that the comments added are a gift of God will receive benefit [Lefèvre continues]; but the benefit they receive will come not from themselves but from grace. They, however, who are attentive to the worldly author, even indeed to Paul himself who is now beyond this world, as though these epistles were his work and not the work of a higher power divinely active in him, and who approach the reading of the epistles with their own understanding, will derive but little fruit.

To recognize the futility of one's own unaided reason, Lefèvre declares, is in itself no small gain. Paul is only an instrument; it is Christ who speaks in him (2 Cor. 13:3), and the doctrine is the doctrine of Christ and of no one else.

Lefèvre, moreover, sees himself as an instrument utterly inferior to the apostolic instrument:

> But if Paul is only the instrument of this divine knowledge, what can those who come after him be, if indeed they can be said to be anything, unless it is a very frail and insignificant subinstrument [subinstrumentum], something less than and inferior to every instrument? Even so, it is a great thing to be in this way a subinstrument, and something far surpassing

---

1. Renaudet, p. 624.

human abilities. Accordingly, it is not St. Paul or anyone else, but Christ and his exceedingly good Spirit who will be of prime importance for those who piously approach the reading of these epistles in order that they may benefit from their piety.

Lefèvre then gives some account of the contents and the structure of the volume. Following the custom of many centuries, Lefèvre accepted the Epistle to the Hebrews as a composition of the apostle Paul (the authorship of which would soon be questioned by Erasmus and denied by Luther and, later, Calvin) which accounts for his reckoning the Pauline epistles as fourteen in number. Lefèvre begins by presenting the "canons" or summarized contents of each epistle in turn, chapter by chapter, set out in ornamented pillared columns, two per page. Following this he tabulates both "canons of the articles of faith," references in the epistles confirming the credal affirmations of belief, and "canons against heretics and heresies," references that refute particular false doctrines. Then he gives the Latin Vulgate text of the epistles together with his own Latin revision based on a comparison with the original Greek text. These are in two columns as well, but Lefèvre's version is in smaller type and its column is narrower than that of the Vulgate. Thereafter the main body of the volume is devoted to the commentary on the epistles. He first quotes a passage consisting of one or more verses and then comments on it, and at the conclusion of each chapter critically examines textual questions that arise, particularly with reference to the Greek original. Accordingly, this volume is a trail-blazing work not only in the discipline of modern exegesis but also in the textual criticism of the New Testament.

Lefèvre included, in addition to the fourteen canonical epistles, several apocryphal opuscules. These were: 1) the epistle claiming to be that of St. Paul to the Laodiceans (cf. Col. 4:16), but actually a pastiche of sentiments from the genuine Epistle to the Philippians, placed by Lefèvre between Colossians and First Thessalonians; 2) the correspondence consisting of fourteen letters purporting to have been exchanged between Paul and Seneca, in all probability a fabrication of the fourth century that had persuaded Jerome that Seneca was a Christian,[2] which he placed between Philemon and Hebrews; and 3) two short writings attributed to Pope Linus on the martyrdoms of Peter and Paul respectively, which he placed at the end of the volume.

As in the *Fivefold Psalter* where Lefèvre had sought to correct the Latin version of the Psalms by comparing it critically with the Hebrew text, so now in this commentary on the Pauline epistles he amended the Latin of the Vulgate with references to the Greek of the original. His revision of the Latin of the Psalter had met with a hostile reception in certain circles and he was aware that he could well be inviting further misunderstanding

---

2. Jerome, *De viris illustribus* 12.

and condemnation for now daring to question the accuracy of the Vulgate version of the New Testament. He was not unfamiliar with the strange mentality that obstinately preferred a version to the original and treated the former rather than the latter as sacrosanct. In an attempt to forestall misapprehension, however, he added, immediately after the prefatory epistle, a special "Apologia" in which he pointed out, with every justification, that Jerome's work in the fourth century was precisely that of a critical revision of the Old Latin version. But, more than that, he contended that the contemporary Vulgate text was not in fact the product of Jerome's revision, but rather a version already in existence, which as such had come under Jerome's scrutiny. This being so, Lefèvre, far from attacking or belittling Jerome's work, was doing no more than follow his example. Lefèvre's reconstruction may need some qualification, but his argument is that of a scholar, not a sophist.

Not caring whether his work should be praised or condemned, Lefèvre was determined not to be diverted from what he believed to be the right course. Referring to this and other matters connected with the plan and content of the volume, he writes:

> It may be that some will commend our diligence in all these things. But whether they do or not matters little. For it should be of no concern to a servant, much less a subservant [*subservus*] and one less than a subservant, whether others approve or censure, so long as his labor is acceptable to the one who is Lord of all and his own Overlord [*superdominus*].

Then, with direct reference to his critical revision of the Vulgate text, he says:

> Perhaps some will be not a little surprised that I should have dared to add the sense of the Greek to Jerome's version, judging me to have acted arrogantly, and will not so much question as condemn me for my rashness and audacity.[3]

This prognostication would soon prove correct.

Lefèvre, of course, was not exactly breaking new ground by calling into question the accuracy of the Latin Vulgate. In the course of the centuries it was only to be expected that errors and corruptions would find their way into the text of this (or any other) version, and from time to time, from as early as the sixth century onward, scholars took steps to rid the Vulgate of such blemishes—for example, Flavius Cassiodorus Senator (sixth century) in Italy, Isidore of Seville (seventh century) and Theodulf (eighth century) in Spain, and Alcuin (eighth century) and Stephen Langton (twelfth century) in England. In the thirteenth century, thanks to the influence of Robert Grosseteste of Lincoln, a new Latin translation—not a revision—of the Old Testament was made directly from the Hebrew. In the fifteenth

---

3. For the Latin of the quotation from the prefatory letter see Rice, pp. 296ff.

century the reliability of the Vulgate was vigorously assailed by Lorenzo Valla in his *Annotations on the New Testament*,[4] a critical examination of the Vulgate text, in which he exposed numerous errors by comparing it with a number of Greek and Latin manuscripts. Written in 1444 but not published during Valla's lifetime, the manuscript was discovered sixty years later, in 1504, by Erasmus in the Premonstratensian Abbey of Parc near Louvain. Undoubtedly, it was a discovery of crucial importance for Erasmus, who, already an admirer of Valla's acute scholarship and elegant latinity, published it the following year in Paris. Its publication at this time (four years before the appearance of the *Fivefold Psalter*) and in this city must mean that it was known to Lefèvre and we can assume that reading it influenced the development of his own critical studies.

In 1516, a few years after the appearance of Lefèvre's Pauline commentary, Erasmus, angered by the carping criticisms of those who objected to any attempt to correct the Latin of the Vulgate version then current, asked this question:

> Did the truth of the Gospel lose any of its authority when Lorenzo [Valla], who was a specialist in rhetoric rather than theology, condemned certain passages as mistranslations? Do we now read the Pauline Epistles with any less confidence because Jacques Lefèvre d'Etaples, a man admirable no less for character than for learning, has denied that the version of them in common use can be by Jerome, and because he has followed Lorenzo in altering many passages that were corrupt or wrongly translated?[5]

Some thirty years later (in 1547) Calvin would protest vigorously against the obduracy of the Council of Trent in decreeing that "the Vulgate edition, which by the long usage of so many ages has been approved in the Church, should be held as authentic in public lectures, disputations, preachings, and expositions," and that "no one is to dare or presume to reject it under any pretext whatsoever."[6] This drew from Calvin the following expostulation:

> Farewell now to all who have devoted much labor and time to the study of languages in order to seek the genuine sense of Scripture from the fountainhead itself! . . . What! Are they not ashamed to make the Vulgate version of the New Testament authentic, when all have in their hands the writings of Valla, Lefèvre, and Erasmus, which demonstrate precisely, even to children, innumerable places where it is corrupted?[7]

---

4. Lorenzo Valla, *Adnotationes ad Novum Testamentum*.

5. *The Correspondence of Erasmus, 1514-1516*, trans. R. A. B. Mynors (Toronto, 1976), p. 71.

6. Council of Trent, Session IV: Decree concerning the edition and the use of the sacred books.

7. Calvin, *Acta Synodi Tridentinae cum antidoto, Calvini opera* (Amsterdam, 1667), VIII: 229, 231.

JUSTIFICATION BY FAITH

Beginning his study of Paul's epistles with Romans, Lefèvre found himself confronted with the cardinal question of the sinner's justification before God. We have already seen, in the prefatory epistle, the emphasis he placed on the unfruitfulness of human reason when it is not enlightened by divine grace. Indeed, according to the apostolic teaching, the sinner's incapacitation is such that he is quite unable to justify himself before God. The doctrine that justification comes not by human works but solely by divine grace appropriated through simple faith is central to the gospel proclaimed by St. Paul, now to be recovered from virtual oblivion by Lefèvre and thereafter to become a cornerstone of the theology of the Reformation. This doctrine is grasped and summarized in his comments on Romans 3:19-20.

> Let every mouth be stopped; let neither Jew nor Gentile boast that he has been justified by himself or by his own works. For none are justified by the works of the law, neither the Gentiles by the implanted law of nature nor the Jews by the works of the written law; but both Gentiles and Jews are justified by the grace and mercy of God.[8]

Lefèvre, it appears, is prepared to grant the possibility of a certain "legal," this-worldly righteousness, which seems to be the same as what is sometimes called social righteousness in relation to one's fellow man, but which is something other than the righteousness necessary for justification before God. Thus in the same place he writes:

> Since all, whether Jews or Gentiles, are found guilty in their works before God, no flesh will be justified in his sight by the works of the law. But let him who keeps the works of the law throughout his life be troubled. By those works, indeed, he will be righteous, but by a legal righteousness— I say "legal," whether it be of the law of nature or of the written law. But he is still not justified, still not the possessor of that righteousness from which he is able to have eternal life; for it is God alone who provides this righteousness through faith and who justifies by grace alone [sola gratia] unto life eternal.

Lefèvre then explains more fully his understanding of the distinction between these two kinds of righteousness:

> The former righteousness is called the righteousness of the law, the latter the righteousness of faith; the former is of works, the latter of grace; the former is human, the latter divine; of the former man is the author, of the latter God; the former pertains to earthly and transitory blessings, the latter to divine and eternal blessings; the former prepares, the latter consummates; therefore the former is the road, the latter the destination; the

---

8. Page numbers are not given for quotations from Lefèvre's commentaries, since these can be readily located through the biblical references that are cited.

former is a shadowy vestige and sign, the latter is the light and the truth; the former causes one to know sin for what it is and death as something from which to flee, the latter causes one to know grace for what it is and life as something to be pursued. Let us therefore be eager to have the former, but above all let us aspire to the latter. Though the sacred authors speak of both, it is of the latter especially that they speak, whereas the philosophers speak of the former.

Plainly, Lefèvre is struggling to understand the relationship between faith and works in the biblical perspective. He has grasped the truth insisted on by St. Paul that by the works of the law (legal righteousness) no person is justified and that the sinner's justification is "by faith apart from the works of the law" (Rom. 3:28; Gal. 2:16). This principle, he points out, is illustrated by the case of the penitent thief who had no time left for the performance of good works: it is obvious that "he was justified by faith alone [*sola fide*]." But it would be wrong to conclude that works are of no significance. Indeed, good works are expected of a Christian, but not for his justification. Lefèvre warns, however, that "if we do not perform them when we have the opportunity of performing them we lose the grace of justification." This conclusion is open to objection. It is reminiscent of the medieval tenet that the commission of mortal sin involves the loss of salvation. Lefèvre would have stated things in a manner more compatible with apostolic teaching had he spoken not of losing the grace of justification but of questioning whether it had ever been received. This criticism applies equally to the support adduced (in these comments on Rom. 3:28) from the Epistle of James concerning the importance of works; for St. James says nothing about losing saving faith or the grace of justification, and much about the deadness and spuriousness, in effect the nonexistence, of a pretended faith that does not produce good works. He argues that works are the evidence of a true and lively faith, as in the case of Abraham whose faith was manifested by his works.

Lefèvre, moreover, sees works, and even faith, as in some sense a preparation for the grace of justification, though he has discarded the notion that they are meritorious. "Neither faith nor works justify," he writes, "but they prepare for justification. . . . Works as it were prepare and purge one's life; but faith is as it were the terminus and the gateway of divine entry." The relationship between faith and works as he describes it here does not accurately reflect the position either of Paul or of James, for whom faith is the root from which works pleasing to God spring and works are the fruit and evidence of faith. Yet Lefèvre is very clear in his emphasis that in the sinner's justification all is of grace and therefore that the glory belongs entirely to God and not at all to man and his works. In his comments on Romans 3:21, for example, he maintains that saving righteousness "flows solely from the mercy of God," and therefore that "men ought to give the glory to God alone [*soli Deo gloria*], since it is impossible for them to be saved of themselves and by their own works."

This principle of forgiveness through grace applies, Lefèvre explains, no less to sins committed after justification than to those committed before. When expounding Romans 3:24, where St. Paul says that sinners are "freely justified by God's grace, through the redemption which is in Christ Jesus, whom God set forth to be a propitiation through faith in his blood," Lefèvre asks what this means, "unless it is that God has set Jesus before himself as the placation and peace between himself and sinners." And he continues:

> For he is our peace, so that when we have faith that we are redeemed through his blood he manifests his righteousness, the righteousness, namely, of faith and grace, by forgiving us our sins which we committed before we came to faith. Indeed, if we who have faith fall into serious error, our sins are not forgiven except through that propitiation set before God and interceding on our behalf by the blood of redemption, which was shed in the great sacrifice on the wooden altar. All these things are given to us freely: it was he alone who trod the winepress. And thus Isaiah says: "He bore our griefs and he carried our sorrows; the Lord laid on him the iniquity of us all; the chastisement of our peace was upon him; and by his bruising we have been healed" [Isa. 53:4-5]. And who is the sinner that, turning to the contemplation and heartfelt invocation of such great goodness of God, does not, with so great a Mediator, find pardon? And when the Apostle speaks of God as justifying him who has faith in Jesus he shows that this righteousness and justification are from God and not from men. Therefore no one should glory in himself and in his own works as though he could be saved by them; for there is no cause for glory save in God alone, in the wounds of Christ, and in his blood.

The same clarity and firmness are present in the exposition of the fourth chapter of Romans, where Lefèvre affirms the harmony of Paul and James in their doctrine of justification. He comments, for instance, on St. Paul's assertion in Romans 4:2 that "if Abraham was justified by works he has something to boast about, but not before God," as follows:

> It would have been the praise of Abraham but not of God if Abraham had worked and his own works had justified him. But when we say that God justified Abraham by faith, this glory of justification belongs to God, not to Abraham. But perhaps you will say here that the Apostle James[9] nonetheless states that Abraham was justified by works, for he says: "Was not Abraham our father justified by works when he offered his son Isaac on the altar?" This, however, is in no way contrary to what the inspired Paul denies; for Paul denies that Abraham was justified by works, in the way that those who trust in the works of the law imagine, as though righteousness were by works and works themselves justify; but he affirms that he was justified, rather, by God because of faith. This St. James also

---

9. Lefèvre is presumably using the designation "apostle" loosely here and in the next quotation, since the author of the Epistle of James was the brother of Jesus, but not one of the twelve.

perceives, for he says: "Every good gift and every perfect gift is from above.". . . Now who would deny that justification is a perfect gift?

Lefèvre's understanding that the different emphases of Paul and James present not contradictory but complementary teaching is admirable, as the following passage shows:

> Formerly there were two sects: the one consisted of those who trusted in works as, in their judgment, sufficing for justification; the other consisted of those who trusted in faith, without having any concern for works. The latter the Apostle James refutes, the former the Apostle Paul. And you (if you have spiritual understanding) trust neither in faith nor in works, but in God, and, following Paul, attribute to faith the first place in obtaining salvation from God, and then, following James, add the works of faith, for they are the sign of a living and fruitful faith. But the absence of works is the sign of a useless and dead faith.

In his commentary on the Gospels (published some ten years later in 1522), Lefèvre, expounding John 1:29, postulates two justifications. This is really a variation on the same theme, although his manner of expression can easily lead to misunderstanding. The analogy he uses is that of the sun, whose rays are a combination of light, which dispels darkness, and of heat, which dispels cold. "The first justification," he explains, "comes by faith, as by light; the second by love, as by heat, but heat joined to light. For if love, if charity, is not constantly and inherently united to faith and to the Author of faith, it justifies no one." He goes on to define a "double justification" of a different kind as he points out that Christian justification is not only general and universal—sufficient for all—but also particular and personal—efficient for those who believe. He is still dealing with John 1:29: "Behold, the Lamb of God, who takes away the sin of the world."

> You see, therefore, that the Author of our salvation takes away sins, both universally and in particular, and justifies with a double justification. And let John the Baptist speak here of universal justification, through which particular justification is understood without difficulty (for the one accompanies the other as heat accompanies light). John the Evangelist in fact expressly mentions particular justification in his first epistle, when he says: "If any one has sinned, we have an advocate with the Father, Jesus Christ the righteous, and he is the propitiation for our sins; and not for ours only, but also for the sins of the whole world" [1 John 2:1–2]. And Peter in his first epistle says: "He himself bore our sins in his own body on the tree, so that, dead to sins, we might live to righteousness" [1 Pet. 2:24]. Notice how on the cross he bore not only that sin which is universal, but also particular sins, in order that we might hope in him alone who bore our sins before we sinned.

And this brings Lefèvre back to the theme of faith and love. "What therefore remains for us to have?" he asks; and then answers: "Only faith and love.

. . . For faith and love are the death of sin and the life of righteousness.''

In 1527, another five years later, when discussing the passage in question from James (2:18ff.) in his commentary on the Catholic Epistles, Lefèvre displays a surer grasp of the relationship between faith and good works:

> Every good tree, according to the Saviour's doctrine [Matt. 7:17ff.; 12:33], bears good fruit. And, contrariwise, it is impossible for him to have good works who does not have faith, whose works do not spring from faith. For everything which is not of faith is sin [Rom. 14:23]. If, then, you do not have faith you are an unbeliever and a bad tree. . . . But the Lord tells us that a bad tree cannot bear good fruit. Therefore both the man who says that he has faith but has no concern for works, and also the man who says that he has good works but has no concern for faith, is deceiving himself. But he who has faith must necessarily, while there is time for working, have good works; and he who has good works must have faith. Thus James says: "I will show you my faith by my works." For good works are signs of faith. . . . They are good fruit, declaring the tree to be good. But other works which do not spring from faith, even those performed through love, human love however—the works, according to the philosophers, of moral virtues—even though they seem to be good, are really not good.

FAITH AND MERIT

In Romans 4:3ff., St. Paul explains (with reference to the affirmation of Gen. 15:6 that "Abraham believed God and it was reckoned to him as righteousness") that "to one who works his wages are not reckoned as a gift but as his due," whereas "to one who does not work but trusts him who justifies the ungodly his faith is reckoned as righteousness." In his commentary on this passage Lefèvre shows how decisively he has turned his back on notions of human merit.

> If anyone should be justified by works his justification would be something owed to him and would not be the gift of God's grace. Indeed, he who says that justification is owed to him removes all grace from God and makes men ungrateful to God and for that reason unworthy of justification. If, for example, you dig in the garden and receive wages as a reward for the day's work, what thanks do you owe to him who pays you?—for he has paid what he owed; he has shown you no grace: you have earned it. Because you have earned it, he has paid you. Let us not say, then, that we are in this way justified by works. Those who say this have respect to themselves, they attribute merit to themselves, and pay themselves what they have earned. What comes by grace they regard as something owed. They are ungrateful and puffed up, and they glory in their works. But we should say that it is by faith that anyone is justified, so that we may see that justification is the gift and the grace of God, and not something owed by him.

It is because "justification is grace and not the reward of works," without there being any place for human merit and deserving, that St. Paul cites the opening sentences of Psalm 32 here in Romans 4:7-8: "Blessed is he whose transgression is forgiven, whose sins are covered; blessed is the man against whom the Lord will not reckon his sin." The penitent sinner, who acknowledges that he has offended God and turns to God through faith in Christ, Lefèvre explains, discovers that "justification is by the grace of God alone [*Dei sola gratia*]." He then continues:

> Those who say this have respect not to themselves but to God; they do not ascribe merit to themselves; they do not say that justification is a reward that is owed, but that it is truly by grace; they are not ungrateful, but with ardent devotion they constantly give thanks to their justifying God for a gift so ineffable and beyond all possibility of being earned; they do not glorify themselves and they are not puffed up; but they humble themselves before God with complete submission of mind and heart, knowing that they owe him everlasting gratitude. . . . Let us then turn to God; let us not trust in ourselves, but in his goodness alone and in the gift of his grace and good will. . . . Goodness is of the Lord, grace is of the Lord, mercy is of him. What he does for us is not our merit, not what he owes to us, but the gift of his superlatively generous goodness [*superexuberans bonitas*] and only a gift. Ever blessed be that all-transcending goodness [*supereminens bonitas*] beyond all thought, which is so great that it can owe nothing, but only give.

In his exposition of the concluding section of Romans 4 (vv. 18ff.), Lefèvre exhorts his readers to learn from the example of Abraham that justification comes to us by the grace of God and is appropriated by faith:

> So also (when we speak about righteousness and justification) we ought with faithful Abraham to have faith respecting the obtaining of the promise of an everlasting possession, and we ought to give glory to God, knowing that these things are from God and not from ourselves or our works, and praising his redeeming grace and his omnipotent truth and faithfulness as he truly and faithfully fulfills for men of faith every promise of his grace. For when it is said, "It was reckoned to him for righteousness," although this is true with reference to Abraham, yet it was not written for his sake alone, but also for our sakes, so that we might have a firm faith in God, knowing that he justified Abraham by his grace, and believing that, because of the abundance of his grace, he will also justify us, and much more than Abraham, since he has now delivered up his only begotten Son for the expiation of our sins, and has raised him to immortality for our justification. . . . Therefore to the Author of such great benefits be praise and honor and thanksgiving for evermore!

In Romans 5:1, St. Paul writes: "Therefore, since we are justified by faith, we have peace with God through our Lord Jesus Christ." The peace of which he speaks is, as his argument shows, the consequence of the total sufficiency of Christ's death as an atonement for the sins of humankind. Lefèvre expounds this theme as follows:

> Through the death of Christ our sins are blotted out, that is, they are remitted and pardoned to Christ for us; and in him they are remitted and pardoned as often as we sin and turn to him in repentance and with true faith. Thanks to his resurrection, after the remission of our sins justification is granted to us in him, that is, to him for us. There follows peace with God and reconciliation, so that together with Christ we may receive an eternal inheritance, which in this world we possess in hope, but in the next in the fruition of external blessings.

Here, again, as in his comments on Romans 3:24,[10] we see how Lefèvre asserts the efficacy as well as the sufficiency of Christ's death for the remission of all sins, past, present, and future, sins committed after as well as before coming to faith.

He later emphatically reaffirms this doctrine in his work on the Catholic Epistles. Thus, when commenting on 1 Peter 2:24 ("He himself bore our sins in his body on the tree, that we might die to sin and live to righteousness. By his wounds you have been healed"), he says:

> On him he placed the sins of us all, the satisfaction of all our sins, and all the sins of believers were nailed with him to the cross and died there. Through the supreme and incomprehensible kindness, mercy, and compassion of the eternal Father they were pardoned, remitted, deleted in his death, so that through it we, having died to sins and been justified in his resurrection, might live to righteousness. By his stripes the stripes of our souls, which we deserved to suffer for our sins, were healed, as it is written: "He was wounded for our iniquities, he was bruised for our transgressions, and with his stripes we are healed" [Isa. 53:5].

To take another example, in expounding 1 John 1:8-9 ("If we say that we have no sin we deceive ourselves, and the truth is not in us. If we confess our sins, he is faithful and just, and will forgive our sins and cleanse us from all unrighteousness"—words addressed by the apostle to Christian believers), Lefèvre writes:

> Since the Lord knew that we could not pass our life without sins when left to our own resources, he taught us to pray to the Father, "Forgive us our debts, as we also forgive our debtors." And if by the grace of God sins are not imputed to us, but are forgiven and covered by the presence of the light and Spirit of Christ, yet we have sins, and in this life the mass of concupiscence, which is all sin, remains, but washed and purged by the sprinkling of his blood, if we follow this faith and the Spirit, and not the flesh. And thus, if we look to ourselves, as also we ought to do, we should acknowledge that we are nothing but sinners, because

10. See p. 76 above.

to the extent that it is of us that is all that we are; but when we are justified we look not to ourselves but to Christ and his grace, to whom, not to ourselves, we ascribe all that we have received. . . . Therefore, in order to witness that God is true, in order that his word, which is the word of truth, may abide in us, let us confess that we are nothing else than what we are of ourselves, namely, sinners; and if we are something else, this is not our doing, but his; and let us truly feel with Paul that all have sinned and come short of the glory of God [Rom. 3:23], to the end that we may glorify God who alone has mercy, who justifies and liberates from sins, and whose glory is to be merciful to sinners and to justify them quite freely by his grace and mercy. To him therefore be all glory for ever and ever!

The complete adequacy of Christ's sacrifice is also stressed in the commentary on the Gospels, for instance in Lefèvre's explanation of the significance of Luke 24:46-47, as he declares that "all the sins of all who have faith, past, present, and future, have been forgiven, because by this sacrifice the Father of mercies has forgiven all believers their sins." Lefèvre cites Hebrews 9:13, and then continues:

He therefore who does not believe that his sins are forgiven in the passion of Christ, at that moment when Christ suffered and was sacrificed, dishonors God, who gave him for us all, and the Son of God, who freely gave himself up to be sacrificed, and the Holy Spirit, who offers him in the fire of infinite love for the all-sufficing salvation of the world, indeed an infinite number of worlds (if such there be). Contrariwise, he who firmly believes honors God, Father, Son, and Holy Spirit, marveling at their ineffable work and ineffable clemency and goodness, and at the still more admirable plan for the salvation of all men by faith in the unique sacrifice. Those persons, then, who believe and trust in their own sufferings, which they call penances, neither believe nor trust that their sins are forgiven by the one sole true sacrifice, which alone is acceptable to God; and they make their own penitence in their own estimation superior to and more powerful than the Son of God and his passion, which is irrational and stupid; nor do they understand what it is for repentance to be preached in his name for the remission of sins. Therefore when we call to repentance it is only to this faith that we call. . . . His cross is powerful to save; yours is powerless.

In *The Epistles and Gospels for the Fifty-Two Sundays of the Year* (1525), we find it clearly affirmed, in the exhortation based on the Epistle for the Eleventh Sunday after Pentecost (1 Cor. 15:1-10), that St. Paul is reminding the Corinthians especially of two things "which are the foundation of all Christian faith, assurance, and hope":

The first is that Jesus Christ died for our sins. This is a word which certainly ought to be imprinted on the heart of Christians, without which no one is worthy to be called a Christian. Jesus Christ died for our sins, says St. Paul. Accordingly, we owe nothing more for our sins, since Jesus Christ has made satisfaction and paid the price for us.

The second fundamental truth is that Jesus Christ "was buried and has been raised"; and this leads to the admonition that "the person who loses the hope of resurrection loses all spiritual consolation."

The passage from the commentary on Luke (see above) makes it clear that by 1522 (the date of the publication of the commentary on the Gospels) Lefèvre had decisively rejected any notion that the performance of penances possessed meritorious efficacy for the canceling or expiation of sins committed by baptized persons. In point of fact, as Bedouelle has shown, as early as 1509 Lefèvre propounded in his *Fivefold Psalter* "a rigorously contrasted opposition between grace and merit in tones close to the writings of the Reformers." According to Bedouelle, he emphasized that "justification does not come from works but from the pure mercy of God welcomed and received by the believer"—so much so that his perspective was then already that of *sola gratia*.[11] However, the position he was making his own ahead of the Reformers was not gained in a day. Although purgatory is in effect an extension of the concept of penance to the intermediate state of the believer between death and resurrection, Lefèvre seems to have discarded the idea of purgatory rather more slowly. This was due, apparently, to his belief (at least for a while) that, though all sin is freely forgiven by the grace of God, the forgiven sinner may still need to contribute some compensatory suffering.

The 1522 work on the Gospels reflects Lefèvre's state of indecision regarding this question. For example, in expounding the parable of the rich man and Lazarus (Luke 16:19ff.), in which the former, after his death, is described as being tormented by flames, he writes as follows:

> The indications Luke gives show that the rich man was a bad man. . . .
> There is a reversal of the situations after death: now Abraham and the poor man Lazarus are exalted with Christ. The rich man pleads for his five brothers, a good action which cannot be performed by the damned: therefore the place where he is is purgatory. God indeed is able to pardon the transgression and to set free from the punishment of the transgression, especially since the suffering of Christ. But he is able equally to remit neither the one nor the other, and in this case some pass directly from the first death to the second death.[12] But in the case of others God is able to remit only the transgression and they then have to make expiation, as David did for his adultery.

In connection with the history of David, Lefèvre had in mind 2 Samuel 12:13-14, where, in response to David's confession that he had sinned against the Lord, the prophet Nathan declared that the Lord had put away his sin, but that because he had "utterly scorned the Lord" the child born

---

11. Guy Bedouelle, *Le Quincuplex Psalterium de Lefèvre d'Etaples* (Geneva, 1979), pp. 190, 191, 192.

12. See Revelation 2:11; 20:6, 14; 21:8; Matthew 10:28.

to Bathsheba would die. Sin undoubtedly brings its own tragic consequences, but the distinction proposed by Lefèvre between the remission of sin and the remission of punishment for sin is inadmissible. Punishment cannot be required for a sin that has been pardoned, for punishment is precisely the penalty for unremitted sin, so the remission of sin without the remission of its punishment is a contradictory concept. But, even apart from this consideration, the unwelcome effects of his sin (which are nowhere described as expiatory) were experienced by David in this life, not in purgatorial flames after death.

In the Sermon on the Mount Christ warned his hearers that to be angry with one's brother was to be "liable to judgment," that to insult one's brother was to be "liable to the council," and that to insult one's brother was to be "liable to the gehenna of fire" (Matt. 5:22-23). In his commentary on this passage Lefèvre explained it as a warning against three kinds of sins with varying degress of seriousness: liability to judgment he took to mean liability to "the eternal punishment of mortal sin," whereas liability to the council and to the gehenna of fire he understood as a reference to "other kinds of sins which can be expiated by the fires of purgatory." Claiming, precariously, that "the Psalms distinguish between a hades below and a hades above," he asserts that "the latter is purgatory." It is surprising to find him interpreting "the gehenna of fire" as signifying purgatory, especially as the expression has traditionally been understood as a designation of "hell-fire." Furthermore, Lefèvre thought that another allusion to purgatory could be detected in the parable of the debtor who was forgiven an immense debt by his master and then, himself refusing to forgive a small debt owed him by a fellow servant, was delivered to the jailers "till he should pay all his debt" (Matt. 18:23ff.). In his commentary Lefèvre asserts that "the place of expiation"—represented by the jail into which the unforgiving servant was cast—"is not hell from which people do not return, but purgatory." Here again, however, the notion of purgatory is alien to the context and lies awkwardly with the principle of *sola gratia* that he so emphatically advocates.

But when we turn to *The Epistles and Gospels for the Fifty-Two Sundays of the Year* (which is essentially the work of Lefèvre),[13] published three years after the commentary on the Gospels, we discover the significant fact that in his exhortations on these same three passages Lefèvre makes no mention at all of purgatory. In the first (Luke 16:19ff.), the rich man after his death enters the torment of hell, where he is beyond all help since "it is now too late for him." In the second (Matt. 5:20ff.), a quite different interpretation is now offered:

The men of old were commanded not to commit murder and they imagined that it was sufficient for them not to commit the outward act. But it is

13. See p. 128 below.

not so. For he who is inwardly angry with his brother will be condemned; and he who expresses his anger by calling him brainless, or something similar, will be appropriately punished by the judges; and he who calls him a fool will be punished with the gehenna of fire. The reason for this is that the righteousness of God, which is by faith and charity, is not of the kind that commits murder either outwardly or inwardly, that is, by anger, hatred, and malevolence against one's brother; it does not sanction the utterance of anything that has to be censured and punished by the judges of this world, or anything for which after this world the gehenna of fire should be feared, which is the punishment ordained by the Great Judge.

In the third passage (Matt. 18:23ff.) the unforgiving servant is now condemned to endless punishment from which there is no possibility of release:

God is so clement and merciful that if only we entreat him he pardons every sin and every offence, however great it may be, on condition that, in imitation of his clemency and mercy, we pardon our brother a small offense against ourselves. But if we are not forgiving he will demand from us the great debt we owe him and we will be in torments without end, unable ever to pay it off. Therefore, my brothers and friends, since all the offenses of the world against us, insofar as they are against us, amount to nothing in comparision with a single offense against God, insofar as it is against God, let us be readily forgiving, not simply by word of mouth and externally, but with a good will and internally in our hearts. . . . And God will pardon our offenses which are so great—for who has not offended him innumerable times?—and we shall be children of God, imitators of his kindness, clemency, and mercy, which this great King, to whom we are all such great debtors, wishes to bestow on us through our Lord Jesus Christ, through whom he has shown and continues to show all mercy.[14]

It is worthy of remark, moreover, that in 1512, when commenting on 1 Corinthians 3:10–15, where St. Paul speaks of the testing of each man's work by fire, Lefèvre makes no attempt to explain this as a reference to purgatory, even though this passage was commonly adduced in support of the teaching of purgatorial fire. It is surprising, however, that he should have understood that those whose work survives the test represent the just (or justified) who are saved and that those whose work is burned up represent the unjust (or unjustified) who are condemned to everlasting torment; for the distinction St. Paul is making here is clearly not between the saved and the lost but between different categories of believers, who are all building on the one foundation that is Jesus Christ (v. 11). Thus St. Paul affirms that "if any man's work is burned up he will suffer loss, *though he himself will be saved*, but only as through fire" (v. 15)—an affirmation whose significance Lefèvre seems to have missed.

14. For these quotations see the Gospels for the First, Sixth, and Twenty-second Sundays after Pentecost.

GRACE AND RESPONSIBILITY

One who reads Lefèvre's expositions of the New Testament cannot fail to be struck by the manner in which the theme of the all-sufficient grace of God freely and simply appropriated by faith resounds constantly and joyfully throughout the commentaries and exhortations. This the following excerpts will further help to illustrate.

> Christ truly forgives our sins, setting us free from them in this life's pilgrimage. . . . But he who trusts in works trusts in himself and leans on a cane which breaks of itself.[15] . . . By grace alone [per solam gratiam] can we be saved. . . . For we are saved by his grace through faith—saved not because of ourselves, but by God's grace. For grace is a gift, not a work. And lest we should think that the faith by means of which we are justified is ours, even this is God's gift. Therefore we should attribute everything to God and nothing to ourselves, and so we should glory neither in ourselves nor in works, but in God's grace and mercy alone.[16]

Explaining the parable of the Pharisee and the tax collector, he says:

> The Pharisee symbolizes all who trust in their own works and believe that they are righteous of themselves and deserving of the best from God. The tax collector symbolizes all those who atribute no part of their justification to their own works, but everything to the grace and goodness of God. The former claim merit; the latter do not. The former regard God as their debtor, and least of all regard themselves as debtors; the latter, on the contrary, regard themselves as debtors, and indeed such debtors that they can never make satisfaction for their debts, but they do not imagine that God is their debtor or that he could ever be such. The former expect eternal joy as something owed to them; the latter as the mere gift of God's grace. The former consider themselves worthy; the latter consider themselves unworthy. . . .The former attribute some good to themselves; the latter, nothing but evil. The former are proud; the latter humble. The former seek perfection in themselves; the latter seek it in God alone, but only imperfection in themselves. . . . Let us, then, be truly humble, like the tax collector, as often as we pray, and let us look for the righteousness by which we are saved, attributing it not to ourselves but solely to God's grace [soli gratiae Dei].[17]

Also worth citing is this admonition:

> Whoever looks for true salvation through his works or through any creature otherwise than through Jesus Christ alone is saying, "Jesus is anathema," which is to call him accursed, and does not have the Holy Spirit. For the

---

15. PE, on Galatians 3:6–10.

16. PE, on Ephesians 2:8–10.

17. CG, on Luke 18:9ff.

Spirit gives a man a living and sure knowledge through faith that Jesus Christ is his sole Lord, and that man gratefully acknowledges that it is through his grace that he has everything he has in this world and everything he will have in the world to come.[18]

The emphasis on the free bestowal of divine grace without regard to human works and merit does not, however, cancel out the importance of responsibility and earnestness in the living of the Christian life. All the New Testament writers insist that the believer must persevere in the struggle against the forces of evil and conduct himself in a manner that is honoring to God and considerate of others. They plainly teach, moreover, that this too can be done only by the power supplied by God's grace. Lefèvre had a firm grasp of this doctrine. It is the theme, for example, of the exhortation on Philippians 1:6–11:

> The apostle teaches us that we must look to God for the accomplishment of every good work that has been started, saying that it is for him to complete the work he has started. . . . Accordingly, we can readily understand that of himself man can do no good thing, and that all who boast of their ability are in error and blaspheme against God when they attribute to themselves what belongs properly to God, from whom comes our ability to do any good thing. . . . The apostle was quite right to be confident concerning the Philippians that God would grant them this grace to enable them to persevere to the end. . . . Here, then, St. Paul causes us to understand how good work in its entirety, from beginning to end, should be attributed to God.[19]

Similarly, in Philippians 2 human responsibility ("work out your own salvation with fear and trembling") goes hand in hand with divine grace ("for God is at work in you, both to will and to work for his good pleasure"). Commenting on this passage, Lefèvre says:

> When we will some good thing, especially something godly and spiritual, and perform it, looking to God for the will and the deed, it is God who according to his own good pleasure operates within us that will and that action and performance, while we are God's instrument. . . . God therefore operates the will and the energy and the action and the performance in spiritual persons; and they, as children of God, irreproachable, single-minded, undefiled, and free from all blame, have received from him the ability to live and shine in the dark world like luminaries and stars in the sky, apart from whom (like the sky without luminaries and stars) the whole world would be in darkness.[20]

---

18. EG, Epistle for the Tenth Sunday after Pentecost (on 1 Cor. 12:2ff.).

19. EG, Epistle for the Twenty-second Sunday after Pentecost (on Phil. 1:6–11).

20. PE, on Philippians 2:12ff.

"We are transformed by the renewal of our mind," Lefèvre writes elsewhere, "when, having mastered carnal desires, we concentrate our attention on spiritual virtue, not, however, attributing this to ourselves but to the gift of God's all-surpassing grace [*dono supereminentis gratiae Dei*]."[21]

EUCHARISTIC TEACHING

By 1512 Lefèvre's independent studies had led him to develop sacramental views that anticipated the receptionist doctrine that later gained the approval of Calvin and Bullinger in Switzerland and of Cranmer and his colleagues in England. Indeed, in some respects his eucharistic position appeared to draw close to the commemorative teaching commonly associated with Zwingli, due, it would seem, to his reaction against the prevalent sacerdotal concept of the ministerial office. The commentary on the Epistle to the Hebrews affords clear evidence of the extent to which Lefèvre had moved away from that concept:

> What those other priests[22] used to do every day for their own sins and for the sins of the people Christ did, not for his own sins—"for he did no sin and deceit was not found in his mouth" [Isa. 53:9; 1 Pet. 2:22]— but for the whole world, when by a single offering he made satisfaction, a single priest offering a single sacrifice more powerful than innumerable offerings infinitely repeated.[23] Therefore the things which are now done in the ministry of his priesthood[24] are not repeated offerings, but rather a remembrance and recollection [*memoria ac recordatio*] of the same one victim who has been offered once only. "As often as you do this," he said, "you do it in remembrance of me" [1 Cor. 11:24–26; Luke 22:19]. Thus he made satisfaction once for all. Nor does the sacrament contain any mystery other than the remembrance effected by the presence of the body and blood formerly offered in that divine offering and satisfaction which is all-sufficient for salvation. This is more acceptable to God than every other sacrifice and offering to the end of the world. . . . Walking therefore in the light of our new priest and new sacrifice, let us ever be dedicated to him, enlightened by his grace who is the true Son of God, the sole eternally perfect and supreme priest, who cleanses us, redeems us, converts us, hostile and hateful though we are, and reconciles us to God the Father, in remembrance of that offering in which he offered himself to him for us.[25]

The theme of the absolute uniqueness of the priesthood and sacrifice

---

21. PE, on Romans 12:2.

22. I.e., levitical priests under the Mosaic system.

23. I.e., under the Mosaic system of the Old Testament.

24. I.e., in the Christian church.

25. PE, on Hebrews 7:26–28.

of Christ and the perfect satisfaction effected by his once-for-all self-offering
on the cross is one to which he willingly returns:

> In the old law the victims were ceaselessly offered over and over again
> year after year. . . . This served to admonish them that their sins were
> not removed by these former victims. Nor was there a true remission of
> sins until the coming of the true victim and the shedding of Christ's blood,
> which was symbolized by the blood of bulls and goats and other victims.
> For then, by virtue of that blood and that offering, sins were perfectly
> and universally remitted. Not that thereafter men would not sin, and sin
> gravely, but that those sins are not taken away except by that offering
> and that sacrifice which Christ offered for the world. It was for this reason
> that Christ poured out his own blood as a victim only once; for that unique
> outpouring was universally and absolutely sufficient for the washing away
> of all sins which will be forgiven and which have ever been forgiven.
> And if some do not find forgiveness, this is because they do not turn to
> this universal fount where sins are washed away, and do not know or are
> unwilling that they should be cleansed in it.[26]

This theme provides the foundation for Lefèvre's understanding of the
eucharist.

> The offering of many sacrifices by Christ would have meant that there
> was no truly universal and truly efficacious offering. But the offering of
> Christ is truly universal and absolutely efficacious. Therefore it is but one
> offering and only once offered. For if he had offered himself twice, either
> the first offering would not have been absolutely universal and completely
> sufficient, or the second offering would have been to no purpose and
> superfluous. The action of priests in the new rite[27] is not a repeated offer-
> ing, but a remembrance and imitation of that same offering. Therefore
> in the second and new rite everything is in truth performed by virtue of
> the one sole offering, which the old could not achieve by an infinite number
> of offerings. Nor does the symbolic rite[28] add anything by an infinite
> number of remembrances, but until the end of the world it imitates the
> innumerable benefits of that unique offering.[29]

Lefèvre was prepared to speak of the eucharist as a sacrifice, but
specifically as a sacrifice of praise or thanksgiving. In the commentary on
the Gospels, for example, he describes the sacrament as "a sacrifice of
praise, indeed eternal praise," citing the support of Psalm 50:23, "The
sacrifice of praise will honor me, and this is the way by which I will show
him the salvation of God."[30] At the institution of the eucharist, he says,

---

26. PE, on Hebrews 10:1ff.

27. I.e., the eucharist.

28. I.e., the eucharist.

29. PE, on Hebrews 10:11–12.

30. The translation follows the Vulgate Latin version quoted by Lefèvre.

Christ gave his disciples "that body which a short time afterwards was sacrificed on the cross, but in a sacramental and spiritual mode, under the veil of bread to be eaten, and his blood, a short time after to be poured out, to be drunk likewise under the veil of wine." He propounds a distinction between the "spiritual and impassible mode" of Christ's body in the sacrament and the "sensible and passible mode" of his body that was then visibly before the apostles, at the institution of the sacrament, and which soon would endure suffering and death on the cross. The physical body, he asserts, was not shut up within the elements, nor yet was it in a spiritual sense excluded. While impassibly "hidden" under the "sacred signs" of the sacramental elements, Christ himself "was truly passible, and afterwards truly suffered and died on the cross."

> But what was the effect of the sacrament [he asks] for them then when the Lord was in their midst? Surely it was a token [*indicium*] of unspeakable love, for by giving his body and blood for them he was intimately uniting their bodies with his body and their blood with his blood, and indeed their soul with his soul and their spirit with his spirit, and was embracing them most profoundly as friends, in an incomprehensible manner, while he was still mortal, and was inviting even the most treacherous Judas to be the companion of his divinity, if he would but receive his body and blood by faith. For the appropriation of his body and blood is the most profound uniting of Christ with those who receive him and the closest binding of his ineffable love to us.[31]

His declaration elsewhere—"He eats who perfectly believes: therefore he ever eats who ever perfectly believes"[32]—is reminiscent of Augustine's position: "To what purpose do you make ready teeth and stomach? Believe, and you have eaten already,"[33] though there is no indication here that Lefèvre was dependent on Augustine. Judas and many apostates ate, Lefèvre points out, but defectively, because they did not do so with pure faith. Referring to Jesus' affirmation "I am the living bread which came down from heaven; if any man eats of this bread, he will live for ever; and the bread which I will give for the life of the world is my flesh" (John 6:51), Lefèvre observes that "many eat the sacred sign and will not live forever, because they do not eat perfectly." This leads him to conclude that "it is the spirit therefore that eats, not the body"; the sacrament itself is "a sign of this eating." But he insists that "the sacrament does not effect anything without faith, whereas faith without the sacrament is quite possible." Lefèvre further explains that Christ's saying that his flesh was the bread he would give for the life of the world "opens the mystery of the passion in which he gave his flesh, that is, the human nature he had assumed, for the life of

---

31. CG, on Matthew 26:26–28.

32. CG, on John 6:51.

33. Augustine, *Tract*. 25, on the Gospel of John.

the world, for those who are, were, and will be in the world, otherwise dead and lost, unless brought to life by that eternal life." It was "with reference to that suffering that the sacrament was instituted." Consequently, the eucharist is "a monument of the ineffable and all-transcending love which caused him to give his life for the world."

> Whoever truly believes that Christ's humanity was offered in death for the life of the world [Lefèvre proceeds], and that the world was redeemed by that sacrifice and given life by his death, eats his flesh; and whoever believes in the blood of Christ shed on the altar of the cross, and that he himself and the world, that is, believers who come to Christ from the world, are washed, drinks his blood. . . . He who has not thus eaten and drunk before the reception of the signs neither eats nor drinks when he receives the signs; whereas he who constantly believes constantly eats and drinks.[34]

Lefèvre carefully distinguishes between the sacrament and "the truth of the sacrament," that is, the truth of which the sacrament is a sign. To come with faith to the sacrament is to receive the truth of the sacrament and to find that the sacrament is a means of grace; but to receive the sacrament without faith is to turn it into a means of condemnation.

> If faith is not present, the recipient eats and drinks judgment to himself, by partaking only sacramentally and not spiritually; and by receiving the sacred sign of faith he lies to God. And because he is already judged (as the Lord said in chapter 3: "He who does not believe is already judged because he has not believed in the name of the only-begotten Son of God" [John 3:18]) he eats and drinks to the increase of judgment to himself. That is why Paul admonished that a man should examine himself [1 Cor. 11:27ff.]. But this examination consists most of all in faith; for if faith is present, I mean living faith, bringing with itself the love with which it is fervent, he has passed the test; and if he comes and eats in this manner, this leads to the increase of grace, and in him the sacramental eating and drinking are a true sign and the truth of the sign is efficacious. He abides also, both previously and now, in the Son of God—previously through the truth of faith, now, however, both through faith and also through the truth of the solemn and sacred sign, and the Son of God abides in him.[35]

It is possible that in finding his way to this position Lefèvre had originally been stimulated by the inquiring mind of Pico della Mirandola; for in his *Apologia* Pico had proposed, with reference to the wording of 1 Corinthians 10:16 ("The bread which we break, is it not the communion of the body of Christ?"), that we are not meant to understand

---

34. CG, on John 6:51ff. Lefèvre's interpretation is apparently controlled by Jesus' explanation "He who comes to me shall not hunger, and he who believes in me shall never thirst" (John 6:35).

35. CG, on John 6:51ff.

that the substance of the bread or the species of the bread is truly and really Christ or the body of Christ, nor that the body of Christ is correctly predicated of the substance of the bread or of the species of the bread; but the sense is this, that the bread which we break in the sacrament, that is, the participation of the bread broken on the altar, is the participation of the divine body, that is, it makes us to be one with Christ.[36]

Pico, significantly, showed himself to have been acquainted with the opinions of Berengar of Tours who, in the eleventh century, had opposed the concept of transubstantiation and declared that the words spoken by Christ at the institution of the sacrament were to be understood in a symbolical sense. He had maintained that there is no destruction or annihilation of the elements of bread and wine, that it was material bread that Christ broke and distributed at the Supper, that Christ's bodily presence is in heaven, not multiplied on a million earthly altars every day, and that the sacrament received into the mouth was the sign and pledge to the believer of the whole heavenly Christ received into the heart.[37]

Mere outward participation in the sacraments guarantees nothing, Lefèvre stresses, and it must not be imagined that "it is enough to have been baptized or sacramentally to have received the body of Christ" for us to obtain "the prize of eternal blessedness."

For, despite the fact that all the children of Israel without exception passed through the Red Sea (which was a figure of baptism) and also partook of the manna (which represented the body of Jesus Christ), yet of so great a multitude there were very few that entered into the promised land. This story was a figure of what would happen to Christians, few of whom, despite the fact that they have been externally baptized, will be saved if the works of faith do not follow. If, then, my friends, we are all in the race, it is important for us to do so well that we may please him who gives the prize, namely, our Lord Jesus Christ, otherwise it is impossible to have the prize of eternal blessedness.[38] But as there are many things to hinder us from reaching this goal we should follow the example of the

36. *Opera Pici*, pp. 181ff.

37. See A. J. Macdonald, *Berengar and the Reform of Sacramental Doctrine* (London, 1930), pp. 300ff.

38. The expression "the prize of eternal blessedness" occurs in the letter that Pico wrote to his nephew on 15 May 1492 in a context of comparably earnest exhortation, for Pico was urging on his nephew the necessity of pleasing God rather than men. "Finally," he wrote, "I wish to advise you—as I did frequently when you were here with me—that there are two things which you should never forget: firstly, that the Son of God died for you, and, secondly, that you too, however long you live, will surely die. With these, as with two spurs, the one·of fear and the other of love, urge forward your horse through the brief course of this fleeting life to the prize of eternal blessedness" (*Opera Pici*, pp. 340ff.). As there had been six editions of Pico's *Opera Omnia* (including his letters) by 1519, one of them published in Paris in 1505, and eleven editions of his letters by 1520, four of them published in Paris, Lefèvre must almost certainly have been familiar with this letter, and he may well have borrowed the phrase "the prize of eternal blessedness" from it, perhaps unconsciously.

competitor in the physical race, who keeps himself from all things that
might hinder his running. If one shuns all hindrances for the obtaining
of a temporal prize, how much more, my friends, for the obtaining of
the eternal prize, which is the glory of God and true blessedness, should
we shun everything that hinders us from gaining it! And if you wish to
know what these hindrances are, I tell you that it is your will alone. Shun
your own will, therefore, and follow the will of God, and then nothing
will hinder you from obtaining the great prize.[39]

ANOINTING AND CONFESSION

During the medieval period the practice known as "extreme unction,"
the priestly anointing of those who were at the point of death, gained acceptance as one of the ecclesiastical sacraments. Support for this practice
was largely based on a particular interpretation of James 5:14-15, where
the author advocates anointing the sick with oil, accompanied by prayer.
Lefèvre, however, cleared a different path as he propounded what he
regarded as a more appropriate understanding of the sense of the passage.
The healing oil intended by St. James, he maintained, was not physical but
"spiritual oil," the oil of God's mercy, though at the same time he admitted
that "James does not forbid physical oil to be provided as a sign of the
spiritual oil for those who trust in the mercy of God." Once again, he insists
on the necessity of the presence of faith:

> By faith and perfect trust in Christ, who heals all our sicknesses, and
> whose name is oil outpoured, those who were ill often felt the allevia-
> tion of their infirmity through this unction, and the prayer of faith
> restored many to health, and, if they were fast bound by sins, the faith
> both of those who prayed and of those who were ill in the mercy of
> God obtained remission of sins.

He then proceeds to criticize the customary administration of extreme
unction:

> But now the sick show how little faith they have when they call for the
> elders of the Church as late as possible and not at all for counsel and con-
> solation of soul to the strengthening of faith against the taunts of evil per-
> sons. . . . But when survival in this present life is despaired of, then, in-
> stead of summoning the elders of the Church, by whom the apostle means
> men full of the Spirit and faith who faithfully declare the word of God
> and the Gospel of salvation, they call for a special kind of presbyter (for
> that is how they designate those who administer the sacraments) and it
> is then, when they are at the point of death, that they are anointed, and
> nothing or very little of what the apostle advises here is done.[40]

---

39. EG, Epistle for Septuagesima (1 Cor. 9:24–10:4).

40. CE, on James 5:13ff.

Lefèvre maintained that St. James was not proposing extreme unction for those who were passing from this life to the next, but anointing with confession of sins and prayer for healing, in accordance with the exhortation of verse 16: "Therefore confess your sins to one another, and pray for one another, that you may be healed." In his exposition of this verse Lefèvre deplored the lack or loss among Christians of brotherly confession of sins one to another. He stressed, moreover, that confession must first be to God:

> Unless you first confess to God (since this should be done in faith, and faith has respect to God and his word) I judge confession of this kind to men, whether as it was formerly or as it is now, will be of little worth. Therefore he who confesses sins should above all intend to confess to God.

Scripture, Lefèvre affirmed, teaches a twofold confession: 1) confession from the heart to God, and 2) confession between Christians to each other for the reconciliation of offended and offending brothers. He objected that "the method of confessing sins which now prevails has superseded that which used to be practised, since men . . . do not make confessions in the primitive manner."[41]

The development of the confessional and priestly absolution was dependent on the interpretation of two texts granting authority to the clergy for the binding and loosing of sins. The texts were Matthew 16:18–19 ("You are Peter, and on this rock I will build my church, and the powers of death shall not prevail against it. I will give you the keys of the kingdom of heaven, and whatever you bind on earth shall be bound in heaven, and whatever you loose on earth shall be loosed in heaven") and John 20:22–23 ("He breathed on them and said to them, 'Receive the Holy Spirit. If you forgive the sins of any, they are forgiven; if you retain the sins of any, they are retained' "). The former passage was taken to mean that St. Peter was the rock on which Christ declared his church was to be founded, and that the power of the keys had been entrusted to St. Peter, and therefore to his successors by lineal transmission. Lefèvre, however, maintained that the rock of which Christ spoke was not St. Peter but his confession of Jesus as the Messiah and the Son of the living God (v. 16). This, as it happens, coincides with Aquinas' understanding of the verse.[42]

> From this solid confession of the truth, which is from God the Father and firmer than any rock [Lefèvre wrote], Simon received the designation Peter—and on this rock, the faith of unshakeable truth that Christ is the Son of the living God, the Lord founded his Church."

41. CE, on James 5:16.

42. See Thomas Aquinas, *Summa Theol.*, Part II. ii, Q. 174, Art. 6; also the commentary on Ephesians 2:6.

As for "the keys of the kingdom of heaven," they are, Lefèvre explained,

> the keys of faith, and the authority they convey is essentially the authority of the doctrine learned from Christ, who is the giver of the keys. Therefore Peter did not bind or loose by his own authority, but by the authority of Christ whose will is superlatively good and can never err. Nor did Peter alone receive them from the Lord, but all others also who have been built as the Church in faith on Christ, in accordance with the will of Christ the Lord.

That the keys were entrusted not to Peter only but to all the apostles was apparent, Lefèvre pointed out, from John 20:22-23; and that the keys should be understood to mean "the doctrine of faith, the doctrine of Christ, and the word of God" was shown by Luke 11:52, where Christ speaks of "the key of knowledge" that opens the way into the kingdom of heaven. Christ himself was seen using the keys when, after his resurrection, he opened the minds of the apostles to understand the Scriptures (Luke 24:45); but, Lefèvre adds, their understanding was unlocked "especially and most richly when the Holy Spirit was sent from heaven after the ascension" (cf. John 14:26; 15:26; 16:13-14). Lefèvre observed that "there are those who understand the keys as the pontifical power of binding and loosing"; but it was his conviction that "Christ is speaking here of this faith that he is the Son of the living God, which is one of the keys of heavenly doctrine and which he wished to be foundational."[43]

To the same effect, in his exhortation on John 20:22f. Lefèvre states that those who announce the forgiveness of sins do so in the name of Christ, since they are not themselves the source of forgiveness. The one basis of this announcement is the gospel, and the declaration of forgiveness is made specifically to those who believe the message of the gospel. "The forgiveness of the apostles," he affirms, "was only a sign of the true forgiveness which was already a reality on high"; and to the question, "And who are those who do not receive remission?", he answers, "Assuredly, those who do not believe in their message."[44] No ministry, then, can be more important than that of evangelism: "The most noble function and the most worthy office of any in this world is to proclaim the Gospel and to preach Jesus Christ, . . . for the salvation or the damnation of the soul depends on it."[45]

GUILLAUME FAREL

The intensity of Lefèvre's devotional life is graphically described by Guillaume Farel, the aristocratic Dauphinois who as a young man enjoyed

---

43. CG, on Matthew 16:18-19.

44. EG, Gospel for the First Sunday after Easter (Quasimodo) (John 20:19-30).

45. EG, Gospel for the Eighth Sunday after Pentecost (Matt. 7:15-21).

the benefit of Lefèvre's tutelage at the monastery of Saint-Germain-des-Prés and experienced an evangelical conversion under his instruction.[46] Some two decades later (in 1530), Farel, looking back on this time, wrote of the concentrated reverence with which Lefèvre used to pray and recite the offices. Deeply impressed by his dedicated spirituality, Farel told how he frequently and gladly kept him company in his devotions, and how Lefèvre had encouraged him to become a preacher of the gospel and had "often said to me that God would renew the world and that I would see it." Farel stated, further, that the manner in which Lefèvre (who had no doctorate) was defamed and persecuted by the professors of Paris, although "he knew more than all of them put together," destroyed the esteem with which he had previously regarded such academics.[47]

Farel graphically depicted the profound and indeed crucial influence Lefèvre's life and teaching had on him in a letter he wrote on 7 September 1527 from Aigle to Noel Galéot in Lausanne. His time as a student in Paris, he told Galéot, was a time of spiritual crisis. "The more I endeavored to advance and improve myself, the more I slipped backwards." He read many religious works, but they left him unsatisfied. "I wished to be a Christian like Aristotle," he explained, "whom virtually all treated as a Christian, hoping to eat good fruit from a bad tree." When he read the Scriptures he found them diametrically opposed to the way of life he was following and he was unwilling to accept what they plainly taught: "And so I, the most unhappy of all men, turned my eyes away from the light lest I should see." All this was changed, however, through what he learned from Lefèvre:

> But when God our most merciful Father . . . made himself known to me through the gentle guidance of a saintly brother [i.e., Lefèvre] and showed me that he is the only God, who alone is to be worshipped and loved, and that there is no other who can save or bless us—that he alone can blot out our sins for his own sake, through Christ our Mediator and Advocate, the propitiation for sins, since all are washed away by his blood—to him, after being driven hither and thither, my soul, once it had reached the haven, clung, and to him alone. Now things took on a new appearance; Scripture began to be full of meaning, the Prophets plain, the Apostles clear, the voice of the Shepherd, Master, and Teacher Christ recognized, asserting that "there is no access to the Father except through Jesus" [John 14:6], so that anyone who puts his whole trust in him, fully persuaded and believing that he is wisdom, righteousness, sanctification, and redemption [1 Cor.

---

46. In the anonymous symposium *Guillaume Farel 1489–1565: Biographie nouvelle écrite d'après les documents originaux par un groupe d'historiens, professeurs et pasteurs de Suisse, de France, et d'Italie* (Neuchâtel and Paris, 1930) one contributor asserts that Farel arrived in Paris in 1509 (pp. 99, 101), but another suggests a date some three years later. Herminjard (I:179) favors the earlier date.

47. *Epistre à tous seigneurs et peuples et pasteurs.* The text in my possession is given in a volume of Farel's writings entitled *Du vray usage de la croix de Jésus-Christ par Guillaume Farel suivi de divers écrits du même auteur* (Geneva, 1865), pp. 162–86.

1:30] has eternal life—so much so that in thanksgiving for the salvation provided through Christ he loves God for himself and in himself
and his neighbor for God and in God.[48]

Also through Lefèvre, Farel came to understand that there is no merit
in anyone except in Christ alone.

> By his instruction [Farel declared in 1530] he drew me away from false
> opinions of merit, teaching me that we have no merits at all, but that
> all comes from the grace and mercy of God alone, without anyone
> else possessing any merit. And I believed this as soon as it was said
> to me. It came about as a result of the manner in which I would con-
> clude my prayers by speaking of the merit of a particular saint; where-
> upon he on whom God had bestowed his grace propounded to me the
> pure invocation of God, and did so most convincingly, by referring
> me to the commandment of God and also to the ancient prayers of-
> fered on Sundays.

In 1519 Lefèvre commenced work on the compilation of a martyrology or
biographical handbook of the saints commemorated in the ecclesiastical
calendar;[49] but soon, struck by the dangers inherent in the cult of saints,
he abandoned the project, having completed no more than the first two
months of the calendar. Farel, with him at the time, recalled the occasion:

> When he understood the gross idoltry associated with prayers to the
> saints, and that these legends could be used like sulphur to light the
> fire, he left it all and after that devoted himself completely to Holy
> Scripture.

Farel described how he had at first found himself torn between respect for
the saints and respect for Lefèvre; but, he wrote, ''at last God enabled me
to acknowledge that he alone should be invoked and that all invocation of
the dead and of all those who are beyond this world, by which prayers are
offered to those absent as though they were present, is sheer idolatry.''
It was then, he added, that ''the holy word of God began to have first place
in my heart.''[50] Farel's reminiscences shed light on the theological formation of Lefèvre's mind and show him to have been a man who was concerned that his practice should match his conviction.

LEFÈVRE'S EVANGELICAL THEOLOGY

The evidence from Lefèvre's own writings sufficiently demonstrates
that the theological position he established for himself was distinctively

---

48. Herminjard, II:42ff.

49. *Agones martyrum.*

50. *Epistre à tous seigneurs et peuples et pasteurs.*

evangelical in character. Not only did he, like others in his day and before it, deplore the hypocrisy, the superstition, and the corruption that were so crippling to the church's effectiveness, but he also knew, by his own experience, that the grace and power of the gospel provided the dynamic remedy for these ills. He was possessed by the all-absorbing objective of making this remedy available, through his work of biblical exposition and translation, to all the people of France. Bedouelle, as we have noted,[51] has drawn attention to the fact that his teaching on justification, as early as 1509, anticipates that of the Reformers. The commentary of 1512 on the Pauline Epistles gives ample proof that before Luther, Zwingli, and Calvin had appeared on the scene, he had firmly grasped and propounded that evangelical faith which has commonly been regarded as the preserve of the theologians of the Reformation, and, what is more, that he did so in the precise terms or formulations that were destined to become the distinctive hallmarks of Reformed theology—in particular, "by grace alone" (*sola gratia*), "by faith alone" (*sola fide*), and "to God alone the glory" (*soli Deo gloria*).[52] Biblical truth and piety he now declares to be the only authentic truth and piety. He warned, for example, against those who wish to entice one to practice "a silly pietism contrary to the teaching of Christ," and against putting one's trust in the observance of Lenten fasts and the payment of church dues.

> What use is it [he asks] to trust in footling formulations whose authorship is uncertain and to leave undone the apostolic requirements? What use is it to die in a monk's cowl when you have lived your whole life in secular clothing? Such things are not commanded by Christ's teaching, which teaches that we should give heed for our salvation to the grace and mercy of God, and not to many other things which may be more superstitious than religious.[53]

If anything is plain, it is that Lefèvre and the Reformers were of one mind in their understanding of the fundamentals of the gospel. They were agreed that the sinner is justified by faith alone, through divine grace alone, solely on the basis of Christ's merit and the perfection of his atoning sacrifice, with the consequence that all the glory goes to God alone. They were at one in their acceptance of the authority of Holy Scripture as the word of God and in their demand that sincerity of believing should be attested by sanctity of living. There is an essential harmony in these matters that they held to be of central significance.

Regrettably, some scholars—seemingly governed by their private predispositions—have made Lefèvre's evangelicalism an issue of conten-

---

51. See p. 82 above.

52. See the passages quoted on pp. 74, 75, 79, and 85 above.

53. PE, on Romans 16:17-18.

tion. To assert, as François Wendel does, that "there was never any common measure between Lefèvre's religious aspirations and the dogmatics
of the Reform," and that "whatever has been advanced to show that Lefèvre
ever really adhered to the Reform or to its theological principles can be
cast into the limbo of contentious legend," is an example of the cavalier
manner in which Lefèvre is dismissed by a number of modern historians;
and when one is advised that this conclusion was reached "after an impar-
tial examination of Lefèvre's writings,"[54] one can only wonder whether
Lefèvre's biblical commentaries and expositions have been read and taken
into account.[55] W. G. Moore, when comparing Luther and Lefèvre, observes
with greater fairness that the latter "not only travelled the same road as
the German Reformer but at times was in advance of him," and he
deprecates the injustice of the opinion that in contrast to ardent spirits like
Luther and Farel Lefèvre was timid and unwilling to take risks: "He was,"
he declares, "above all a scholar, with an extremely open spirit, and
endowed with the same evangelical passion as Luther."[56] This is even more
true of the affinity between Lefèvre and Calvin. As Kenneth Strand has
stated, "one cannot but be impressed by the parallels between the religious
thought of Lefèvre and the Northern reformers [i.e., the Brethren of the
Common Life], on the one hand, and of Lefèvre and the later Protestant
Reformers, on the other." He rightly points out that "there are particularly striking similarities regarding such fundamental doctrinal matters as
the authority of Scripture and the meaning of justification by faith, as well
as in relationship to practices such as the use of the vernacular"; and he
adds that, "in some respects, Calvin's thought is even more similar than
Luther's to that of Lefèvre and the Dutch reformers."[57]

Today it serves little purpose to argue whether Lefèvre should be
claimed for Protestantism or for Roman Catholicism, or for one side to
denounce him as a compromiser and the other as a heretic. While it is true
that he never deserted the Church of Rome,[58] is is also true that he
wholeheartedly dedicated himself to the cause of biblical doctrine and felt
a deep affinity of mind and purpose with those who were promoting the

54. F. Wendel, *Calvin: The Origins and Development of his Religious Thought,* trans.
Philip Mairet (London, 1963), pp. 130, 42.

55. Cf. the surprising assertion of T. H. L. Parker that "Lefèvre did not teach, and was
not even moving towards, the Pauline and Lutheran doctrine of justification by faith alone,"
in *John Calvin: A Biography* (London, 1975), p. xiv. R.-J. Lovy is a Protestant author who
seems incapable of being sympathetic to Lefèvre; see *Les origines de la Réforme française,
Meaux, 1518-1546* (Paris, 1959), pp. 40ff. and passim.

56. W. G. Moore, *Réforme allemande et littérature française* (Strasbourg, 1930), pp.
70f. For a discussion of Lefèvre and Lutheranism see pp. 131f. below.

57. Kenneth A. Strand, "John Calvin and the Brethren of the Common Life," *Andrews
University Seminary Studies* 13 (1975):76.

58. The reasons for this are discussed below, pp. 189f.

reform of the church in other places (as his correspondence shows). It was not his nature, however, to resort to compromise or to give personal comfort precedence over faithfulness to evangelical truth. Guy Bedouelle, himself a Roman Catholic, has placed Lefèvre in what we consider to be the right perspective, seeing him neither as a Catholic with a bad conscience nor as a crypto-Protestant, but rather as an *evangelical* who firmly believed that the truth when positively proclaimed would triumph over error. He writes as follows:

> In no way do we deny the designation "evangelical" to Lefèvre, with all the connotations proper to the sixteenth century: it would without doubt have appeared to Lefèvre a special honor to be known as a man of the Gospel. His writings on the interpretation of Scripture, his letters that we still have, and his life in its entirety bear witness to this.

And we concur with Bedouelle's insistence that Lefèvre's thought should be regarded as "a heritage common to the Christians of the West," and that to understand it better will make it possible for us to understand each other better.[59]

---

59. Bedouelle, op. cit., pp. 234f.

Opposition and Controversy

LEFÈVRE AND REUCHLIN

The antipathy of the Sorbonne theologians toward Lefèvre, whose emphasis on authenticity constituted a judgment on their uncritical acceptance of the elaborate artificialities handed down from the medieval schoolmen, gathered momentum when he came to the defense of Johann Reuchlin in the agitation that followed the Pfefferkorn affair. Inspired, like many others, by Pico's confident affirmation that the cardinal doctrines of the Christian faith were fully approved in the secret tradition of the Jews known as the cabala, Reuchlin, as was mentioned earlier,[1] took up the study of Hebrew when he was approaching middle life and went on to become the leading Hebraist of the age. His Hebrew grammar, *The Rudiments of Hebrew*,[2] published in 1506, was eagerly used by scholars throughout Europe, including Lefèvre. Among those whom he instructed in the Hebrew language was his grandnephew Philipp Schwarzerd, who became famous as Melanchthon—the Greek equivalent of his German surname, which was given him by his great-uncle. (Reuchlin himself, while often referred to as Capnio and infrequently as Fumulus, Greek and Latin equivalents respectively of his surname, was not so successful in shedding his German patronymic.) In 1509 a Jew named Johann Pfefferkorn, who had been converted to the Christian faith, managed to persuade the Emperor Maximilian of the desirability of banning and burning all Hebrew books with the exception of the Bible. When Reuchlin expressed his opposition to such senseless destruction, observing that books that are not there to be read cannot be refuted, Pfefferkorn denounced him as a traitor to Christianity.

On 10 November the Alsatian scholar Beatus Rhenanus, one of Lefèvre's devoted disciples, wrote a letter to Reuchlin in which he praised Lefèvre as "a man beyond compare in every age and the most abundant

---

1. See pp. 21f. above.
2. *De Rudimentis Hebraicis.*

source of every kind of learning," describing him as responsible for the opening of a new day for philosophy "when it was suffering from excessive neglect and deprived of its native splendor;" he encouraged Reuchlin by informing him that Lefèvre had spoken of him as "the most elegant and beyond doubt the most learned of the Swabians."[3] Nearly four years later, Reuchlin started corresponding with Lefèvre, sending him a letter from Stuttgart dated 31 August 1513. After expressing admiration for Lefèvre's writings and appreciation of his cordial attitude of good will toward him, he expressed regret that, though he would have preferred to write of more pleasant matters, he must speak of the vexations that had beset him. These he attributed to the "new plague" that over the past two years had attacked him and could "be driven back neither by virtue nor by the weapons of verbal warfare"—and all this despite the fact that he had ever sought to benefit all and harm none. "This contagion," he wrote, "originated in Cologne where there is a certain species of most inhuman men called theologians. They consider no one learned other than themselves and regard themselves as the pillars of the Church." Moreover, they had a shocking record for the disgraceful persecution of worthy and learned persons.

> Now at length [Reuchlin complained] they have turned their attention to me, a completely innocent individual, with the purpose of besmirching my good name and reputation. This may be, in part, because they see that I have planted the seeds of Hebrew learning in Germany, although I have done so completely freely and without hope of financial reward, just as you, Lefèvre, consummate philosopher, have been the first to restore the falling ramparts of Aristotelianism.

Reuchlin remarked that, since distinguished German scholars acknowledged that they owed their familiarity with Greek and Hebrew to his initiative, the haughty pride of the hostile "barbarians" could not tolerate the spreading of his reputation, fearing that a posterity imbued with more illustrious scholarship would despise the puerile studies and effete disciplines that for so long had been accepted in his country. This was the reason, Reuchlin declared, that they had dared to calumniate him in a manner that was scandalous and abominable. The defense that he had prepared[4] accompanied this letter to Lefèvre. Rightly anticipating that among the Parisian professors hostility would show itself in accusations of insolence and rashness and even infidelity, Reuchlin appealed to Lefèvre to display his friendship by circulating this defense and supporting his cause.[5]

Lefèvre took up the cudgels on Reuchlin's behalf with vigor, but could make little headway against the prejudices of the Sorbonne academics. In September 1513 Reuchlin was summoned before the court of the Inquisi-

---

3. Herminjard, I:10.

4. *Jo. Reuchlini defensio contra calumniatores suos Colonienses* (Tübingen, 1513).

5. Herminjard, I:9ff.

tion, presided over by Pfefferkorn's friend Hoogstraten, and was charged
with heresy because of what he had written in his work entitled
Augenspiegel—his rejoinder to Pfefferkorn's *Handspiegel*, which had
accused him of treacherously favoring Judaism rather than Christianity.
Reuchlin appealed to the Pope (Leo X), who in turn passed the case on
to the bishop of Speyer. The latter not only pronounced Reuchlin innocent
of the charge of heresy but also ordered Hoogstraten to pay the costs of
the hearing. Hoogstraten and the Cologne Dominicans then appealed to
Rome against this decision, which in 1516 had been confirmed by the
Vatican, and, after considerable delay, the judgment in favor of Reuchlin
was in fact overturned. That took place in 1520, but, apparently, to little
effect, for by that time the sympathy for Reuchlin's position that flowed
from humanistic scholars had brought about a more tolerant and enlightened
climate of opinion—a climate, however, from which the Sorbonne
scholastics persistently isolated themselves.

Meanwhile, in the spring of 1514, the professors of the Sorbonne
received the dossier against Reuchlin from the professors of Cologne. They
responded by commending them for so zealously defending the faith and
promised a thorough investigation. In June Reuchlin wrote from Stuttgart,
sending a copy of his *Augenspiegel* together with a summary account of
the developments in the affair, and reminding the Parisian professors that
he had formerly been a student in their city. His request that they should
not take the side of his enemies was supported by a letter from Duke Ulrich
of Würtemberg who urged the Parisians not to meddle in an affair on which
a ruling had already been given by the bishop of Speyer in accordance with
the authority delegated to him by the Pope and in which personal animosity
played so large a part. The Dominicans of Cologne, however, exhorted
them all the more strongly to take action and by way of extra ammunition
supplied them with a copy of Reuchlin's *Defense*.

On 2 August the Sorbonne professors met to consider the evidence and
pronounce a verdict. They declared the *Augenspiegel* blasphemous and
suspect of heresy in some of its teachings, favorable to Jewish perfidy rather
than Christian truth, and offensive to the faithful. The lash of their hostility
struck at Lefèvre as well as Reuchlin, not only because he had done all
in his power to vindicate their victim but also because the vigor of his learning and spirituality was in itself a threat to their complacency. On 30 August
Lefèvre wrote to Reuchlin:

> The mob has conquered; they have done precisely what the men of Cologne
> wanted them to do. Your friends have one consolation, however, because
> we hope that this judgment, since it is only scholastic, will do little or
> no harm to your cause. We are all praying that God will grant this. And
> so·we ask you to be of good cheer and to conduct your case boldly before
> your own judges. A victory for you will be a victory for us also.[6]

6. Ibid., pp. 15ff.

THE LATIN OF THE VULGATE

The censorious judgment of the University of Paris against Reuchlin served to stimulate antagonism toward Lefèvre, who had forthrightly supported Reuchlin's cause. The previous accusation of tampering with the venerable Latin of the Vulgate version and presuming to publish a Latin translation of his own[7] now gathered momentum. This antagonism also drew Erasmus into its vortex. In September 1514, Maarten Van Dorp in Louvain had written a courteous but critical letter to Erasmus (which never reached him; however, he did see a copy when he was in Antwerp, which enabled him to reply belatedly to it). Van Dorp advised Erasmus that his *Praise of Folly* (1509) had caused offense, even among those raised in the humanities, and suggested that it might be well to counterbalance it by writing, in a more positive and pleasing vein, a "Praise of Wisdom." He commended Erasmus for working on a corrected edition of the letters of Jerome and on the revision and annotation of the New Testament text, but then warned him against attempting to purge the Scriptures of errors, and in particular to improve on the Latin Vulgate version by comparing it with the Greek, as Valla and Lefèvre had presumed to do.

Van Dorp was unwilling to question the accuracy and integrity of the Vulgate, since he found it impossible to accept that "the whole Church, which has always used and still now approves and uses this edition, has been mistaken for all these centuries," or that "so many holy fathers, so many outstanding men, were deceived when they relied on this version as in the general councils they resolved the most difficult questions, defended and expounded the faith, and published canons to which even kings submitted." He maintained, indeed, that the infallibility of the general councils depended on this version. Furthermore, he asked, by what criterion did Erasmus conclude that copies of the Greek text were impaired by fewer errors than the Latin? Considerations of this kind prevented Van Dorp from entertaining a high opinion of the labors of Valla and Lefèvre, nor did he see that the immense toil involved had contributed anything, except for those places where the sense of a passage was clarified. Meddling with Scripture could be expected to have only an unsettling effect on the populace, arousing doubts about its reliability and crippling its authority.[8]

In his response to this letter, written from Antwerp in May 1515, Erasmus took the critical comments of Van Dorp in good part. Though he wasted no time in replying, he explained that he was fatigued by his travels by sea and on horseback and was busy preparing to set off again, with the result that, to his regret, he was unable to write at leisure. Nonetheless, he wrote an extremely lengthy missive. The first and longer portion is a

---

7. See pp. 71ff. above.
8. Allen, II:11ff.

sustained defense of his *Praise of Folly*. In the concluding section he demonstrated without difficulty the flimsy character of Van Dorp's cavils concerning the correction of the Vulgate, as the following excerpts show:

> You consider it indefensible to dislodge in any respect something that has enjoyed approval by the agreement of so many centuries and by so many synods. I ask you, most learned Dorp, if what you write is true, why do Jerome and Augustine and Ambrose so frequently cite a text different from the one read by us? Why does Jerome find fault with many things and correct them one by one—corrections which are still present in our edition? . . . If there is one thing that cries out and is abundantly plain, even, as they say, to a blind man, it is that through the incompetence or negligence of the translator the Greek has been rendered incorrectly, that the genuine and authentic reading has been corrupted by ignorant scribes, something we see happening every day, and often enough altered by persons who are half-taught and half-asleep. Who encourages falsification more, he who corrects and restores these passages, or he who would rather see an error added than removed?—bearing in mind that it is the nature of such corruptions that one error generates another. . . . It is not unusual for the text to have gone completely astray; and whenever this happens, where, I ask you, do Augustine, Ambrose, Hilary, and Jerome take refuge if not in the Greek original? . . . When, moreover, you write that there should be no departure from an edition that enjoys the approval of so many councils, you are behaving like one of the popular theologians, whose custom it is to attribute to the authority of the Church anything that has somehow slipped into common usage. Just produce one synod for me in which this edition was approved.

In any case, it would be hard to imagine a synod approving a text of unknown authorship; "for that it is not Jerome's is attested by Jerome's own prefaces." (Thus Erasmus stood by the position previously propounded by Lefèvre.)

But even if it be granted that some synod approved it, did it do so in such a way that to correct it by comparison with the Greek original was completely forbidden? And did it approve all the errors that in one way or another might creep in, affirming perpetual complaisance with any distortion, corruption, addition, or omission for which incompetent copyists might be responsible? How, furthermore, is one to handle the fact that different copies of the Vulgate itself are not in agreement with each other?

Erasmus went on to speak scornfully of "those most falsely named theologians whose sole outlook is that what they themselves have learned should alone be treated as of any value."

> But what have they learned that is not the most inept and confounded rubbish? Should they ever gain control, the world would be compelled to accept their absurd drivelings as oracles in place of the best authors of antiquity. . . . These are the persons who do not wish any text to be

restored, lest it should appear that there is something of which they are ignorant. Such persons block my way with the feigned authority of synods; they pile up a great threat to the Christian faith; they proclaim that the Church is in danger (presuming to support it on their own shoulders, when they would be better occupied supporting a farm-wagon) and spread rumors to this effect among the untutored and superstitious mob, by whom they are taken for learned theologians—a reputation they have no desire to lose. They are fearful that when they misquote Scripture, as they frequently do, the authority of the genuine Greek or Hebrew text will be cast in their teeth and it will rapidly become evident that what they propounded as an oracle is worthless nonsense.

Erasmus assured Van Dorp that he was well aware that Valla had occupied himself with similar studies, for it was he who had first published Valla's *Annotations* (in 1505), and that he was also familiar with Lefèvre's commentary on the Pauline Epistles. He considered Valla worthy of the highest praise because, despite the fact that his field was that of rhetoric rather than theology, he had taken pains in his biblical studies to compare the Greek original with the Latin versions, "while there are any number of theologians who have never read the New Testament right through in its entirety." He (Erasmus) had indeed been anticipated by Lefèvre, whose commentary on the Pauline Epistles was completed while he was still preparing his own work on the New Testament. He also expressed his wholehearted approval of Lefèvre's achievement.

That Van Dorp should have drawn attention to Valla and Lefèvre as though they were obstacles in his way puzzled Erasmus. He refused, however, to be deterred, pointing out that their labors were not identical. Valla had annotated only a limited number of passages, and not in any depth, and Lefèvre's commentary was confined to the letters of St. Paul, with his own translation and the addition of critical notes where there might be some discrepancy; whereas he was translating the whole New Testament, carefully scutinizing copies of the Greek text, giving the Greek original and his Latin version side by side so that all could make their own comparison, and adding separate notes to explain and justify his emendations. He was confident that his work would be welcomed by responsible persons in the church, starting with the pope.[9]

During these same years the distinguished Primate of Spain, Cardinal Ximenes de Cisneros, himself a serious scholar and patron of sound learn-

---

9. Ibid., pp. 91ff. In the third of the prefaces "to the reader" in volume 2 of his edition of the works of Jerome, dated a couple of months prior to Van Dorp's letter, Erasmus had drawn attention to the fact that Jerome did not hesitate to correct his own translation, and he asked in what way Lorenzo Valla had detracted from the truth of the gospel because he, "a rhetorician rather than a theologian, took exception to a number of passages that had been falsely rendered by the translator." He observed, also, the Lefèvre had followed Valla's example when "he altered many places affected by corruption or bad translation" (Allen, II:57).

ing, had assembled a team of scholars at the University of Alcala (of which he was the founder). It was this team that produced the celebrated Complutensian Polyglot Bible (Complutum being the old Roman name for Alcala). The New Testament, based on a careful comparison of numerous Greek manuscripts, was completed first and printed in January 1514. The Old Testament was ready and printed in July 1517. The whole Bible consisted of six large and superbly crafted volumes in a limited edition of 600 copies. However, due to the procrastinations of ecclesiastical officialdom, the actual publication was held up until 1522. The delay allowed Erasmus and his printer Froben to produce with unseemly haste their own edition of the New Testament and to place it on the market in advance of the appearance of the Complutensian Bible. Erasmus's volume even followed the format of the Complutensian New Testament; but the Greek text was prepared from a collation of only six or seven late and incomplete manuscripts, and the hurry to be first in bringing it out led to the presence of many errors that proper scholarly oversight would not have left uncorrected. Thus, in 1516, when the Complutensian New Testament had been in print but unpublished for more than two years, Erasmus's New Testament appeared and was greeted with enthusiasm in the academic circles of Europe.

Like Lefèvre, Erasmus desired to liberate the scholarship of his day from the sophistries of medievalism and to direct it back to the study of the sources, in particular to the study of the text of Scripture as the source essential for purging the church of corruption. And like Lefèvre, Erasmus was not spared the attention of hostile critics. As an integral part of his New Testament (*Novum Instrumentum*) he published an addendum of explanatory notes (*Annotationes*), thus following Valla. These notes are interesting and valuable, but they are quite different from the extensive theological exposition of the sacred text that Lefèvre gives in his commentary on the Epistles of Paul. For Erasmus, as for Lefèvre, the "philosophy of Christ" was the absolutely pure source; unlike Lefèvre, however, Erasmus was more the philologist than the theologian.[10]

The nature of the opposition to his work is disclosed in a letter written to Henry Bullock in Cambridge during the latter part of August 1516, a letter which, as Allen observes, in places closely resembles the *Apologia* prefixed to the first edition of his New Testament earlier that year. Erasmus complains that his critics make no attempt to refute or correct what they consider is wrong in his writings, but simply condemn him for having written at all, denying the propriety of undertaking any revision of the biblical text without the authorization of a general council of the church. He charges that such persons condemn and tear to pieces a book that they have not read, or, if they have, that they are incapable of understanding.

---

10. See John William Aldridge, *The Hermeneutic of Erasmus* (Zürich and Richmond, 1966).

> What [he complains] could be more unjust than this? These are the very persons who daily pervert the sacred writings, having nothing to offer except their own reckless ignorance. Shall we not be permitted to restore what has been corrupted by reference to the mind of the ancient authors apart from the calling of a council of the whole Christian world?

They are unwilling to sanction even the correction of textual errors so obvious that they make nonsense if allowed to stand.

> They cry out hysterically, "O heaven, O earth, this fellow is correcting the Gospel!" How much more just it would have been to exclaim against the one responsible for the corruption, "O sacrilege, he is the one who is perverting the Gospel!" We have not in fact produced a new edition, but according to our ability have restored the old.

Erasmus points out that in doing this he has the excellent company of Lefèvre:

> Our friend Jacques Lefèvre d'Etaples has already done for Paul what I have done for the whole New Testament. Why then should certain persons make such a commotion, as though it were something entirely new? Or are they unwilling to permit me alone to do what they are willing to permit all others to do? Lefèvre has actually been a good deal more daring than I. He has set his own translation over against the old, and that too in Paris, the queen of all universities, whereas I, claiming to be no more than a reviser, offer a number of corrections or explanations. I do not say this to involve Lefèvre in their ill will, for thanks to his glorious reputation he has long since passed beyond the reach of ill will, but in order that it may be plain to all how unjust is the conduct of certain persons who censure in me, as though it were something unprecedented and novel, what for a long time has been practised by many without censure.

In point of fact, as has been mentioned and as will become plainer still hereafter, Lefèvre was by no means beyond the reach of ill will, but he was able to bear it with greater equanimity than the thin-skinned Erasmus. Erasmus, at any rate, was sure enough of his scholarship to issue this challenge:

> In a number of places I show that Hilary made a mistake, and Augustine, and Thomas, but I do it, as one should, respectfully and without being abusive, in such a way that if they were still alive they would be grateful to me for any such admonishment. They were very great men, but nonetheless they were men. Let my critics prove the correctness of their judgment, and let them refute me with arguments, not with abuse, and they will find me sincerely grateful.[11]

A few years later, in 1519, Henry Cornelius Agrippa of Nettesheim

---

11. Allen, II:321ff.

denounced the opposition to Lefèvre and Erasmus, while defending a number of propositions he had published "against a certain Dominican who had attacked them:"

> There is no lack of envious and pestilential detractors who, together with you, defame Erasmus of Rotterdam and Jacques Lefèvre d'Etaples. Certain third-rate Parisian theologians wished to condemn the latter for heresy, because he had asserted, with the support of logical arguments, that the current translation of the New Testament, which you and your fellow pygmy sophists have attributed to Jerome, was not in fact the work of Jerome. In doing this, however, it is themselves they have blackened for ever before the world by the shame of their ignorance and malice, while at the same time bringing disgrace on the whole Sorbonne.[12]

Returning to 1515, we note that with the appearance of the *Metaphysics*, Lefèvre concluded his ambitious project, the publication of an authentic version of the works of Aristotle. The Latin translation was that of Bessarion, done in the middle of the previous century but hitherto unpublished. Included in the same volume were the translation by Argyropoulos of the first twelve books of the same work, completed c. 1460 and previously published in Venice in 1496; Bessarion's translation of the *Metaphysics* of Theophrastus; and Lefèvre's own *Introduction* to Aristotle's *Metaphysics* with the four dialogues that had first been published in 1494, more than twenty years previously. In the dedicatory letter addressed to Robert Fortuné, principal of the Collège du Plessis (who had published the writings of Hilary and Cyrpian in 1511 and 1512), Lefèvre explained that the manuscript of the Bessarion translation had been given to him by Pico della Mirandola. He took the opportunity to commend Fortuné for the manner in which he always endeavored to effect a combination of learning and morality and to engage professors whose instruction was marked by authenticity and not at all by silliness and barbarity—a thrust by Lefèvre at the ineptitude of his adversaries at the Sorbonne.[13]

This, to all intents and purposes, was Lefèvre's farewell to Aristotle; though it should be mentioned that in 1518 an edition of Aristotle's works on natural philosophy was brought out by the young scholar François Vatable, Lefèvre's disciple and fellow Picard, who had undertaken the preparation of this edition at Lefèvre's instigation (as the prefatory letter addressed to Guillaume Briçonnet, in which Vatable describes Lefèvre as "my Mycaenas and mentor," makes clear).[14] The Latin translation was

---

12. Herminjard, I:58; cf. also the similar denunciation by the anonymous editor of "The First Part of the Works of the reverend father and doctor of sacred theology Martin Luther," in the preface addressed to "authentic theologians"; ibid., pp. 61f.

13. Rice, pp. 355ff.

14. Ibid., pp. 406ff.

Vatable's. Lefèvre's energies were now being fully devoted to the translation and exposition of the biblical text.

LEFÈVRE'S FRIENDSHIP WITH ERASMUS

Erasmus and Lefèvre, who were revered by their contemporaries as the leading scholars of the age, were alike in their aversion to the meretricious artificialities that passed for scholarship in many academic circles and to the superstitions and corruptions that stifled the effective witness of the church; they both labored for the revival of sound learning and pure religion; and they were attracted to each other by sentiments of friendship and respect. Endowed with a more equable temperament and a more profound mind than Erasmus, Lefèvre, who had penetrated deeply to the evangelical heart of things, was much more bold and positive in his championing of the gospel. Though he could express himself plainly, and on occasion scornfully, when referring to those whom he regarded as promoters of error, Lefèvre was free of the savage satirical vein that was present in the make-up of Erasmus. Erasmus, however, was the more urbane and elegant, the more polemically incisive, and also the more personally sensitive to criticism of the two. He seemed to be braver on paper than in direct encounter. Moreover, his facetiousness did not always become his dignity.

The cordial feelings of esteem and affection that Erasmus had for Lefèvre are not infrequently expressed in his writings. For example, in March 1515 he wrote of Lefèvre as "a man admirable no less for the integrity of his life than for his learning," and affirmed, "I hold Lefèvre in the highest esteem as a man extraordinarily erudite; I venerate him as the very best of persons; I cherish him as a very dear friend."[15] That these feelings were fully reciprocated is apparent, again by way of example, in a letter of 5 August 1516 sent to Erasmus from Paris by Thomas Grey,[16] who passed on Lefèvre's greetings in the following terms:

> He required me to salute you in his name with the utmost warmth and to say that he has not written to you for any other reason than that he is unable either to write or to dictate anything [owing to the illness with which he was then stricken]; but, as I say, he holds you in the greatest affection, he praises you before all as not only most learned but also most diligent, and, if I am any judge, he is genuinely devoted to you.

Believing, in fact, that Lefèvre had not much longer to live, Grey assured Erasmus that "the nearer he draws to the death of the flesh, the more he

---

15. In the third of the prefaces addressed "to the reader" published in the second volume of his edition of the works of Jerome; Allen, II:57.

16. The letter has already been alluded to on p. x above.

is alive in spirit.''[17] As things turned out, however, Lefèvre recovered his strength and survived for another twenty years.

But it was just at this time that a cloud cast a shadow over their friendship. In the second (1515) edition of his commentary on the Pauline Epistles Lefèvre added a lengthy excursus after the exposition of the second chapter of the Epistle to the Hebrews.[18] This excursus discussed the interpretation of Psalm 8:5, "Thou didst make him a little lower than *elohim*," an assertion that in Hebrews 2:5-9 is applied directly to Christ. The question under discussion revolved primarily around the translation of the Hebrew term *elohim*, which in the Old Testament is commonly an appellation of God but is also on occasion used of exalted spiritual—that is, angelic—beings. In his own Latin translation Lefèvre has "lower than God,"[19] despite the fact that the Greek reads quite unequivocally "lower than angels." This Greek reading, however, he attributed to Paul's translator, maintaining that Paul had written the epistle in the Hebrew language and that the translator had mistakenly followed the Greek of the Septuagint, which renders the expression "lower than the angels."[20] Lefèvre added this excursus because Erasmus had stated in his *Annotations* that "lower than angels" (the Vulgate rendering in both Ps. 8 and Heb. 2) was the correct and appropriate translation. Both Erasmus and Lefèvre agreed that the passage in the Epistle to the Hebrews referred to the self-humiliation of the incarnate Son. Certainly, the rendering "lower than the angels" suits the context, in which the author of the epistle is demonstrating the Son's superiority over the angels. After humbling himself for the redemption of humankind, the Son, and with him our humanity, was exalted to glory far above the angels. But this is a consideration that Lefèvre apparently failed to take into account.

Lefèvre, on the other hand, was concerned lest making Christ "lower than the angels" should humble him too far and thus pose a threat to the reality of his divine dignity. The issue, as he saw it, was one of Christology. But Christology reaches downward as well as upward, and Lefèvre's position might be seen in turn as posing a threat to the reality of Christ's humanity. Erasmus, in fact, charged Lefèvre with tending toward a docetic position in the *Apologia* that he hurriedly wrote and published as a rejoinder to Lefèvre's criticisms.[21] Both scholars, however, were essentially orthodox in their Christology, and this dispute is a good example of the way in which academic controversy can promote an exaggerated polarization. Erasmus

---

17. Allen, II:287f.

18. PE, fol. 225v–229v.

19. Ibid., fol. 56v; this is the rendering he adopts in the commentary on Hebrews 2:7, fol. 224v.

20. The Pauline authorship of the Epistle to the Hebrews was commonly accepted at that time, and had been since the fifth century.

21. *Apologia Erasmi Roterodami ad eximium virum Iacobum Fabrum Stapulensem.*

claimed the support of both Scripture and the patristic authors for his assertion that Christ in his incarnation had been humbled "below even the most
abject of men," citing the messianic 22nd Psalm ("I am a worm and no
man, scorned by men and despised by the people;" v. 6) and Philippians
2:5ff. ("who, though he was in the form of God, . . . emptied himself,
taking the form of a servant . . . he humbled himself and became obedient
unto death, even death on a cross").

Something else Lefèvre took exception to was Erasmus's understanding
of the expression "little" in a temporal sense, so that he translated the
passage to read "Thou didst make him for a little while lower than the
angels." This was a perfectly legitimate way of taking it, but Lefèvre
objected strenuously, insisting that the expression denoted the degree of
Christ's humiliation. Accordingly, he rendered the sentence "Thou didst
make him to a small degree lower than God"—also, grammatically, a
legitimate interpretation. Erasmus's was the stronger position, however.
Lefèvre, for his part, assailed Erasmus's interpretation "with passion as
impious and totally unbecoming to Christ and God, and as opposing the
spirit and adhering to the letter which kills."[22] The accusation of literalism
may seem somewhat surprising in view of the fact that Lefèvre himself
devotes considerable space in his excursus to the discussion of the literal
meaning of the terms around which the dispute revolved. But he was undoubtedly motivated by a desire to be true to his own principle of interpretation, which postulated not only the barrenness of the bare literal sense
but also the coincidence of the literal and spiritual senses by which one is
led in particular to the christological significance of the text.[23] Understood
in this light, the accusation of literalism was in effect a charge that Erasmus's
exposition was christologically inadequate.

This consideration helps us to comprehend the other accusation, namely,
that, of impiety. The concept of "impiety," and indeed the very term, is
little used in our day; but at the time of this controversy it denoted an act
or attitude of ungodliness that could be regarded as virtually heretical.
Erasmus reacted vigorously: he regarded the charge as outrageous; it
impugned not only his theological perception but also (though Lefèvre could
hardly have intended this) the genuineness of his profession as a Christian;
it demanded a response and a refutation. And so he sat down and wrote
his *Apologia*, which was published on 5 August 1517. He recognized that
Lefèvre was certainly not impelled by any feelings of personal animosity.
In fact, at the beginning of his excursus Lefèvre speaks of the different
opinion held by "my friend Erasmus." Nor does Erasmus cease to describe

---

22. PE, fol. 226v. Lefèvre's wording reflects a common misconception of the meaning
of the assertion of 2 Corinthians 3:6 that "the letter kills but the spirit gives life," which
is surprising since in his commentary on that passage he has no place for this interpretation,
but rightly defines the distinction as being between the old (Mosaic) and the new covenants.

23. See pp. 58f., 60ff. above.

Lefèvre as his friend. In the *Apologia* he recalls the "frequent, prolonged, and intimate conversations" he had enjoyed in Paris with Lefèvre. Soon afterward he wrote from Louvain to Louis Ber in Basel:

> I am sad about Lefèvre, who has compelled me to respond to him in a hateful disputation. . . . May I perish if I would not much rather fill a huge volume praising instead of refuting him.[24]

A couple of weeks later, on 7 September, in a letter to Marc Laurin of Bruges, he claimed a distasteful victory:

> All are agreed that I have got the better of Lefèvre, but, as God loves me, it is a victory that I loathe. Would that anything had entered his mind other than to provoke me to this contest! I love the man with all my heart, but in this matter he did not do himself justice.[25]

And the next day he wrote in similar terms to John Fisher, bishop of Rochester:

> I am sending you the *Apologia* in which I reply to Jacques Lefèvre. All theologians, even including all Lefèvre's supporters, are unanimous in judging me the winner. But I hate the necessity that drew me into this contest; I hate gaining a victory over a man so dear to me.[26]

Erasmus let another three days pass and then sent the following letter to Lefèvre:

> Those who wish us both well, most excellent Lefèvre, are sad for both of us. I cannot imagine what divinity so perversely put it into your mind, when there was no call for it, to provoke me to a disputation so hateful, and to do so in such a way that it would have been blameworthy for me to remain silent, short of pleading guilty to all those accusations. . . . Though fully occupied with other concerns, and though this kind of authorship is especially abhorrent to me, I find myself compelled to do battle with a man for long particularly dear to me. This, moreover, is a cause of rejoicing to those who are ill disposed to us and to the worthier kind of studies. They now have an excuse for reproaching us both, for assailing our reliability, for finding comfort in their own ignorance. May Christ be displeased with me if I do not hate not only this necessity but also this victory, which all unanimously grant me. Therefore, my dear Lefèvre, I beseech you by all that you hold sacred, let there be an end to this ungodly conflict.

Erasmus advised Lefèvre that with this letter he was sending him a

---

24. Allen, III:50.

25. Ibid., p. 73.

26. Ibid., p. 75. The claim that he had been unanimously awarded the victory may be regarded as an Erasmian exaggeration.

copy of his *Apologia;* he asked him to read it through carefully and to reconsider the whole issue; and he begged that "genuine and truly Christian sincerity" should prevail between them. "In me," he concluded, "you will find no deception."[27]

At the end of November Erasmus wrote again to Lefèvre:

> I sent you my *Apologia* in which I reply to your disputation or rather accusation. If it caused you offense, the fault is yours. There were so many and such atrocious charges that I could not and ought not to overlook them. This is the unanimous judgment of all who have read what you have written. If you do respond, I beg you to keep in mind what is worthy of Lefèvre, if you have any concern for our friendship, which, I assure you, I could not value more highly. You see how many resort to the insanity of spreading slanders: let us not provide such persons with an opportunity. I am ready to be taught and to be corrected; but I will not endure the charge of impiety against Christ when I do not deserve it. Farewell, most excellent man; continue to love me, as you have in the past, for I love you with all my heart.[28]

The following February Erasmus sent a long letter to Guillaume Budé, much of which was devoted to discussing the controversy with Lefèvre. Here, too, he showed how deeply he felt the threat posed by the conflict to his friendship with Lefèvre. "I do not imagine," he wrote, "that there are many who wish Lefèvre well more cordially than I."

> I was aware of the very inequitable condition of this contest, in which, if I should be conquered, I would have to acknowledge the guilt of impiety; whereas, if I should conquer, I would be liable to the charge of inhumanity since I would seem to be fighting with a close friend. . . . But I beseech you, as a just man, what would you wish me to do, when he has attacked me with so many atrocious statements in books distributed throughout the world and has publicly accused me of blasphemy and impiety?

Lefèvre, Erasmus insisted, was a friend on whom he had inflicted no injury; indeed, he had shown himself in this business to be on his side rather than against him, and only wished that his own injury had been of such a kind that he could have ignored it or endured it with restraint.

> I would gladly have condoned it whether for the sake of our friendship or in the interests of Christian propriety or for the benefit of sound learning. But piety itself particularly prohibits toleration of the calumny of impiety.

---

27. Ibid., p. 81f.
28. Ibid., p. 152.

Erasmus protested his own innocence and deplored Lefèvre's attack as a lapse of friendship. He objected, moreover, that, even if he had happened to be at fault, Lefèvre should have honored their friendship by keeping the matter private and admonishing him with personal letters. He insisted that he himself would never contend against Lefèvre over the New Testament unless he were convinced that his friend's reputation would in no way be besmirched. "Even though injured and provoked, I have not violated our friendship, nor, as far as in me lies, will I ever do so." Even now, when he felt obliged to refute an intolerable calumny, he wished to do so without occasioning his friend any sort of harm.[29]

That Erasmus felt ill used is plain. The sincerity of his protestations of friendship for Lefèvre need not be doubted. Evidently Lefèvre, carried away by a misconceived zeal, was guilty in this instance of exaggeration. He had made a great issue out of a small question that should have been readily and amiably resolved. Yet it is only fair to conclude that his disagreement, however excessive the language in which it was expressed, was not at all intended to damage his friendship with Erasmus. The latter's *Apologia* was no less hard-hitting and no punches were pulled. How was it, Erasmus asked, that through all the preceding centuries no one had denounced the rendering "lower than the angels" as a dreadful affront to the glory of Christ? Furthermore, if this rendering was in fact "false, impious, heretical, and contrary to Holy Scripture," why did Lefèvre delay to demand the summoning of a general council to regulate this matter for the whole of Christendom by the abolition of an error so gross and so universally accepted? There is an interesting comment on this controversy in a letter from Luther to Spalatin dated 18 January 1518, which concludes with these words:

> I shall say nothing about Erasmus's *Apologia*, but I am very sorry that such a conflict should have broken out between these great princes of learning. Erasmus is certainly by far the superior of the two, and he is a greater master of language. However, he is also more violent, though he makes a great effort to preserve friendship.[30]

The force of this *contretemps* soon subsided, and deservedly so. The friendship survived, little if any the worse for it, and was reinforced by the development of crises of a more serious nature in which the two scholars mutually aided each other. Moreover, his earlier denunciations notwithstanding, Lefèvre was apparently humble enough to withdraw from his position and to come to the same mind as Erasmus, for in his translation of the New Testament into French, published in 1524, he followed the Greek

---

29. Ibid., pp. 223ff.

30. *Luther's Works*, Vol. 48, Letters I (1963), p. 55, trans. G. G. Krodel. For the Latin: WA Br.1,134.

(and the Latin of the Vulgate) by rendering Hebrews 2:7 "a little lower than the angels."[31]

Meanwhile the indignation against Lefèvre for meddling with the text of the Vulgate had not died down. We have already seen how Erasmus defended his friend in response to the disapproval expressed by Maarten Van Dorp of Louvain.[32] At the same time, George Civis,[33] canon of the cathedral of Tournai, listed in a letter (of 12 December 1514) to Josse Clichtove the four main objections to Lefèvre's treatment of the Vulgate as propounded by the theologians of Louvain. Civis, who had been friendly with Clichtove since their student days together at the Sorbonne, was favorably disposed toward Lefèvre and his work, but felt himself unable to reply in a satisfactory manner to the objections alleged against him, and so he turned to Clichtove for an adequate rejoinder. Clichtove, one of Lefèvre's many notable disciples (though he later sided against his master), promptly composed a defense, which he sent to Civis on 26 February 1515.

But Louvain was not the only center of opposition (as will become increasingly apparent). Denunciations, in fact, were already being voiced in Rome itself and these drew forth a defense of Lefèvre, simultaneous with that of Clichtove, from the Franciscan cardinal Marco Vigerio, as we learn from a letter of 29 May 1515 to Beatus Rhenanus from Michael Hummelberg, who was then studying law in Rome. "I considered the *Apologia* of the cardinal of Senigallia[34] on behalf of our friend Lefèvre d'Etaples not unworthy of your perusal," Hummelberg wrote to Rhenanus. He observed that there was "a numerous army of those who, since they are incompetent

---

31. Lefèvre's French reads "un peu moindre que les anges." One question remains as yet unresolved: how is it that the second edition of Lefèvre's commentary on the Epistles of St. Paul, which is dated 1515—at the conclusion of the section on the Epistle to the Hebrews (fol. 258r)—contains the excursus discussed above on Erasmus's New Testament and *Annotations*, which were not published until the beginning of March 1516? One solution proposed is that it was simply a matter of misdating, so that 1515 should read 1516. Another is that the printer, Henri Estienne, was following the old style of dating, so that 1515 would in fact be the equivalent of 1516 by our present reckoning. Neither of these suggestions, however, is really satisfactory. It is more likely that Lefèvre received prior information or had a preview of what Erasmus had written for his printer, Froben, who is known to have commenced the printing at the beginning of October 1515. Lefèvre, we may suppose, hurriedly composed his excursus for inclusion in the second edition of his commentary; indeed, Estienne may be assumed to have had the type set for the new edition, with the dating 1515, and then to have delayed publication so that he could make adjustments for the insertion of the excursus. This could have been done with relatively small inconvenience since the Hebrews commentary comes near the end of the volume. A reconstruction of the sequence of events along these lines, admittedly hypothetical, would allow for the actual appearance of this second edition being held up until some time after the beginning of the year 1516.

32. See pp. 104ff. above.

33. "Civis" may well be the Latin equivalent of the name "Bourgeois," as Renaudet and Massaut suspect.

34. Vigerio had been bishop of Senigallia since 1477.

to produce from themselves anything of note, spend their time finding fault with men of learning and repute,'' adding that ''those who are attempting to trump up charges of heresy against Lefèvre'' belong to their company.[35]

Clichtove's *Apologia* remained unpublished, but the manuscript is preserved in the Bibliothèque Mazarine in Paris and the Latin text, together with a French translation, has recently been published by Jean-Pierre Massaut.[36] In the introductory section, Clichtove stated his approbation of the manner in which Civis cites the example of Jerome as a pattern to be followed by commentators, whose task is to recover the clear and authentic sense of Scripture by comparing faulty Latin translations with the Greek original. This, he affirmed, was precisely what Lefèvre had done, as all who read him attentively and without prejudice must acknowledge. That Jerome and Lefèvre should offer different interpretations of a number of passages was not surprising, because a particular word may have a variety of significances and different commentators may form their judgment on the basis of different considerations. This was obvious enough in the history of exegesis. Jerome and Augustine, for instance, disagreed over their understanding of the significance of Paul's rebuke to Peter (Gal. 2:11ff.). ''What then should prevent our commentator from departing from Jerome in a number of places when he has a compelling reason to do so or follows a reliable author with whose judgment he concurs?'' The formulation of the four specific objections and Clichtove's refutation of them need not detain us here. Suffice it to say that the nature of the objections could scarcely be said to have posed a threat to the method or the credibility of Lefèvre.[37]

More menacing was an attack that came from Spain a few years later, In 1519 Diego Lopez de Zuñiga (known as Stunica), one of the scholars responsible for the preparation of the Complutensian Polyglot Bible, published a work entitled *Annotations against Jacques Lefèvre d'Etaples*[38] in which he condemned Lefèvre for presuming to offer his own Latin translation of the Pauline Epistles. He expressed respect for Lefèvre as a Christian and a scholar—Lefèvre's reputation in Spain stood high—but suggested that he was outreaching himself in moving from philosophical to biblical criticism, and especially the criticism of Jerome's Vulgate version (though Lefèvre, it will be remembered, had maintained that the Vulgate version then in use was not the work of Jerome). Stunica seems to have held Jerome's translation to be virtually inspired from above, and even the order of his words to be endowed with mystical significance. It was true that Jerome

---

35. Renaudet, pp. 654f. Vigerio died the following year (1516). Renaudet remarks that ''the *Apologia* on Lefèvre's behalf was undoubtedly destroyed after his death,'' for ''the historians of the Franciscan order have no knowledge of it.''

36. Jean-Pierre Massaut, *Critique et tradition à la veille de la Réforme en France* (Paris, 1974), pp. 126ff.

37. For a useful discussion of the subject see Massaut, pp. 50ff.

38. *Annotationes contra Jacobum Fabrum Stapulensem.*

had been commissioned by the Pope, which could not be said of Lefèvre; but the arguments advanced by Stunica hardly became him as a man of learning. After all, Lefèvre was doing only what Jerome had done many centuries earlier, namely, eliminating, by reference to the original language, errors that by one means or another had found their way into the Latin version of the Bible. If that was necessary in Jerome's day after three centuries, how much more so in Lefèvre's day so many more centuries later![39] Stunica actually cited Jerome's own defensive question: "Why should we not refer to the Greek original for the purpose of correcting those things that have been wrongly altered by perverse interpreters or recklessly 'corrected' by incompetent and presumptuous persons or added or changed by sleepy copyists?" Richard Cameron justly observes that "it does not seem to have occurred to Stunica that this last argument might be used (as it was) to support subsequent translations, including Lefèvre's, also."[40]

ONE MARY OR THREE? FURTHER CONTROVERSY

At the same time the blasts of opposition increased in intensity because of the publication, in one volume, of two treatises by Lefèvre early in 1518 with the title *Discussion concerning Mary Magdalene and Christ's Three Days* (i.e., in the tomb).[41] The queen mother, Louise of Savoy, had requested the royal almoner, François du Moulin de Rochefort, to compose a life of St. Mary Magdalene for her devotional use. Du Moulin in turn had consulted Lefèvre, under whom he had studied, as to whether the cult of the Magdalene had not in fact combined three Marys into one. Lefèvre's researches, which were encouraged by the queen mother, confirmed that this was indeed the case and led to the writing of the first of the two tracts in the publication mentioned above. He contended, on the basis of the evidence of the New Testament and the patristic writings, that the Mary Magdalene celebrated in the church calendar was a figure compounded of three different women, namely, Mary of Bethany, the sister of Martha and Lazarus (John 11:1ff.; Luke 10:39), Mary Magdalene out of whom seven demons were cast (Luke 8:2), and the unnamed woman who had been forgiven much and had anointed Christ's feet with ointment (Luke 7:37ff.).

Lefèvre carefully explained that it was not his intention to place the human witness of the patristic authors on the same level as that of Holy Scripture, to which they were necessarily subordinate. Submission of their writings to the supreme authority of Scripture, however, did not require

---

39. Understandably, in view of his circumstances, Stunica was not disposed to place a contemporary Frenchman on a level with so celebrated a church father as Saint Jerome.

40. Richard Cameron, "The Attack on the Biblical Work of Lefèvre d'Etaples, 1514–1521," *Church History* 38 (1969):12.

41. *De Maria Magdalena et triduo Christi disceptatio.*

their rejection, except of course where they were evidently in conflict with the biblical record. There were, moreover, two traditions: one much more ancient and consonant with the gospel account, and the other less venerable and inconsistent with the evidence of the New Testament. Furthermore, piety demanded that the reputation of Mary of Bethany should be rescued from the disgrace of confusing her with the woman of Luke 8 whose career, prior to her experience of Christ's forgiveness, was traditionally held to have been that of a prostitute.

The second of the two treatises attempted to resolve the question regarding the length of time Christ spent in the tomb between his death and resurrection. Matthew's Gospel speaks of Jesus being raised "on the third day" (Matt. 16:21; 17:23; 20:19), as also do Luke's Gospel (Luke 9:22) and St. Paul (1 Cor. 15:4). But the First Gospel also contains the prediction that the Son of man would be three days and three nights in the heart of the earth (Matt. 12:40); and to the same effect the Second Gospel refers to the resurrection as taking place "after three days" (Mark 8:31; 9:31; 10:34; cf. John 2:19–22)—though in Lefèvre's day both the Vulgate and the Greek text then received read "on the third day" at Mark 10:34. Traditionally, the apparent problem had been explained, in a reasonable and satisfactory manner, as arising from the practice of speaking of any part of a day as though it were a whole day (a manner of speaking known as synecdoche). Augustine, for example, wrote:

> This figure of speech, which puts the part for the whole, explains also the great question about the resurrection of Christ. For unless to the latter part of the day on which he suffered we join the previous night, and count it as a whole day, and to the latter part of the night in which he arose we join the Lord's day which was just dawning, and count it also as a whole day, we cannot make out the three days and three nights which he foretold that he would be in the heart of the earth.[42]

Lefèvre's solution was far from compelling. Dismissing the classical interpretation as false and incompatible with the tenor of Scripture, he maintained that the proper sense of the Greek commonly rendered as "after three days" was "in three days."[43] To inquire about the understanding of the "three days and three nights" of Matthew 12:40 was, he insisted, indicative of human curiosity rather than a genuine seeking for the truth, and of concern with the mere computation of hours instead of the apostolic method of interpretation, which was "according to the Scriptures" (1 Cor. 15:3-4).

---

42. Augustine, *De doctrina christiana*, III.xxxv.50 (J. F. Shaw's translation). Particularly significant in this connection is the Jewish concept of the "night-day," νυχθήμερον, as a unit (see 2 Cor. 11:25).

43. He argued that as μετὰ χεῖρας could mean "in the hands" (*in manibus*) so μετὰ τρεῖς ἡμέρας could mean, and in these instances did mean, "in three days" (*in triduo*) — a very insecure deduction!

"Paul," he maintained, "is telling us that he rose the third day, not according to your manner of thinking and your presuppositions, but according to the Scriptures, according to the sense and logic of Scripture, that is to say, according to the Spirit."

It is not surprising that Erasmus was dismayed at Lefèvre's argumentation in this second tract, though he thoroughly approved the position defined in the first. Early in 1518 he wrote the following to the Englishman Edward Lee, who was in Louvain:

> I am sending you a new booklet of Lefèvre's. Its contents I find generally pleasing, except that I cannot help wondering why he should wish to lower the disputation to the level where he maintains that anyone affirming that Christ rose after three days is speaking against the Church, against the articles of the faith, against all truth—notwithstanding the fact that for so many years the Church has understood it in this way. The alternative he presents is that either he silences all or else he himself must be silenced. Nor do I see what forbids our saying that Christ rose after the third day, that is, by the use of synecdoche, which no one disallows, that he rose after the third day had begun. But you will be better able to judge this. Nor does it seem to me that there is a correspondence between μετὰ χεῖρας "within the hands," and μετὰ τρεῖς ἡμέρας.[44]

At about the same time Erasmus also sent a letter to Henry Glareanus in which he spoke of Lefèvre as a man of learning, integrity, and culture, whom he loved "ex animo," and deplored the intemperate manner in which Lefèvre had joined issue with him (over the interpretation of Heb. 2:9). "He has not done much harm to my reputation," Erasmus told Glareanus; "but his own he has served ill—and this truly distresses me more than you would believe." He went on to say that Lefèvre's "little book on the three Magdalenes" had pleased him, but, as in the letter to Edward Lee, explained his disagreement with Lefèvre's treatment of the passages referring to the period between Christ's death and resurrection.[45] Similar sentiments were expressed by Erasmus in his letter to Guillaume Budé of 22 February 1518.[46] The plain truth is that linguistics was not one of Lefèvre's strengths.

In the middle of 1518 a second edition of the two treatises appeared, and now bound together with them was a third with the title One Mary from Three,[47] in which Lefèvre assailed the ecclesiastical tradition that St. Anne, the mother of the Virgin Mary, had had three husbands in succession and three daughters, one from each husband, each of them called Mary. The tradition he was opposing found no support in the New Testament, which does not even mention the parents of Mary. However, it was very popular

---

44. Allen, III:203f.

45. Ibid., pp. 204f.

46. Ibid., pp. 226f. See p. 114 above.

47. *De Maria Magdalena, Triduo Christi, et ex tribus una Maria disceptatio.*

in the medieval period, despite the criticism of a number of scholars, including Thomas Aquinas. It had even gained a place in the liturgy in the form of a hymn.

Lefèvre affirmed that those who value the truth should not occupy themselves with collections of cheap legends whose origin was unknown and content manifestly false. Moreover, he attacked this particular legend as altogether impious, the fabrication of an evil man who served as an instrument of Satan. It was, he contended, a demonic assault on the purity of St. Anne, implying on her part an inability to endure the condition of widowhood and saddling her with a character of lustfulness and incontinence that required three husbands to satisfy. This could only mean that the doctrine of the immaculate conception was demolished, for Christ would then have had for his mother one who was the child of a monstrously voluptuous woman. Already, in his commentary on Romans 7:8ff., Lefèvre had postulated the immaculate conception as a guarantee of Christ's freedom from concupiscence, in conjunction with the virgin birth, which, in addition, meant that Christ's conception by Mary was not accompanied by the concupiscence common to the ordinary marital union of husband and wife. Now he took things a stage further back, to Anne, insisting on her purity as the wife of one husband. This kind of logic, however, can only lead to an endless regress when consistently applied, and raises more and greater difficulties for the biblical theologian than those it is intended to solve. But before long Lefèvre would see things very differently.[48]

The publication of Lefèvre's opinions met with a furious response. He was thunderously denounced as the enemy of Christian piety, ecclesiastical tradition, and the sacred liturgy, indeed of God, who, it was asserted, would never have allowed his church to remain in error for so long a period. He was well aware, and his friends had warned him, that the new treatise on the Virgin's mother would expose him to further frenzied abuse and hostility. But, confident that in this controversy truth and piety were on his side, not on the side of his opponents, he remained unmoved and unafraid. "I do not imagine that there can be any danger in driving error from the heart of the faithful and exposing the truth," he declared. He was simply being loyal to the principle he had long since adopted of returning to the source, in this case the Gospels, so that erroneous accretions might be removed and the original teaching recovered in all its purity.

Lefèvre denied that he was attacking the church, which he held to be holy. "Therefore," he stated, "if things sung in the churches are fictitious, false, or ridiculous, I shall not hesitate to deny that the holy Church appointed, sanctioned, or approved them, but rather that they are the invention of someone deceived by excessive naivety." How could it be imagined that the church was the perpetrator of such absurdities? "Far be

---

48. See p. 127 below.

it from us to make the Church, the mother of the faith and the instructress of the truth, into the mistress of error!'' It was Lefèvre's prayer that God would raise up in his church watchful and enlightened leaders who would be champions of the truth and would diligently instruct the people in the authentic faith.

For the edition with all three treatises Josse Clichtove provided a protective introduction addressed to François du Moulin de Rochefort, to whom Lefèvre had dedicated the two earlier treatises, but without a prefatory epistle. Observing that while the earlier publication had not received a wide welcome among theologians, Clichtove pointed out that there were nonetheless many, especially those who had an interest in seeking out the truth, who thought highly of it. ''Ours is an age,'' he explained, ''in which people are pleased with what they are accustomed to hearing, whereas unaccustomed things, though true, are not readily accepted.'' As for himself, he too had been of the opinion that there was only one Mary, not three; but the arguments offered and the evidence adduced by Lefèvre had persuaded him to change his mind. He now saw that Lefèvre's position was in harmony with the consensus of the early centuries, so that it could not be said that he was in conflict with the mind of the church. ''Was not the Church in existence in the days of Irenaeus, Origen, Eusebius, Chrysostom, Jerome, and Ambrose?'' That Gregory the Great held the opinion assailed by Lefèvre was of no consequence, for not only was Gregory later but he was also unreliable as a teacher. Furthermore, it does not follow that singing something in church makes it true. Ecclesiastical chants and patristic homilies belong to ''a class of writings that come a long way behind the dignity of the Holy Scriptures which are known as canonical.'' As for the objection that the populace would be scandalized if now instructed that there were three Marys and not one as they had always been told, Clichtove rejoined that ''it is not the truth but falsehood that scandalizes,'' and that ''the light of the truth illuminates souls and builds up to salvation.'' To the further complaint that even if the populace should not be scandalized their devotion would be diminished, he maintained that on the contrary their devotion would increase as the spiritual significance of the three biblical women came to be appreciated.[49]

Not long after this Lefèvre published a ''second discussion''[50] in which he affirmed that he was in no way opposed to piety and that he thought no ill of those who did not accept his conclusions. All he was endeavoring to do was to give first place to the gospel, for the Word and the Spirit of God come before the words and the opinions of men, and popular sentiment, when misguided, must give way to the truth, which is stronger than all else. A victory for the truth could only be to the benefit of piety. Pro-

---

49. For the text of Clichtove's introductory epistle see Rice, pp. 400ff.

50. *De tribus et unica Magdalena disceptatio secunda*, 1519.

ceeding by way of discussion, he was not being contentious; nor was he propounding some new position, but only that held by the church fathers of old. Above all, it was to the gospel that he went as the source of his knowledge: "My reasons are drawn from no other fount than that of the Gospel." Moreover, he had expressed his judgment in plain, not involved, language. To cite any number of authors was not enough. The gospel was more powerful than an infinity of authors, and the truth more than the most venerable of observances. Had not the light and truth of the gospel dispelled at one stroke idolatrous worship with a history of thousands of years? At the same time he submitted his conclusions to the pope, confident that the Spirit of God and the church and the truth belong together.

But, peaceable though his motives were, Lefèvre was unable to still the controversy to which these publications had given rise. On his side, François du Moulin had written two booklets (which were not printed); the first, written before the appearance of the first of Lefèvre's "discussions," was on the life of the Magdalene; the second, written after Lefèvre's treatise, was on St. Anne. Both were favorable to Lefèvre's position. Du Moulin's approach was not at all polemical, but rather devotional in character. But in September 1518 Marc de Grandval, an Augustinian canon of St. Victor who had become prior of Athis, near Versailles, wrote and published a defense of the traditionalist position. In it he condemned Lefèvre as an innovator and, in the fashion of the Parisian scholastics, held to the biblical interpretation of Gregory the Great.[51]

At the instigation of Etienne Poncher, the bishop of Paris who was soon to become archbishop of Sens, John Fisher, bishop of Rochester and chancellor of the University of Cambridge, joined the fray in February 1519. In three books, Fisher launched an attack on Lefèvre, contending that the revision he had proposed must be expected to undermine the faith of the populace and threaten the authority of the church: so many authors would have to be condemned, so many books corrected, so many sermons revoked. Trust would be driven out by doubt, and inevitably our common mother the church, which for so many centuries had sung and taught the same thing, would come under a cloud of suspicion. Fisher seemed to be a champion of expediency rather than truth, of prevailing tradition rather than of a proper understanding of the original.[52]

Clichtove reentered the arena to side with Lefèvre against the accusations of Grandval, whose book he described as an incrimination rather than a defense. Grandval retorted with a "safeguard and anchor" of his

---

51. *Marci de Grandval theologi, ecclesiae catholicae non tres Magdalenas sed unicam colentis: apologia seu defensorium.*

52. *Reverendi Patris Johannis Fisscher Roffensis in Anglia Episcopi, necnon Cantabrigien. academiae Cancellarii dignissimi, de unica Magdalena, Libri tres.*

Defense.[53] Still in 1519, Fisher produced two more compositions, an "over-throw" of Clichtove's position[54] and a "refutation" of Lefèvre;[55] and in November 1519 the opposition was augmented by the publication of a "scholastic declaration" by Noel Béda,[56] which was intended to supplement and improve what Grandval and Fisher had written; this was followed the next year by a "defense of the daughters of the blessed Anne."[57] Béda denounced Lefèvre's insistence on the literal sense as the only proper sense of Scripture and reaffirmed the traditional fourfold method of interpretation. He postulated the divine inspiration of Gregory the Great, whose judgment that there was but one Mary was thus not open to question, and the inviolability of long entrenched tradition.

Others, however, wrote in support of Lefèvre, notably Symphorien Champier in his *Harmony of the Gospel Writers*[58] and, from Germany, Willibald Pirckheimer, who published a "dissertation" on Mary Magdalene.[59] The last two contributions to the controversy were made in 1521, also from abroad, by members of the hostile Dominican order, one a Spaniard, Balthasar Sorio,[60] and the other an Italian, Giovanni Maria Tholosani delle Colle, who wrote two treatises which remained unpublished.[61]

That Lefèvre maintained a serene frame of mind despite the buffetings of this controversy is further attested by an exchange of letters between him and Cornelius Agrippa of Nettesheim in 1519. At the end of April Agrippa wrote from Metz, affirming his unwavering friendship, with the assurance that he could count on him as a loyal advocate and defender against all who wished to impugn his honor. "There are indeed many such," Agrippa remarked, "but they are men of inferior intellect and paltry abili-

---

53. *Apologiae seu defensorii Ecclesiae Catholicae non tres sive duas Magdalenas sed unicam celebrantis et colentis tutamentum et anchora, per ipsius auctorem apologiae Marcum de Grandval.*

54. *Eversio Munitionis quam Iodocus Clichtoveus erigere moliebatur adversus unicam Magdalenam.*

55. *Confutatio Secundae Disceptationis per Jacobum Fabrum Stapulensem habitae in qua tribus foeminis partiri molitur quae totius ecclesiae consuetudo unicae tribuit Magdalenae.*

56. *Scholastica declaratio sententiae et ritus ecclesiae de unica Magdalena per Natalem Bedam . . . contra magistrorum Iacobi Fabri et Iodoci Clichtovei contheologi scripta. . . .*

57. *Apologia pro filiabus . . . Beatae Annae.*

58. *Evangelistarum symphonia,* November 1519.

59. *Willibaldi Pirckheimeri dissertatio sive* 'ΑΝΑΣΚΕΥΗ *historica et philologica de Maria Magdalena, quod falso a quibusdam habeatur pro illa peccatrice seu* (undated).

60. *Fratris Balthasaris Sorio sacre theologe professoris Apologeticus: pro unica Maria Magdalena: pro vera sanctorum assignatione tridui Christi in corde terre: pro duabus quoque sororibus virginis Marie matris Dei, Christique materteris: adversus maledicta Jacobi Fabri in illas.*

61. *De Maria Magdalena* and *Disceptatio in Jodoc. Clicht. Jacobi Fabri defensorem.*

ty and hostile to all good studies—who no doubt impress the ignorant populace with their façade of learning and hypocritically gain their confidence—with the result that it is difficult, in fact dangerous, to resist them." However, he added, this consideration in no way deterred him from what he saw to be his duty.[62] Lefèvre responded, on 20 May, that Agrippa's letter had given him great pleasure and urged him not to take it ill that there were many who opposed his works on Mary Magdalene and Anne. "I believe the day is coming," he said, "when the truth of these things will be more clearly seen. I offer them only for discussion and avoid rash dogmatism. . . . Falsehood withers away by itself and at length collapses without an attacker."[63]

On 22 May, before he had received Lefèvre's reply to the letter mentioned above, Agrippa wrote again to his friend in Paris, saying that he had doubtless received the earlier letter and with it the propositions with which Claude Dieudonné, the bearer of the letter, had been entrusted. The propositions in question had been composed by Agrippa in support of Lefèvre's treatises on Anne and the Magdalene.[64] "The reason which compelled me to compose these propositions," Agrippa explained, "was precisely that I might have an opportunity of withstanding those who calumniate you, men who assuredly are the enemies of all learned scholars."[65] Lefèvre wrote on 20 June acknowledging the safe arrival of both the correspondence and the propositions. Regarding his own work Lefèvre expressed himself as follows:

> I would have preferred the matter concerning Anne to be debated without contention among scholars. Since this is not possible because of the present ill will and the perverse temper of men, and you have felt it right to join the conflict, see that you do this not out of zeal for my honor but only for the sake of safeguarding the truth and out of devotion to Mary the Mother of God and her mother the most blessed Anne. But no honor can come to you by joining issue with those barbarous men who busy themselves with the defamation of others, nor do I consider their trifling and hostile and tasteless ineptitudes worthy of refutation. All such things will collapse of themselves and at length the truth will be acknowledged. It is better not to contend at all than to contend for the victory of my opinion.[66]

In October Agrippa dispatched another letter to Lefèvre informing him that he had completed a defense of his own propositions and promising to

---

62. Herminjard, I:46f.

63. Ibid., p. 49.

64. *H. C. Agrippae de beatiss. Annae monogamia ac unico puerperio propositiones abbreviatae ac articulatae juxta disceptationem J. Fabri Stapulensis in libro de tribus et una.*

65. Herminjard, I:50ff.

66. Ibid., pp. 52ff.

let him have either a manuscript or a printed copy. He ventured the suggestion that Lefèvre would not be displeased with it, especially "because it was least of all pleasing to those sophists who engage unavailingly against us in open warfare." Lefèvre and Agrippa were even being accused of heresy.[67] On 14 November Lefèvre wrote and commended Agrippa for the nobility of spirit that had brought him to the defense of Anne, the parent of the Virgin Mother of God. He also commiserated with him over the harassment he was suffering from the malice of many persons, and reminded him that Reuchlin, "a most excellent as well as a most learned man," had endured much affliction.[68] Because of the unscrupulous character of their opponents, he warned Agrippa to be cautious and precise in everything he wrote.[69]

Four weeks before this, on 17 October 1519, Erasmus wrote from Louvain to the bishop of Rochester, deploring the manner in which Lefèvre, "beyond question a most excellent man," was being attacked in Paris with immoderate hostility, most of all by the Dominicans, because he had given his support to Reuchlin and had expressed the wish that theologians might show concern for reconciliation instead of injuring one another.[70] Lefèvre's spirit, as we have seen, was irenic, not militant. Béda and his faction, however, were implacable and unwilling to let things rest. An opportunity for decisive action presented itself in the summer of 1521, a short time after Lefèvre had left Paris for Meaux. On St. Mary Magdalene's Day, 22 July, Martial Mazurier took advantage of the Christian calendar and preached a sermon in the cathedral of Meaux in which he propounded Lefèvre's opinion that popular tradition had mistakenly combined three different persons into one. The theological faculty of Paris was convoked and an official investigation was approved. Mazurier was summoned to attend in person, but on 1 October, the day before he was due to appear, Clichtove gained a hearing and succeeded in persuading the professors against prosecuting (which would have involved Clichtove himself and Lefèvre as well as Mazurier). The views to which they objected had been advanced, Clichtove urged, only for discussion and not in a dogmatic manner, and his offer to prepare a report on the matter was accepted. Clichtove, apparently, was in a state of transition, actually moving away from his position of allegiance to Lefèvre to that of collaboration with the Sorbonne professors. His report, ready in early November, was designed to put an end to the "scandals" caused by Lefèvre and to lay the whole controversy to rest. That he and Lefèvre would henceforth desist from their opinions, which the document at least implied, may have been agreeable to him but hardly to Lefèvre.

---

67. Ibid., pp. 57f.

68. See pp. 101ff. above.

69. Herminjard, I:59f.

70. Allen, IV:92f.

Clichtove's statement was accepted and Lefèvre's views were formally censured at the beginning of December. The popular tradition was reaffirmed as authentic.

But Béda was not yet satisfied. He was determined to get the Parlement to take action against Lefèvre. For the present, however, his hopes of doing so were disappointed. Influenced by the intervention of Guillaume Budé, the King referred the matter to his confessor, Guillaume Petit, whose sympathies were strongly with Lefèvre and his principles of reform. Petit advised Francis that there was no ground for a charge of heresy against Lefèvre and that, as the point at issue was a question of personal judgment rather than crucial doctrine, freedom of interpretation should be permitted. Accordingly, the King instructed the Parlement that Lefèvre was not to be charged with heterodoxy or otherwise troubled on this account. It was not the only time that there would be a royal intervention on Lefèvre's behalf.[71]

Lefèvre's treatise of 1518 on Anne gives some indication of the extent to which he was at the time devoted to the cult of the Virgin Mary. This devotion is confirmed by his publication in 1519 of a work entitled *The Contemplations of an Idiota*,[72] the second part of which comprised "contemplations made in honor and praise of the most holy Virgin Mary." This section was prefaced by a letter of Guillaume Briçonnet addressed to the abbess and sisters of Faremoutiers in the diocese of Meaux, of which he was now bishop. Briçonnet himself had translated this second part into French. In this introductory letter he extolled Mary as having become "above all creatures (after him who is the truth of all self-abnegation and humiliation) the paragon of humility," and as having been "exalted and elevated by the divine goodness not only above men but above every hierarchical order of angels and made queen of heaven and earth."[73] The appearance of this work denotes little if any change by Lefèvre from his position of twenty years previously, when he included in his publication of Ramon Lull "The Book of Praises of the Blessed Virgin Mary." But, as we have seen,[74] in the same year (1519) Lefèvre experienced a radical change of attitude: coming to the realization that the invocation of creatures, however memorable they might be as instruments of divine grace, was dishonoring to God, and that our petitions should be addressed to God alone through the mediation of our Redeemer Jesus Christ, he abandoned the work on which he was engaged commemorating the saints of the church's calendar (*Agones martyrum*) and bade farewell to the cult of creatures.

---

71. For this controversy see Jean-Pierre Massaut, *Critique et tradition à la veille de la Réforme en France* (ut supra), chs. V-IX; Anselm Hufstader, "Lefèvre d'Etaples and the Magdalen," *Studies in the Renaissance* 16 (1969):31ff.; Richard Cameron, "The Attack on the Biblical Work of Lefère d'Etaples, 1514–1521," *Church History* 38 (1969):9ff.

72. *Contemplationes Idiotae.*

73. Rice, p. 413.

74. See p. 50 above.

The reality of this change is attested by his commentary on the Gospels, which was published three years later, in 1522. He still held to the doctrine of the Immaculate Conception (see on Matt. 1:18ff.) and of the perpetual virginity of Mary (see on Luke 2:22–24), but there is no trace of any mediation between God and man except through the incarnate Son. Thus he now insists that it is mistaken to imagine that, in approaching Jesus Christ, one will gain access to him by reason of the goodness of someone else (see on Matt. 15:21), and, still more specifically, that "if anyone who is praying places his confidence in the intercession of the blessed Virgin or of all the saints, whoever they may be, rather than in Jesus Christ alone, he is not praying as he ought" (see on Luke 21:5). Again, when expounding the miracle of the changing of water into wine (John 2:1ff.), he observes that it was not the mother of Jesus who was asked to solve the crisis occasioned by the shortage of wine; "but," he points out, "she asks the Son, thus instructing and teaching us that every prayer in matters which are divine must be addressed not to any creature, but to the Son and God alone." It has also justly been observed, with reference to the *Epistles and Gospels for the Fifty-Two Sundays of the Year*, published in 1525, that "the omissions are perhaps as remarkable as the precise affirmations, and that, by way of example, the exhortation on the Gospel for the feast of the Purification of the Virgin (2 February) "offers no praises of the Virgin.""[75]

Throughout the course of the controversy over the Magdalene and St. Anne, Lefèvre was moved by a sincere concern for genuine piety. He had no desire to disturb the peace of the church. But he knew that genuine piety cannot have error as its basis, and that, as Christ himself taught, those who worship God must worship in spirit and in truth (John 4:24). Traditionalism that was contrary to the revealed truth of the Scriptures could not be expected to promote Christian piety. Once he had learned this, Lefèvre was driven by the earnest wish to lead his fellow churchmen back to the pure source of the church's faith, namely, the doctrine of Christ communicated through the apostolic writings of the new Testament. "Back to the source!" is still his watchword, but now it is to *this* source, to the exclusion, in the ultimate issue, of all other, merely human sources. It was not easy for him personally to question beliefs and practices that had been part of his life since childhood, and it was not pleasant to have to endure the animosity of academics and ecclesiastics who did not welcome the disturbance of their routines of thought and worship. But to be faithful to the cause that now obsessed him meant that he could not be silent.

---

75. Margaret Mann, *Erasme et les débuts de la Réforme Française* (Paris, 1934), p. 108.

Meaux

THE DEPARTURE FROM PARIS

Lefèvre had left the Collège du Cardinal Lemoine in 1508 in order to join his influential friend and disciple Guillaume Briçonnet at the abbey of Saint-Germain-des-Prés, following the appointment of the latter as abbot. At the end of 1515 Briçonnet was nominated bishop of Meaux, and in 1517, after a period of service as the French king's envoy extraordinary to Rome, he decided, in accordance with ancient practice but contrary to current custom, to reside in his diocese as the chief pastor of his people. Meaux is some twenty miles to the east of Paris and Lefèvre spent several months there as Briçonnet's guest during the years 1518 and 1519. It was in the spring or early summer of 1521 that he finally departed from the capital and settled in Meaux in response to Briçonnet's urgent invitation to lead the work of church reform in his diocese. No doubt it was with mixed feelings that Lefèvre left Paris, where for so many years he had been the center of a dedicated circle of scholars and researchers; but at the same time it must have been a relief to him to put some distance between himself and the antipathy of the professors of the Sorbonne. In the more congenial environment of Meaux his zeal for renewal would have the enthusiastic collaboration of the bishop and other like-minded colleagues.

Lefèvre's most malicious opponents in Paris, Noël Béda and Guillaume Duchêne (also known as Quercus, i.e., "Oak," the Latinized form of his name), were in turn heads of the theological faculty there. Erasmus, in a letter written in May 1521 from Malines to Nicholas Everard, spoke scathingly of Béda as "a block of wood rather than a man" and of Quercus as "a virulent little old man," explaining that it was these two who were leading the campaign in Paris against Luther.[1] Shortly after this, on 4 July, Glareanus wrote from Paris to Zwingli in Zürich:

---

1. Allen, IV:447f.

Our dunderheads[2] have shown themselves worthy of the honor of filling the shoes of the Pharisees in our day. The Triumvirs, Béda (not, however, the Venerable),[3] Quercus, and Christophorus,[4] have given their condemnation. These monsters are now commonly known as "Belua" [Lat., "the Brute"], "Stercus" [Lat., "dung"], and "Christotomus" [Gk., "one who butchers Christ"].

The stimulus for both these letters was the condemnation of Luther issued by the theological faculty of the University of Paris; in it they equated the German Reformer with Muhammad and demanded the extermination of his followers. Glareanus added in his letter that Lefèvre had left the French capital because "he cannot bear to listen to the slanders against Luther," though Quercus, whom he sarcastically described as "that distinguished theologian," was actually (he remarked) no more temperate in his attitude to Lefèvre and Erasmus.[5]

Lefèvre's fondness for those who were promoting the work of reform, in whatever country, was evident as early as April 1519 in a letter he wrote to his former pupil Beatus Rhenanus in Basel: "Please greet in my name all the learned men who are in your company," he requested. "I hear that there are a great many and I commend them for their doctrine and probity." He mentioned by name "my very dear Michael Hummelberg" (of Ravensburg in Swabia, another of his former students), Wolfgang Fabrus (the Alsatian Wolgang Köpflein or Capito, with whom Lefèvre would stay when he took refuge in Strasbourg), Sapidus (Johann Witz of Schelestadt), together with "all the others whom I love dearly in Christ, also Luther, if ever he comes your way."[6] Again, some five years later, we find him writing to Farel, then in Basel: "My very dear brother, I pray you through Jesus Christ share my letter with the brethren and friends dearest of all to me in Christ"—and he mentioned in particular Ecolampadius (Johann Hussgen, then cathedral preacher in Basel), Pellican (Conrad Kürschner, the hebraist and former Franciscan), and Hugaldus (Huldrich Hugwald, another German scholar then in Basel). "May Christ Jesus, our life, be the eternal salvation of you all!" he concluded.[7]

It is obvious that by 1521 Lefèvre had become very much a marked man. He had bitter enemies who were demanding his blood. Scholastic traditionalists in France were openly denouncing him as an antichrist. In a letter from Louvain to Alexander Schweiss, dated 13 March,[8] Erasmus referred

---

2. I.e., the Sorbonne professors.

3. The allusion is to the Venerable Bede, c. 673–735.

4. This person has not been identified.

5. Herminjard, I:69ff.

6. Ibid., p. 45.

7. Ibid., p. 227.

8. Ibid., pp. 63f. Herminjard corrects the date to 13 May; but Allen argues in favor of the earlier date.

to the papal bull of the previous year requiring preachers to speak against Luther, "that is, to refute his opinions by the testimony of Holy Scripture and to teach different and better things," and drew attention the significant fact there was no one who came forward to do this: "no one proves him wrong; they only revile him, often resorting to lies." He related how at a public service in the presence of the King of France "a certain Carmelite" declared that Antichrist was coming and that he already had four precursors: an unnamed Franciscan monk in Italy,[9] Jacques Lefèvre d'Etaples in France, Reuchlin in Germany, and Erasmus in Belgium. Presumably Luther was intended as the Antichrist of whom these four were the forerunners.[10] A variation on this theme occurs in a communication sent from Annecy later on in that year (10 Sept.) by Claude Dieudonné to Henry Cornelius Agrippa, in which he narrated how some hooded academics of the Dominican order had entered his cell and "spued out their poison" as they declared that there were now four antichrists in the kingdom of Christ, namely, Erasmus, Luther, Reuchlin, and Lefèvre.[11]

LUTHERANISM

The figure of Luther was certainly looming large over Europe during these years and his name more than that of any other person was associated with the mounting desire for spiritual renewal and ecclesiastical reform. "No one would believe how widely Luther has penetrated into the hearts of many nations and how highly he is enthroned through his books spread everywhere in every language," Erasmus remarked in the letter cited above. The enemies of the evangelical movement used the designation "Lutheran" as a synonym for what was doctrinally heretical and ecclesiastically inauthentic. In France, passions were readily aroused by the cry of "Lutheranism," which was an alarm warning against something, however vaguely understood, constituting a detestable threat not only to the stability of the church but also, by reason of its foreignness, to the genius of the Gallic spirit. The cry, when raised against Lefèvre, was an unjust one; for Lefèvre was not a follower of Luther. The principles he advocated and sought to apply had not been imported from alien soil; the movement of which he was a pioneer in France was genuinely and spontaneously a French movement. At the same time he rejoiced to see and was conscious of a true affinity with the spiritual renewal that was being kindled in other lands. Influences were of course exerted and experienced across national boundaries

---

9. This can hardly have been Bernardino Ochino of Siena, as Allen has suggested, and also Bedouelle (Lefèvre d'Etaples et l'Intelligece des Ecritures, p. 93) following Allen's lead, since 1521 is surely too early a date for Ochino to have achieved such notoriety.

10. Allen, IV:453f.

11. Herminjard, I:72.

as the evangelical flame spread. Writings traveled more extensively than persons. But the pioneering character of Lefèvre's work must not be minimized, even though, like all others, he was susceptible to impressions from elsewhere.

There can be little doubt that in course of time at least some of Luther's writings were read by Lefèvre. It is certain, however, that Luther read and, as we have seen,[12] was much influenced by Lefèvre before Lefèvre read Luther. That it would be more just to speak of Luther as a Fabrist[13] than of Lefèvre as a Lutheran was recognized even by so bitter an opponent of Lefèvre as Béda, who, in his polemical *Annotations* (1526)[14] admitted that in many respects Lefèvre and Erasmus "seem to have taught Luther rather than to have learned from him." Later in the same work, Béda wrote of Lefèvre: "He shows himself to be a disciple of the heresiarch Arius and of the Waldensians and Wycliffe and of many other heretics; but Luther's teacher." Aware, indeed, of the priority of Lefèvre to Luther and of the indebtedness of the latter to the former, Béda stated that, "if the sect of wretched Lutherans should, as is proper, take its name from its first head," it might well have been named after Lefèvre rather than Luther.[15]

Béda did denounce as "Lutheran" one proposition, number 10, from among the 209 he classified as objectionable in Lefèvre's commentaries on the Pauline Epistles and the Gospels; but his basis for this judgment seems to have been terminological rather than theological, since it revolved around the use of certain Latin words (*mutatio, conversio,* and *reversio*) in the definition of penitence that are found in comparable passages of Luther. That Lefèvre borrowed these terms from Luther is improbable—indeed, impossible in the case of the commentary on the Pauline Epistles, which was published before Luther had been heard of. The question in any case is not one of any great moment. There can, however, be no doubt that Lefèvre and Luther were of one mind, independently of each other, in their understanding of the fundamentals of the gospel. They were agreed, without ever having met or corresponded, that the sinner is justified by faith alone, through divine grace alone, solely on the basis of the merit of Christ and the perfection of his atoning sacrifice, with the consequence that all the glory goes to God alone. They were as one in their acceptance of the authority of Holy Scripture as the Word of God and in their insistence that sanctity of living must attest sincerity of believing. In a word, the heart of Lefèvre's theology was essentially in harmony with and, as we have shown, in large measure precursory to what came to be known as Reformed theology.

---

12. See pp. 60f. above.

13. The term is formed from "Faber," the Latin form of "Lefèvre."

14. *Annotationum . . . in Iacobum Fabrum Stapulensem Libri Duo et in Desiderium Erasmum Roterodamum Liber Unus.*

15. Noël Béda, op. cit., fol. iv, cxx, and cxxxiii.

THE SITUATION IN MEAUX

When Briçonnet took up residence in Meaux the need for spiritual renewal was obvious on all sides. Some of the parishes were without clergy; others had clergy who were conspicuous by their absence, preferring residence in Paris to the more humdrum life of a provincial district, while at the same time pocketing the emoluments of the cure whose duties they ignored; and some had clergy on the spot who were idle and incompetent. The scene was one of pastoral unconcern and spiritual neglect. Preaching was virtually nonexistent, except that the Franciscans saw to it that one of their number, with but a single sermon in his repertoire, was delegated to preach from parish to parish, for the purpose, however, not so much of edifying the parishioners as of extracting money from them for himself and his confrères. Upon his arrival in Meaux, Briçonnet found that a certain Brother Robert had been giving the same sermon from place to place for the past ten years! Repeatedly, but with little enough success, Briçonnet tried to compel the clergy to reside in their parishes and care for the flock for which they were responsible. He denounced the immorality, debauchery, and desecration of holy things that were prevalent in the diocese. At a synod summoned in 1519 he preached a sermon on Proverbs 27:23: "Be thou diligent to know the state of thy flocks and to look well to they herds," in the course of which he deplored the scandalous neglect of their duty by the pastors of his diocese.

> The Christian populace [he said], formerly so noble and pure, is now no more than a confused crowd of sheep which no longer have shepherds, wandering amid the mountains and the valleys, and daily plunging into the abyss of every kind of vice. As for the shepherds, they are all ignorant and blind, and their behavior is as insensitive as it is culpable. They have not sought the Lord, they have not fulfilled their responsibility, and all the flock has been dispersed. The people of God have been led astray by their own leaders and carried over the precipice edge. False to their vocation, the care of these men is for their own comforts, not for the well-being of their sheep. The brazenness of a courtesan has become second nature to them. They are sound asleep like dumb dogs . . . and while they abandon themselves to this senseless sleep the ship is engulfed by the waves.[16]

During the year 1520 Briçonnet himself personally examined all his curés and vicars for the purpose of discovering the degree of their competence in the understanding of the faith, in personal piety, and in the care and instruction of their parishioners. The results were appalling. Out of a total of 127, only 14 priests were found to be competent; 53 were declared

---

16. See R.-J. Lovy, op. cit., pp. 70f. The sermon was subsequently printed by Henri Estienne.

incompetent, and 60 were on the borderline of incompetence. These last were allowed a year in which to improve themselves and their work, failing which they would suffer the fate of the incompetents, namely, dismissal. The hostile reaction of most of the clergy and monks could hardly have been unanticipated. The Franciscans, who set themselves to secure Briçonnet's overthrow, led the wave of rebellion. Briçonnet, for his part, was no less determined to ride out the storm. To strengthen his position and promote the work of reform he brought in able men to provide the leadership so badly needed throughout the diocese. First and foremost of these was Jacques Lefèvre d'Etaples.

By mid-1521, when Lefèvre departed for Meaux, Paris had become a city of prohibitions, thanks largely to Béda's repressive genius. The Sorbonne had condemned the teachings of Luther and the Parlement had banned the publication of any religious writing that had not first been authorized. Whoever else might be affected, this meant, and was designed to mean, the muzzling of Lefèvre. Under these circumstances the prospect of a diocese with a sympathetic bishop who was also an old friend, together with the promise of freedom to pursue unhindered his own program of biblical commenting and translation and to promote the cause of evangelical reform, must have been most exciting and attractive.

At first Lefèvre was placed in charge of the hospice for lepers. This seems to have been a temporary or transitional appointment, an arrangement of convenience for bringing him into the structure of the diocese. At the beginning of May 1523 Briçonnet appointed him his vicar-general "in spiritual matters" (*in spiritualibus*), and assigned to him responsibility for the development of spiritual renewal throughout the diocese. For the fulfillment of this challenging task Lefèvre was given the enthusiastic assistance of a team of gifted younger friends and disciples whom Briçonnet had invited to Meaux for this purpose.

BRIÇONNET'S ANTI-LUTHERAN INJUNCTIONS

In what at first sight could be judged a surprising development, on 15 October 1523 Briçonnet issued injunctions that seemed to be contrary to much of the reform he himself had been energetically sponsoring. First, in a decree addressed to the faithful of his diocese, he condemned Luther in no uncertain terms:

> Although those who have attempted, but in vain, to defile in some way the Church's purity have been beyond number, yet none has so rashly and so fiercely put the axe to her roots as has Martin Luther, who overturns the whole hierarchical order, subverts and destroys the state which holds others to their duty, endeavors to obliterate the passion of our blessed Jesus, and, despising spiritual marriage, . . . admits to her ranks without discrimination the first to arrive in order to please the populace.

Luther, Briçonnet charged, relaxed ecclesiastical discipline, giving licence to all to sin as they pleased, and allowing each person absolute freedom of judgment, so that the religion of Jesus Christ became no better than the following of Muhammad. "Fearing," he wrote, "lest so venomous a plant should extend its roots into the field which has been entrusted to us, we regard it as our duty to extirpate it completely." Accordingly, every one of the faithful of his diocese was strictly forbidden, on pain of excommunication and other penalties, "to purchase, read, possess, or sell the books of the said Martin, or to approve, defend, and make them known in public meetings and private conversations."[17]

Second, in a similar decree issued simultaneously to the clergy of the diocese, Briçonnet denounced certain persons who, attracting a following by the novelty of their opinions, "dare to maintain and preach, in disrespect of evangelical truth, that there is no such place as purgatory, and that, consequently, one should not pray for the dead or invoke the Blessed Virgin Mary and the saints."

> Since these persons [the decree continues] have been called to share in our pastoral responsibilities and have succeeded, with their pestilential poison, in infecting the pious ears of the sheep committed our care, we most expressly require that you should all deal with this subject over and over again in your sermons and engage your flock in the offering of pious prayers for the dead, in the belief of the reality of purgatory, and in invoking the Blessed Virgin Mary and the saints, by the frequent repetition of appropriate litanies. If it should happen that any persist in preaching, affirming, and inculcating the contrary and in embracing the above-mentioned heresies or other errors, you must immediately summon them before us and forbid them to continue evangelizing your flock.[18]

Briçonnet issued further injunctions to his clergy on 13 December, reminding them that the ancient statutes of the diocese stipulated that no one, whatever his rank and wherever he came from, was permitted to preach in their churches without authorization. "If ever there was a good occasion for the beneficial observance of this holy and inviolable decree," Briçonnet admonished them, "it is now that the Lutheran plague is growing beyond measure and will spread its venom everywhere if the violence of its course is not restrained by the remedy necessary for such an evil." He defined the remedy as follows:

> We therefore command all in general and each of you in particular, expressly forbidding you by the tenor of these presents, under pain of excommunication and anathema, to permit Lutherans of this kind to preach in your pulpits, as well as all others, of whatever rank, prominence, and

---

17. Herminjard, I:171f.

18. Ibid., pp. 156ff.

quality they may be, who hold their doctrine or whose identity is unknown to you.[19]

It is hardly surprising that judgments have differed over Briçonnet's motivation in the issuing of these injunctions. Was his zeal for reform moralistic and administrative rather than truly evangelical? Or was it a mere façade? Or was Briçonnet irresolute and easily intimidated by the thunderings of officialdom? Or were these injunctions no more than a device designed to calm the threatening waves of hostility and to smooth the path of renewal that the was pursuing? There is no evidence at all that he wished to curb the zeal or moderate the teaching of Lefèvre, whom he had brought to Meaux to be the spearhead of diocesan reform; yet the injunctions would seem to oppose and forbid positions embraced and openly affirmed by Lefèvre. As we have seen, Lefèvre had abandoned and deplored the practice of invoking the saints as unbiblical and subversive of the sole sufficiency of the mediation of Christ, and his commentary on the Gospels shows that this continued to be his persuasion after he had moved to Meaux.[20]

There is, rather, every indication that the injunctions were in no way intended to signal a diminution of the favor and friendship of Briçonnet toward Lefèvre and his colleagues. The two parts of Lefèvre's French translation of the New Testament were published that same year (in June and Nov. 1523) with the full approval of Briçonnet, who himself arranged for copies to be distributed without charge to all poor persons desiring them—an action that displays a complete disregard for the Sorbonne's censure, pronounced in the middle of that same year, of Lefèvre's opinion that the Scriptures should be made available in the vernacular so that all people might be able to study them freely for themselves. This does not look like cowardice. When Béda and his fellow academics attempted to persuade the Parlement to place a ban on the distribution of the Scriptures in French, the king intervened again in support of Lefèvre and his work. At this time the court looked with approval on the reforms that were being introduced in the diocese of Meaux, and there was no obvious reason for Briçonnet to resort to compromise or timidity. Some explanation other than inconstancy or insincerity must be sought for the apparently contradictory coincidence of the anti-Lutheran injunctions and the open distribution of the biblical text in the vernacular.

There is, moreover, no indication that Lefèvre felt discouraged or discredited by the promulgation of the injunctions. On 6 July of the following year (1524) he wrote with enthusiasm to Farel, then in Basel, of the progress of the gospel at Meaux:

O gracious God, how great is my joy to see this grace of the pure knowledge of Christ now spreading through so much of Europe! And I

19. Ibid., pp. 171f.
20. See p. 96 above.

am hopeful that Christ will bestow this blessing on our French territories. May Christ hear our prayers, and may these beginnings lead to his triumph everywhere! You would scarcely believe the wonderful ardor with which, after the French New Testament was published, God has been moving the minds of simple people in many places to embrace his word. But you will rightly complain that it has not been sufficiently spread abroad. There was an attempt to get the Parlement to place a ban on it; but our most generous king came to Christ's defense, desiring that his kingdom should freely hear, without any hindrance, the word of God in that language which it understands. Now throughout the whole of our diocese both Epistle and Gospel are read to the people in the vernacular on festal days and especially on the Lord's Day; and if the curé has some exhortation to offer he adds it to the Epistle or Gospel, or to both. It is wonderful how my bishop has been moved by the letter from Ecolampadius, to whom the whole world is indebted as one who, faithful to his name, truly shines in the house, and not just a private house, but the whole Church of God.[21] . . . Stirred, as I have said, by the reading of Ecolampadius's letter, he has commissioned Gérard,[22] now the canon treasurer of our church, to interpret to the populace, both men and women, every day for one hour in the morning the Epistles of Paul published in the vernacular.

Lefèvre adds that Briçonnet had also sent members of their group to do the same thing in other strategic locations of the diocese.[23] What these men were doing, in short, was spreading the evangelical faith through the exposition of Scripture, and they were doing it at Briçonnet's instigation.

Thus, despite his anti-Lutheran injunctions, Briçonnet continued to promote the vigorous propagation of evangelical religion in his diocese. What are we to conclude from this? First, he himself did not fully comprehend that the thrust of reform, with Scripture as its touchstone, inevitably involved the scrutiny and reassessment of the traditions and practices that have accumulated over the years (a consideration that applies to the church not just in the sixteenth but in every century). As history shows, this reassessment is often a gradual process rather than a sudden achievement. In 1523 Lefèvre had rejected the cult of the saints but not yet the belief in purgatory; by 1525, however, he had turned away from the doctrine of purgatory.[24]

As for Briçonnet, his theological perspective was also changing, as his correspondence with Marguerite d'Angoulême during the years 1521 to 1524 shows. Briçonnet's letters are often expremely lengthy and as such are virtual treatises on a particular notion or theme that, in many instances, has been suggested by a particular word or phrase used by Marguerite.

---

21. Ecolampadius is the Greek equivalent of the German name Hussgen, which was taken to mean "house-lamp." Ecolampadius, who was then in Basel, had left the ranks of the Lutherans and thrown in his lot with the non-Lutheran Reformers.

22. That is, Gérard Roussel.

23. Herminjard, I:220ff.

24. See pp. 82f. above.

Throughout the correspondence the sincerity and devoutness of his Christian faith is apparent; but his preoccupation with the mystical manipulation of terminology, involving the convoluted use of paradox, inversion, and oxymoron, so characteristic of the earlier letters, is almost entirely abandoned in the later letters in favor of counsel that is much more clearly evangelical and biblical in its presentation.[25]

Second, while animated by a genuine desire for the spiritual revitalization of the church, Briçonnet did not regard the renewal he was fostering in his diocese as in any way linked to Luther and his movement. He was no advocate of ecclesiastical disruption, and he wanted it to be plain to his critics that the reform taking place at Meaux, far from having a foreign origin, was truly and spontaneously French in character. It is within this setting that his comprehensive prohibition of Lutheranism must be assessed. The inconsistency of Briçonnet's position lay in a failure to appreciate that, however serious the differences between Luther and the other leaders of reform might be, they were essentially at one in their emphasis on certain doctrines regarded as central to the evangelical message, such as the authority of Scripture and the justification of the sinner *sola fide* and *sola gratia*.

Third, Briçonnet desired to curb the excesses of the fanatics and extremists whose propensity for destruction did more to damage the cause of the gospel, which they professed to promote, than did all the bitter hostility of its open enemies. The more extreme their iconoclasm, the more they played into the hands of the opponents of reform and brought discredit on the work to with Briçonnet and Lefèvre had set their hands. At the other extreme were the no less fanatical traditionalists who were implacably antipathetic to any program involving change and renewal. Briçonnet's secretary, Jean Lermite, spoke of his indomitable patience in enduring the rebellious insolence of the uncooperative clergy whom he wished to constrain to fulfill their duties, and above all the inexcusable behavior of the Franciscans.[26] The bishop of Meaux's position was far from being a comfortable one: as he moved forward with the spiritual reform of his diocese he was beset, on the one hand, by those monks and clergy who bitterly opposed the disturbance of their complacent ineptitude, and, on the other, by the unrestrained spirit of those zealots who demanded and themselves took drastic action to bring about radical change without delay.

PROPOSITIONS FROM BRESLAU

Lefèvre's fundamental sympathy with the principles of the reform then taking place in other lands is apparent not only from his own writings of

---

25. For the text of this correspondence see *Guillaume Briçonnet et Marguerite d'Angoulême: Correspondance (1521–1524);* édition du texte et annotations par Christine Martineau et Michel Veissière avec le concours de Henry Heller, Vol. I, 1521–1522 (Geneva, 1975), Vol. II, 1523–1524 (Geneva, 1979).

26. Herminjard, I:156.

this period (which will be more fully discussed later) but also from certain things he says in the letter to Farel of 6 July 1524 from which we have quoted above. In it he acknowledged the receipt of letters from Farel, Ecolampadius, Pellican, and Hugwald, a number of books by German authors, and also certain "conclusions" or propositions that had been brought to Zwingli from Breslau and that Zwingli in turn had given to Farel when the latter was visiting Zürich. "It is remarkable," he wrote approvingly of these propositions, "how agreeably everything is expressed concerning the word of God, the supreme priesthood of Christ, and matrimony;" and to this commendation he added the wish: "May Christ reign everywhere! May his word take hold everywhere!"[27] The articles were the composition of Johannes Hess, a theologian of Breslau, whom Zwingli described as "a very precise and acute man" in a letter of 16 May 1524 to Vadian. Herminjard regarded "this adherence of Lefèvre to the doctrine of Johannes Hess" as "so explicit" that he included them in their entirety as an appendix to the letter sent to Farel.[28] The first section, on the word of God, may be summarized in the following statements:

> As all things have been created and are sustained by the word of God, all should subject themselves to that word. . . . Since men's fearful consciences are nourished and enlivened solely by the word of God, that word alone ought to be proclaimed and every man admonished and taught by it. . . . Because the word of God is altogether clean and pure, it ought not to be defiled by human decrees or traditions or by worldly regulations. . . . The light of God's word should not be darkened or extinguished by anyone. . . . The course of God's word, as his herald and messenger, ought to be impeded by no one, but all should strive with all their strength to promote its course. . . . Civil leaders and officials, inasmuch as they are God's ministers, have a special responsibility to provide the word of God for the benefit of those over whom they are placed, and not to hinder its progress. Otherwise they resist God and are unfaithful servants who bring judgment on themselves. . . . Since God's word is addressed to all, all should be able freely, in public and in private, and without any hindrance, to proclaim, hear, discuss, comment on, and expound that word of salvation. . . . As it is food and nourishment needed by all, God's word should be allowed to pass into the hearts and consciences of all without anyone prohibiting it.

The second section consists of nine theses concerning the unique priesthood of Christ. The repudiation of the sacerdotalism of the mass and the emphasis of the necessity of faith for the genuine partaking of Christ in the eucharist have their basis in the teaching of the Epistle to the Hebrews and in the accounts of the institution of the sacrament in the Gospels and in 1 Corinthians 11. We give this section in full:

---

27. Ibid., pp. 220, 225.
28. Ibid., pp. 228ff.

1. Having been appointed by God the Father through the word of an oath a priest for ever after the order of Melchizedek, Christ, the sole victim offered for sins, placed in charge of the household of God, is perpetually seated at the right hand of God and remains a priest perfected for ever, unique and alone, exercising a perpetual priesthood.

2. Moreover, he is able to save to the uttermost those who come to God through him, as he ever lives to intercede for them.

3. In the days of his flesh, when he delivered himself up as an offering for us and a victim to God for a sweet-smelling savor, he was at the same time both priest and victim, high priest and spotless lamb, bearing away the sins of the world.

4. By this unique offering of himself and this single sacrifice of his own body once performed he procured eternal redemption for us.

5. Furthermore, by this same unique offering he overthrew sin and made perfect for ever those who are being sanctified, nor is there any other victim for the sins of the whole human race.

6. Just as he died once for sin and suffered once for sins, the just for the unjust, that he might bring us to God, so also he was once offered and his sacrifice was made once for all, nor was he ever afterwards offered or sacrificed, nor is he being offered and sacrificed or being made a victim, just as he can nevermore die or suffer throughout eternity.

7. Therefore the mass and its performance cannot be a sacrifice (otherwise it would have been necessary for Christ often to have suffered from the foundation of the world, and likewise to have been slain and sacrificed often), but it is a commemoration of his once offered sacrifice and of the covenant made through him as priest and victim.

8. The words of Christ himself and of Paul show this, and Chrysostom agrees.

9. In this commemoration what is needful is not particular ceremonies or vestments, or other external rites, but true faith; for by this alone do we effectively participate in the covenant and the sacrifice.[29]

The "Zwinglian" character of these propositions is obvious. Leaders of reform in Geneva, Strasbourg, and Canterbury, who during the next two decades would be concerned with the formulation of a biblically revised doctrine of the eucharist, would have agreed with what is said in Hess's theses, but they would also have wished to say more. They would have agreed that the celebration of the sacrament is a commemoration (in accordance with Christ's command: "Do this in remembrance of me"), but they would have wished to add that it is also a means of grace, a seal of the gospel covenant, and a pledge of God's unfailing grace to those who draw near with faith—though these considerations may well be implicit in the last of the nine propositions.

29. Passages of the New Testament on which these propositions are based are the following: Hebrews 1:3, 13; 2:9–11; 3:1, 6; 4:14–16; 5:7–10; 6:17–20; 7:20–28; 8:1–2; 9:15, 24–28; 10:10–14; 12:2; Matthew 26:26–28; Mark 14:22–24; Luke 22:19–20; 1 Peter 3:18; 1 Corinthians 11:23–29.

The articles comprising the third section relate to the question of matrimony. They affirm that marriage, which was instituted by God at creation and is shown throughout the Bible to be a state lawful for all to enjoy, should still be lawful, free, and public for all persons, and forbidden to no category of men; that those who prohibit it despise God the Father, from whom every family in heaven and earth is named (Eph. 3:15), and are disobedient to his word; that those who teach the contrary give heed to impostrous spirits and to the doctrines of demons;[30] and that, though it should be permitted to all to marry, yet marriage is not an end in itself, for it points beyond itself to the great mystery that unites Christ and the church (Eph. 5:23ff.). From his approbation of these propositions it follows that Lefèvre now agreed in principle with the opinion that the clergy should be free to marry. It does not seem, however, to have been an issue that engaged his attention. His interest was concentrated on the urgent necessity of evangelism and of providing the Scriptures for the French people in their own language.

GÉRARD ROUSSEL

An interesting letter of 6 July 1524 from Roussel to Farel, who was in Basel, gives further information concerning what was happening at Meaux at this time. "I cannot tell you," Roussel wrote, "how much I wish that our people [in France] had never departed from evangelical simplicity and that they would conform their ways to the simple rule of Christ, as I hear is now happening with you, though there are objections from the wise men of this world"—a reference to the opposition Farel had encountered in Basel from some of the university professors, and also from Erasmus, who was strongly antipathetic to Farel. Roussel spoke of his high esteem for Ecolampadius "who, though he is so abundantly competent in every branch of learning that he is virtually without a rival, has committed himself totally to Christ," and mentioned his desire to meet in person one whose writings he admired so greatly and of whom Farel spoke so highly. Roussel feared, however, that he lacked both the ability and the courage of an Ecolampadius and he expressed his sense of inadequacy to put into effect Farel's proposal that he should draft and publish, as a counteroffensive to the adversaries at the Sorbonne, a number of articles setting forth the essentials of evangelical doctrine.

In order to demonstrate the strength and determination of the opposition, Roussel described the action that had been taken only recently in Paris against the evangelicals. The magistrates had placed a ban on particular doctrines propagated at Meaux; further, they had summoned Martial Mazurier and Pierre Caroli, who then submitted to the demand that they renounce their

---

30. 1 Timothy 4:1f.; v. 3 continues immediately, "forbidding to marry."

evangelical beliefs. This incident, he told Farel, would show him how deficient in ardor and fortitude they were. Roussel narrated, further, that subsequently the Parlement had sanctioned an order for the arrest and imprisonment of four men, two of whom he named as Martial (Mazurier) and Moses (whom Herminjard supposes may be Michel d'Arande). The four fled for their lives, but one of them had been captured and, bound hand and foot, ignominiously brought to Paris and imprisoned in the company of the worst criminals with the intention that he should soon be burnt. Moreover, they were hunting for "Moses" because they were eager to burn him, too. It was reported that they had no intention of sparing Lefèvre and Roussel himself and even the bishop of Meaux; had Briçonnet and the king's sister not taken effective steps, "the affair, which has had a happy conclusion thanks to God's will and his consideration of our weakness, was unlikely to have stopped short of the flames."

"There is no one to be found who will courageously take his stand for God's cause in overthrowing the petty regulations of men," Roussel informed Farel. He insisted that they had no way of counteracting the sanctions imposed on the printing of books by the Parlement, "unless that Spirit who is able to do all things ignites our hearts and strengthens us with a constancy not our own which will enable us not to shrink from persecutions, tortures, fires or any other sort of death"; and he begged Farel to pray that they might be granted the courage they lacked. Roussel should not be censured for this apparent irresolution, for he had a proper estimate of the frailty of the flesh and rightly recognized the need for more than ordinary courage. The history of Christian martyrdom is the history of weak and fearful men and women divinely empowered to endure joyfully the most appalling sufferings. Indeed, the day was fast approaching when the evangelicals in Meaux and Paris and elsewhere would produce martyrs from their ranks.

They did, in fact, find ways of stultifying the Parisian censorship. One was to have books printed outside the country. Lefèvre had already had works printed in Antwerp, and it was a policy he could now pursue advantageously in promoting the cause to which he had committed himself, especially for the publication of his French translations of Scripture. Another possibility was the setting up of an evangelical printing press in Meaux, since the authority of the theological faculty of the Sorbonne did not extend beyond the capital, unless authorized by the king and Parlement—and at this stage the king's sympathies were with Meaux rather than Paris. Farel had actually advocated the setting up of a press, the main purpose of which would be the production of books in the vernacular. Roussel responded to this suggestion in the same letter of 6 July 1524. He told Farel that he and his colleagues had discussed and approved his plan, and that they now intended to establish their own printing house in Meaux and at their own expense to produce books for distribution without charge to the poor.

Because, however, of the unsettling events of the following months, which culminated in the disbanding of Lefèvre's circle in Meaux, the plan never became a reality.

With regard to his own activities in Meaux, Roussel told Farel that besides his customary preaching, in which he was going through the gospel in the order in which it was written, he had started expounding the Epistles of Paul daily to the populace,[31] while also continuing his exposition of the Psalter to persons of education. He then mentioned that Josse Clichtove, "who used to be on our side" *(Clichtoveus olim noster)*, had become a determined opponent of the evangelical movement. In Paris, where he still resided, Clichtove had been Lefèvre's disciple and had collaborated with him in producing many publications. In addition, he edited numerous philosophical and patristic writings and wrote commentaries on some of the works edited by Lefèvre. As mentioned earlier, when he received his doctorate in 1506, Clichtove spoke of his devotion and indebtedness to Lefèvre; and later he came to his master's defense in the controversy over the three Marys.[32] But soon after that, as the hostility against Lefèvre increased, he turned his back on his former loyalties and went over to the opposition. Roussel passed on the news that Clichtove had already completed a number of treatises against Luther, and that their publication was expected soon.[33]

After closing his letter with terms of affection, Roussel added that Caroli was publicly expounding Paul with great acceptance in Paris, in the parish of St. Paul—actually, he was preaching from the vernacular translation of the Pauline Epistles, as Lefèvre stated in his letter of the same date to Farel.[34] This is of interest because, as Roussel indicated earlier in his letter, Caroli had been silenced in Meaux. A month after Roussel wrote this letter, on 5 August, Caroli was arraigned before the Sorbonne faculty to account for his novel style of preaching and also for his use of a vernacular version of the New Testament. Yet just two months later, on 5 October, Jacques Pauvan wrote from Meaux to Farel and reported that Caroli was "assiduously preaching" in Paris: "Although he is in the midst of a wicked and perverse nation, in the midst, I might say, of horned theologians, yet he does not on that account desist from the word of God, which is more powerful than all the enemies of the cross of Christ."[35] Three days after this letter was written, however, the Sorbonne theologians issued a judgment forbidding Caroli to continue preaching. Their position was

---

31. See p. 137 above.

32. See pp. 122f. above.

33. Clichtove's *Antilutherus* appeared on 13 October that same year (1524) and his *Propugnaculum ecclesiae adversus Lutheranos* on 18 May 1525.

34. Herminjard, I: 227. For the text of Roussel's letter to Farel see Herminjard, I: 232ff.

35. Ibid., pp. 291ff.

strengthened by the fact that Caroli had come into the diocese of Paris uninvited and without an appointment to a cure of souls there. Even so, he seems to have been able to preach for a while longer in disregard of the ruling; but after a few weeks he left the capital and took a position in Alençon offered him by Marguerite.

During this same period further developments affected evangelicals and their witness in other parts of France. On 2 August 1524 Pierre Toussain wrote from Basel to Farel, who was then active in Montbéliard, a town some thirty miles west of Basel and the Swiss border, and expressed his gratitude to God that the light of the gospel was daily shining with increasing brightness not only in Montbéliard but also throughout France.[36] On the same date and from the same place Ecolampadius sent Farel a letter saying how greatly he rejoiced over the blessing that was attending his ministry in Montbéliard. (Very soon, however, it would suffer unruly interruption, largely as the result of Farel's intemperate zeal.) Ecolampadius mentioned his grief because of the apparent unproductiveness of his own preaching: ''Perhaps I would have done better had I taught a company of Turks,'' he exclaimed—neglecting, it seems, to apply to himself an admonition he had just given to Farel concerning the necessity for patience, love, and faith. He asked Farel to pray that God's word might not be despised through any cowardice or ill humor on his part.[37]

On 24 August, in another letter to Farel, Roussel ventured the opinion that the comparatively tardy progress of the gospel in France might be attributed to divine overruling. He was hopeful that the time was coming when there would be less need for conflict and also better opportunity for leading the people back from darkness into light—an aspiration prompted by the prospect, still bright, of the evangelical movement prevailing in France, thanks, on the human side, to the favor of the king and his sister and other influential persons. Roussel even warned the headstrong Farel against moving ahead of the operation of the Lord, to whom it belonged— not to Farel or anyone else—to send forth workers, lest from an overemphasis on human freedom he should seem to detract from the divine sovereignty. ''The old serpent is cunning,'' he wrote, ''and if we are not vigilant he easily transforms our otherwise extremely pious zeal into our idol.''[38]

Thus Roussel attempted to curb Farel's impulsive nature and to justify his own hesitancy—though the latter would seem to be overstated, since he was diligently propagating the faith in Meaux, and there is no reason to conclude that he imagined that divine sovereignty provided an excuse

---

36. Ibid., pp. 250f.

37. Ibid., pp. 253f.

38. Ibid., pp. 271ff. On the same date Roussel also wrote to Ecolampadius in a similar vein; ibid., pp. 274ff.

for human passivity. But he had some reason for fearing that the activism advocated by Farel might well prove to be rashness, which would be more harmful than beneficial in the long run. To jeopardize by immoderate conduct what was by no means an insubstantial hope of nationwide renewal would be foolish. This was a time when the issue was still in the balance, weighted, if anything, in favor of the evangelicals. The day, indeed, would soon arrive when Roussel would be preaching boldly in Paris to great audiences.[39] As things turned out, the unbridled actions of some reckless spirits contributed in large measure to the frustration of the hopes of a bright noontide for the gospel in France. In any case, it seemed to be a matter of "more haste less speed" with Farel, who, despite his impatience, was then making less progress elsewhere in France than were his friends in Meaux, who probably felt that having left their ranks he should not now be criticizing them.

THE FIRST BURNINGS

As the year 1524 drew to its close the storm clouds of persecution were building up threateningly over France. The intensification of the opposition to the evangelical movement was indicated in a letter Pierre de Sébiville, a Franciscan friar minor, wrote from Grenoble on 28 December 1524 to Anémand de Coct in Zürich (de Coct, otherwise known as Gallus, a Latinized form of his name, was chevalier of Rhodes and seigneur of Chastelard in the Dauphiné).

> You ought to know [de Sébiville said] that Satan has destroyed the harvest of the Gospel that has been growing in France,[40] and even in Grenoble those from whom you expected much are vacillating, and I alone remain and have been forbidden to preach on pain of death. Nothing has been said about discussing the Gospel in secret, but to speak of it publicly can lead only to burning."[41]

Herminjard is surely right in taking de Sébiville to mean that he had no intention of submitting to the order to keep silent, and there is every likelihood that de Sébiville was the unnamed *cordelier* (Franciscan) "who belonged to the party of Luther" mentioned in the *Journal d'un bourgeois de Paris* as having been burned at Grenoble in February 1525.

De Sébiville related that the Thomists had wished to deprive him of his liberty and that had it not been for "certain secret friends" he would have been delivered into the hands of "the Pharisees." He suggests identity

---

39. See p. 180 below.

40. This must be judged an unduly pessimistic generalization, prompted by the situation in which de Sébiville found himself.

41. Herminjard, I:314.

of these friends by going on to say that when the king was in Lyon—during August 1524—there were two "great personages" in Grenoble, namely, Antoine Papillon, "the *premier* of France and one who knows the Gospel well," and Antoine du Blet, a leader in the business world who was a native of Lyon. He mentioned, further, that Papillon had translated Luther's treatise on monastic prayers for "Madame d'Alençon, the king's sister," and that this had occasioned him a great deal of trouble with the "Parisian vermin." The most influential of the "secret friends" was undoubtedly Marguerite, of whom de Sébiville observed that "there is no one in France more evangelical than Madame d'Alençon."

A short time previously, on 17 December, Anémand de Coct had sent Farel this news: "Meigret has been arrested in Lyon; but Madame d'Alençon is there, praise be to God! De Sébiville has been set free and will preach on St. Paul this coming Lent in Lyon."[42] Aimé Meigret, who had been seized for preaching heterodoxy and for publicly supporting Lefèvre's position on the "three Marys," was not set free. Francis I had gone off to pursue his disastrous campaign in Italy and his mother, Louise of Savoy, was acting as regent in his absence. It was with her approval that Meigret was sent to Paris to be tried before the Sorbonne. A letter of 23 January 1525 sent on behalf of the archbishop of Lyon (François de Rohan) to Noël Béda complained of "heretical, erroneous, and scandalous propositions, emanating from the Lutheran sect, preached by the said Meigret both in this city and in Grenoble." Severe punishment of "this pernicious man" was demanded "for the good of Christianity," together with the condemnation of the offensive propositions "so that our catholic faith may soon be restored to its integrity."[43] In Paris Meigret was censured for having taught *inter alia,* that "academic preachers and professors of our number are openly putting the cart before the horse by giving our works precedence over the grace of God." Sentence was passed requiring him to make a public retraction in Lyon where he had propounded his evangelical doctrines, and the burning of the sermons he had published. Meigret did not regain his liberty until 1527. He died in Strasbourg the following year.

De Sébiville informed de Coct, moreover (in the letter cited above), that three months previously, while visiting his diocese, the bishop of Meaux, accompanied by Lefèvre, had ordered the burning of all images, with the exception of the crucifix; consequently, they had both been summoned to appear in person the following March to answer before the parliamentary and university authorities for their actions.[44] This news, however, reflected the charges that were being made against Briçonnet by the Franciscans of his diocese and other ill-disposed persons rather than the true facts. As

42. Ibid., p. 309.
43. Ibid., pp. 323ff.
44. Ibid., pp. 313ff.

already mentioned, there were a few iconoclastic extremists about, but it is inconceivable that Briçonnet was one of them or condoned their actions. His injunctions of the previous year[45] had required the invocation of the saints, and this would ill accord with the destruction of their statues. Iconoclasm would also be incompatible with the admonition Briçonnet issued on 15 January 1525, not long after the writing of de Sébiville's letter, declaring his extreme displeasure and grief over the excesses committed by some intransigent persons "whom we do not hesitate to call children of Satan." He specifically censured their action in slashing with a knife "certain prayers composed in honor and praise of the most holy Virgin and other saints" that had been placed in various parts of the cathedral church. Briçonnet denounced them for "violating by this execrable offense holy places and laying their sacrilegious hands on these tablets consecrated to the Almighty and his temple, with the intention of scandalously defying Christ, his glorious Mother, and the saints, although they are beyond insult and injury." He commanded the clergy to give a solemn warning, publicly and audibly, from the pulpit, to "these miserable children of wrath and perdition, together with their accomplices and all others who know or have learned anything about this matter," that if after six days they had not revealed what they knew they would be excommunicated, and if they obstinately persisted in keeping silent they would be denounced "publicly and in the presence of all, with the bells ringing and the candles lighted, and then extinguished and thrown to the ground, as a sign of eternal malediction."[46] Thus, we must conclude that Briçonnet himself was innocent of any act of iconoclasm, a fact that must have been well known to his accusers. But by depicting him as the champion of "Lutheranism" at Meaux his calumniators were intent on bringing about his downfall without being scrupulous as to how they did it.

The consternation caused by the fact that in many places evangelical preaching was attracting large crowds of eager listeners led to the adoption of measures designed by their drastic character to snuff out this new enthusiasm. The first burning took place in Metz, where the Augustinian monk Jean Châtelain, a powerful preacher and propagator of the evangelical faith in that part of France, suffered martyrdom on 12 January 1525 following an imprisonment of nine months attended by much cruelty. Châtelain's close friend François Lambert of Avignon, a Franciscan who had been preaching the evangelical message in France and Switzerland for some years, described the occasion in a letter written some two months later to Frederick, the Elector of Saxony. He told how Châtelain's preaching had drawn huge audiences and how his exposure of the corruption prevailing in the church had so disturbed the ecclesiastical officials that they planned to put him to

---

45. See pp. 134ff. above.
46. Herminjard, I:320ff.

death. Unmoved by threats and torture, he went to the scaffold, Lambert said, as though he were going to a banquet. "I knew him intimately," he wrote; "we were bound to each other like David and Jonathan. He was about fifty years old; he was a substantial scholar, devoted to the study of theology; his character was reflective, firm, courageous, his appearance imposing, his eloquence ardent."[47] Interestingly, he declared from the scaffold that he had never been a follower of Luther.[48] His violent death aroused the populace, by whom he had been loved and venerated, to frenzied action. Massed angrily against the authorities, ecclesiastical and civil, they demanded and obtained the release of another prisoner, Jean Védaste, for whom a similar fate was intended; and he, after receiving monetary compensation, left Metz to find refuge with Lambert in Strasbourg.[49]

As already mentioned,[50] a Franciscan of "Lutheran" sympathies, probably Pierre de Sébiville, was burned at Grenoble in February 1525. In Metz, though the officialdom had been badly shaken by the reaction of the crowd to the execution of Châtelain, the determination to stamp out the evangelical presence persisted. Writing to the senate of the city of Besançon on 15 August, Lambert (in Strasbourg) reported that certain preachers who had come to Metz with the intention of carrying on the work of Châtelain (two of whom were Toussain and Farel)[51] had found it expedient to flee unceremoniously for their lives. Subsequently, however, Jean Leclerc, a citizen of Meaux (whence he had been expelled), who spent much of his spare time distributing portions of the French Scriptures and Lutheran tracts from house to house, had been arraigned before the Parlement and punished with public flogging both in Paris and in Meaux, and then, after being branded, had arrived in Metz, intending, it seems, to settle there. The city officials, Lambert related, "combined a sort of idolatrous mania with their cruelty and, contrary to the commandments of God, demanded that worship should be paid to images." Leclerc, "incensed by such sacrilge," proceeded to smash a number of images in the cemetery and chapel of St. Louis, including two of the Virgin and Child. The next day he was arrested and thrown into prison. At his trial he vigorously defended his action and thereby invited the pronouncement of the death sentence. On 22 July he was burned to death in the central square of the city (the Champ-à-Seille). Before the flames were kindled he boldly addressed the multitude that had gathered to witness his execution, and when urged to request the people to recite a *Paternoster* and an *Ave Maria* for him, he replied: "I ask you to recite the Lord's Prayer for me, in order that he may enable me to be faithful."

---

47. Ibid., pp. 344ff.; J. Crespin, *Histoire des martyrs* (Geneva, 1554), pp. 247ff.

48. M. Mousseaux, op. cit., p. 56.

49. Herminjard, I:344ff.; R. Lovy, op. cit., pp. 115ff.

50. See p. 145 above.

51. Herminjard, I:338.

When asked why he had not also requested an *Ave Maria* to be said, he responded: "If anyone wishes to recite it, let him do it, but I do not ask for it—not because I despise the Blessed Virgin, but because I cling to the Lord Jesus Christ who died for me: he is the sole mediator and advocate between God and men."[52]

Meanwhile, the situation in Meaux was becoming increasingly difficult for Lefèvre and his colleagues. In February 1525 an attempt was made to indict Roussel for leading the common people into error through the use of scriptural texts in the vernacular, for insulting the pope by contemptuous treatment of a bull of indulgence recently issued, and for failure to use the *Ave Maria* in public worship. In March the iconoclastic Jean Leclerc was (as already mentioned) banished from the city. At the end of March, Jacques Pauvan,[53] accused of disparaging the Virgin Mary and the saints as powerless to help those who call upon them, was arrested and brought before the Parlement in Paris, and then imprisoned in the Conciergerie together with Matthieu Saulnier who had been his fellow pastor in Meaux. With them in the same place was Aimé Meigret who (as described above) had been sent from Lyon to stand trial. Pauvan and Saulnier were charged with heresy on the basis of certain doctrines they had been propounding. Denounced as Waldensian, Wycliffite, Bohemian (Hussite), and Lutheran in origin, the articles to which objection was taken declared, in part, that "there is no such place as purgatory, since the Gospel affirms that there is no forgiveness of sins apart from the death and sacrifice of Jesus Christ"; that "God has no need of a vicar"; that "to make the Virgin a queen of mercy and a source of life and salvation is to proclaim a vain faith, since there is no salvation except in Jesus Christ"; that "images and candles are conducive to idolatry" and "it is better to destroy the images of the saints than to see the simple people led astray by them"; that "masses cannot ensure the forgiveness of sins"; that "the sacrament of the eucharist is for the living and not for the dead"; that "it is better to hear one good sermon than a hundred masses"; that "God alone pardons sins" and "the pope can have no power to pardon sins if he does not have the Holy Spirit with him"; and that apart from faith baptism amounts to nothing. Pauvan and Saulnier were sentenced to death by burning.

This sentence was set aside, however, when Martial Mazurier persuaded Pauvan to recant publicly his evangelical views. Mazurier, as we have seen, had recanted some months previously; it was to his delation Pauvan and Saulnier owed their present plight. At Christmastide 1525 Pauvan submitted to the humiliating procedure of making amends for his faults in front of

---

52. Ibid., pp. 371ff.; Lovy, op. cit., pp. 117ff., who gives the day of Leclerc's execution as 29 July; Crespin, op. cit., pp. 244f., who gives the year incorrectly as 1524. For the last statement see 1 Timothy 2:5.

53. There is a wide variety of spellings for this name: Pauvan, Pauvant, Pavannes, Pavanes, Pouent, Povan, Pavan.

the cathedral of Notre-Dame, petitioning God and Our Lady to pardon him for having proclaimed heretical doctrines. His death sentence was commuted to seven years of confinement on bread and water in the prison of Saint-Martin-des-Champs. But, filled with remorse at having compromised his convictions in this way, Pauvan withdrew his recantation and presented his judges with a written profession of his evangelical faith. The sentence of death was reimposed, and on 22 August 1526 he was burned alive in the Place-de-Gréve, but not before he had addressed the assembled crowd with an eloquent affirmation of the beliefs for which he was now suffering.[54]

ERASMUS AND PARIS

We have noticed that not only were the names of Luther and Lefèvre anathema to the Sorbonne and other centers of traditionalism but so also was the name of Erasmus, who had brought disfavor on himself because of his scathing and irreverent mockery of ecclesiastical casuistry, pomposity, and superstition in his *Praise of Folly* and *Colloquies*. In 1522 the prior of the Carmelites in Louvain complained that the *Colloquies* contained "Lutheran" heresies and should be consigned to the flames.

Among the French admirers of the writings of Erasmus was Louis de Berquin, a gentleman of good family and education from Artois, who resided in Paris and had been influenced by Lefèvre's doctrines. He came under the displeasure of the Sorbonne professors because he had translated and circulated "Lutheran" works, including some by Erasmus. Action to put a stop to such unwelcome conduct was first taken in 1523 when, on 15 June, Berquin was summoned before the theological faculty and convicted of heretical activity. The writings that had been discovered in his home were ordered to be publicly burned and he was imprisoned in the *Conciergerie* and would, it seems, also have been committed to the flames had not the king intervened and obtained his release. But it was only a matter of time before the scaffold would claim his life.

For Paris and the French, Erasmus had little liking, notwithstanding his friendship with scholars like Lefèvre and Budé. We have already noticed his low opinion of Béda and Duchêne (Quercus).[55] In the middle of 1523, when Berquin was under investigation, the theologians of the Sorbonne, led by the indefatigable Béda, had judged portions of Erasmus's publications to be heretical. Then in August his Latin translation of the New Testament had come under condemnation. During the first part of 1524, Béda, at the faculty's request, was busy preparing a "censure" of particular teachings of Erasmus derived from an examination of his *Paraphrase of*

---

54. Herminjard, I:293f., 390f.; Crespin, op. cit., pp. 263f.; Lovy, op. cit., pp. 127ff. The subsequent history of Matthieu Saulnier is not clear.

55. See p. 129 above.

Luke's Gospel and *Exposition of the Lord's Prayer*. Erasmus responded from Basel by writing a letter on 28 April 1525 to Béda. His tone was polite and restrained. Criticism, he assured Béda, was welcome, even though his works had been highly praised by notable scholars.

He did take exception, however, to the intemperate manner in which Pierre Couturier (known also as Sutor)[56] had attacked him in a small book he had published, which was full of "slander, scorn, stupidity, and ignorance." His ineptitude was such that it reminded him of the old proverb, "Let the cobbler stick to his last" *(Ne sutor ultra crepidam)*. Couturier did not have enough sense (and this was as much a thrust at Béda) to see that to denounce Erasmus's Latin translation of the New Testament was in effect to denounce the pope, "who approved our labor with his commendation, not to mention Adrian VI[57] who, far from condemning my industry, actually urged me to do the same for the Old Testament as I had done for the New." Erasmus also drew attention to the applause his work had received from "innumerable persons outstanding for their virtue no less than for their learning."[58]

Béda would have been blind indeed not to see that his own actions brought him under the lash of Erasmus's scorn, even though Erasmus referred to the stupidity of others; but the tone of his response was no less polite. His criticisms, he protested, were prompted by a wholehearted desire for the salvation of Erasmus's soul, which compelled him to point out that many of his opinions were pernicious and a cause of serious offense to Christian people. He mentioned in particular Erasmus's views on such things as clerical celibacy, monastic vows, fasting and the prohibition of meat, the observance of festal days, the evangelical counsels, the translation of Scripture into the vernacular, and the symbols of the church. With regard to providing the populace with the Scriptures in their mother tongue, Béda remarked that the bishop of Meaux had found to his own cost "what sort of benefit the illiterate populace of his diocese has gained from the sweatings of Jacques Lefèvre in this matter"—a reference to the troubles then confronting Briçonnet. In conclusion, Béda mentioned Berquin's translations of certain of Erasmus's treatises, which had met with the disapproval of the theological faculty of Paris.[59]

Erasmus replied on 15 June 1525 with a long and interesting letter, extending to some 10,000 words, which was in effect an *apologia* for himself and his works. He was clearly deeply annoyed at the Sorbonne's condemnation of his writings. He complained of critics in Belguim who had loudly denounced him as an antichrist and his works as heretical, but who, when

---

56. Erasmus used "Sutor," i.e. "cobbler," the Latin equivalent of Couturier's name.

57. Pope Adrian VI had died in 1523.

58. Allen, VI:67ff.

59. Ibid., 81ff.

challenged to point out the errors that needed correction, had been forced
to admit that they had not even read the books they so harshly condemned.
Nor were Béda and his colleagues in Paris innocent of similar obscurant-
ism, for (Erasmus contended) Couturier's hostile booklet showed him to
be a man who needed an exorcist rather than a doctor, and yet it carried
the approval of Béda (sanctioned as it was on the title page by the faculty
of theology). How could Béda excuse this, since it caused many to make
a mouse into an elephant? Erasmus complained, further, that it was unfair
for him to be condemned because of Berquin's translations of some of his
writings, which were made without his knowledge.

He also seemed anxious to keep some distance between himself and
Lefèvre: "You will see, I think, that Lefèvre and I are very different,"
he told Béda. "He strongly asserts things; I do no more than discuss, always
leaving the judgment to others"[60]—a self-assessment that reflects his self-
protective cautiousness but is far from true of much of his writing. Again,
a year later, in a letter of 23 June 1526 to the theological faculty of Paris,
he protested that Béda "has in fact more just cause for raving against
Lefèvre, and yet he deals gently with him" (a far from accurate statement);
"but when he turns to me he becomes the censor and belches out nothing
but charges of blasphemy and heresy."[61] This controversy culminated in
the publication by Béda in 1529 of a work with the title *Apologia against
Clandestine Lutherans*,[62] among whom he assigned Erasmus a prominent
place.

In the letters he wrote to Berquin during these years Erasmus is evidently
more concerned to guard his own reputation by dissuading the Frenchman
from continuing to translate and distribute his compositions than to express
any compassionate sentiment of warmth and gratitude for the way Berquin
placed himself at risk by spreading Erasmus's teachings. Even after Berquin
had been cruelly executed (on 17 April 1529, following his third trial),
Erasmus maintained an almost callous detachment, unwilling to commit
himself by any appearance of taking sides. "If he did not deserve it, I am
sorry; if he did deserve it, I am doubly sorry," he wrote to Willibald
Pirckheimer on 9 May 1529. "I have insufficient knowledge of the real
facts of the case, nor did I know Berquin except from what he wrote and
what some have told me about him."[63]

It was actually in response to Berquin's prompting that Erasmus sent
letters to the Parlement and to the king of France in mid-1526. In the former,
dated 14 June, he complained of the reckless manner in which Béda and
Couturier had attacked and condemned him and Lefèvre, though he

60. Ibid., pp. 88ff.

61. Ibid., p. 365.

62. *Apologia adversus clandestinos Lutheranos.*

63. Allen, VIII:160.

disclaimed any involvement with Lefèvre and his affairs. They raved against him, he protested, "much more virulently than they do against Luther himself"; and he affirmed that in Béda's censures of his work there were more than a hundred obvious falsehoods and calumnies.[64] In the letter to Francis I, dated two days later, Erasmus began by expressing his pleasure that the calamity of the king's capture was now a thing of the past and that he had been restored to his own country and people. He then turned to the Parisian scene, using graphic language that left no room for misunderstanding about his own feelings or his exasperated contempt for the theologians of the Sorbonne.

> By writings no less unlearned than venomous [he complained], they lay themselves open to the derision of the world, raving in particular against Jacques Lefèvre and myself with scurrilous clamorings. They are the laughing-stock of men who are learned and wise, but at the same time they damage our reputation among unskilled and simple folk, and they defraud us of the fruit of our studies which we have pursued with such diligence. Lefèvre will answer for himself.

After giving examples of their slanders, he continued, "And these are the very men who pass judgment on heresy! Denounced by them, good men are dragged into prison and thrown to the flames, preferring to suffer death rather than that they themselves should be convicted of false witness." Erasmus warned the king that if such men were allowed to pursue their policy with impunity the celebrated university of Paris would be no better than "a cave of bandits." Indeed, he charged that they were subversively promoting tyranny in defiance of the king's authority, and urged the king to take action against this "gang of conspiratorial monks and theologians."[65]

A new and expanded edition of the *Colloquies* was published in 1529, and in it Erasmus vented his spleen derisively on Béda and his colleagues, who in 1526 had censured an earlier edition, condemning sixty-nine places as erroneous or tending to corrupt youthful morals (a verdict with which Luther would not have been unsympathetic!). His counterattack, however, was more coarse than subtle. The Latin equivalent of Noël Béda's name was Natalis Beda, and, in a characteristic pseudo-etymological pun, Erasmus spoke of a kind of beet the ancients called "swimming beet."[66] It had, he said, "a twisted and knotty stalk," was "remarkably insipid," and emitted "a foul stench if you came in contact with it, as bad as stinking bean-trefoil."

---

64. Ibid., VI:358ff.

65. Ibid., pp. 361ff. On 23 June, a week later, Erasmus wrote to the theological professors of the Sorbonne, expressing his firm opposition to Luther and the Zwinglians and complaining that instead of applauding him they had attacked him, and had done so much more bitterly and violently than they had Luther. See Allen, VI: 364ff.

66. The Latin is *natatalis beta*, a play on the name Natalis Beda.

To the question "Why do they call it swimming?" he replied, "because it grows in damp and rotten places, and never better than in filth or dung," and has "a smell no excrement could beat."[67] Offensive abuse of this kind could hardly be expected to induce a change of attitude on the part of Béda and his fellow professors. The open scurrility of Erasmus's language may in some degree be attributed to the fact that a couple of years previously the French king had issued a public edict forbidding the sale of Béda's *Annotations* in which both Erasmus and Lefèvre were attacked.

To speculate how the course of affairs in Paris might have been affected had Erasmus become the first head of the Collège de France would be tempting. The Collège de France was planned as a royal foundation that would rival other national institutions of learning and culture such as the university of Alcala in Spain and Leo X's College of Young Greeks in Rome. Early in 1517 Guillaume Budé had written to tell Erasmus that the king of France had him in mind for the principalship. Such negotiations as followed, however, came to nothing, partly, it seems, because of Erasmus's own native lack of decisiveness, and partly because, as mentioned earlier, neither Paris nor the French held any strong attraction for him. His correspondence with Budé, which started in 1516 on a note of mutual adulation, ended a dozen years later in mutual aversion, at a time when the Collège de France was becoming a going concern.[68] But his friendship with Lefèvre survived. The events we have been discussing serve to illustrate not merely the fluctuating fortunes of the struggle between the traditionalists and the evangelicals in Paris and beyond, but also the unpredictability during this period of its ultimate outcome.

LEFÈVRE'S BIBLICAL COMMENTARIES
AND TRANSLATIONS

During his brief ministry in Meaux Lefèvre energetically prosecuted his program of preaching, translating, and commenting on the Bible. In June 1522 his Latin commentary on the Gospels[69] was published in Meaux by Simon de Colines. In the preface, addressed "to Christian readers," Lefèvre affirmed that "the word of Christ is the word of God, the Gospel of peace, liberty, and joy, the Gospel of salvation, redemption, and life," for it gives peace "after incessant war," liberty "after the harshest slavery," joy "after unremitting grief," salvation "after total perdition," redemp-

---

67. *The Colloquies of Erasmus*, trans. Craig R. Thompson (Chicago, 1965), pp. 396ff. This colloquy is entitled *Synodus grammaticorum*, which Thompson renders "A Meeting of the Philological Society."

68. See David O. McNeil, *Guillaume Budé and Humanism in the Reign of Francis I* (Geneva, 1975), esp. chapter six.

69. *Commentarii initiatorii in Quatuor Evangelia.*

tion "after the most wretched captivity," and life "after endless death."
It is called the gospel because "it announces to us the infinite blessings
that await us above." Aware that those who do not love Christ and his word
cannot be Christians, Lefèvre expressed the earnest desire that kings,
princes, and peoples of all nations should make "God's life-giving word,
his holy Gospel," their chief concern and delight, indeed that "the sole
study, comfort, and longing of all should be to know the Gospel, to follow
the Gospel, and everywhere to promote the Gospel," since "to know nothing
except the Gospel is to know everything." The word of God has now become
his exclusive and passionate obsession:

> The word of God is sufficient; this alone is enough for the discovery of
> the life which knows no end; this rule alone is the guide to eternal life;
> all else on which the word of God does not shine is as unnecessary as
> it is superfluous.

Lefèvre was firmly convinced that the recovery of the central message
and authority of Holy Scripture was essential for the revitalization of the
Christian church:

> Would that that standard of belief might be sought from the primitive
> Church which consecrated so many martyrs to Christ, which knew no
> rule apart from the Gospel, and which offered worship to none except
> the Triune God! Truly, if we lived according to this pattern, the eternal
> Gospel of Christ would flourish now as it flourished then. They were then
> entirely dependent on Christ; let us also be entirely dependent on him.
> None lived by his own spirit, but by Christ's Spirit; let this also be the
> manner of our living. And so at last we shall go from this life to him,
> as they also for whom Christ was everything have gone before us, all
> of whom we love and praise for Christ's sake; and therefore with them
> we offer all worship and glory to God alone.

Recalling how the gospel spread to many nations in the early centuries,
Lefèvre was confident that a new day of conquest for the gospel had dawned.
For this he prayed and labored, and this commentary on the Gospels was
directed toward the achievement of this end.[70]
    The appearance of this work incited Lefèvre's enemies at the Sorbonne
to take further steps to silence him. An official investigation was instituted
for the purpose of examining the volume and pronouncing on the heretical
elements contained in it; but on 18 June 1523, just two days after the ses-
sions had commenced, the dean of the faculty was summoned before the
chancellor of France, Antoine Duprat, with whom were the bishops of
Meaux, Langres, and Senlis, to hear a communication from the king forbidding the investigation and condemnation of Lefèvre's commentary, except
on the condition that all the articles alleged to be suspect of error should

---

70. Rice, pp. 434ff.

first be submitted to the chancellor and the three bishops mentioned for their examination.

Lefèvre's French translation of the Gospels, which was the first part of his translation of the New Testament, was also published during June 1523, in Paris. The introductory epistle, addressed "to all Christian men and women," confirmed the earnestness with which his mind was set on the renewal of the church through the power of the Scriptures.

> The time has come [he wrote] when our Lord Jesus Christ, who alone is salvation, truth, and life, wishes his Gospel to be purely proclaimed throughout the world, so that people may no longer be led astray by alien doctrines of men who think they are something, when (as St. Paul says) they are nothing and deceive themselves [Gal. 6:3]. Now, however, we can say with St. Paul, "Behold, now is the acceptable time, now is the day of salvation"[2 Cor. 6:2].

He explained that he had translated the Gospels into the common tongue in order to make it possible for all who were familiar with the French language but ignorant of Latin to receive "this present grace, which God, thanks alone to his goodness, pity, and mercy, offers us at this time through the sweet and loving favor of Jesus Christ our only Saviour," with the consequence that "the simple members of the body of Jesus Christ, having this in their own language, can be as certain of evangelical truth as those who have it in Latin." Lefèvre promised that they would soon have the rest of the New Testament, "which is the book of life and the sole rule of Christians " thus matching what was being done for other peoples with their different languages throughout most of Europe.

Lefèvre warned his readers that there was an urgent necessity "that great and small should know the holy Gospel," for, as in ancient times the Babylonians had been the instruments of judgment on God's people, so now divine judgment was impending through the instrumentality of the Turks, the enemies of the Christian faith. If this should happen, the purpose would be "to correct the faults of Christianity, which are very great." It could be avoided, but only if there were "soon a return to God together with the abandonment of all futile confidence in any creature whatsoever and in all human traditions which cannot save, and allegiance to the word of God alone which is spirit and life." Lefèvre accordingly exhorted his readers in the following terms:

> Let us all therefore endeavor to know God's will through the holy Gospel so that in the time of trial which is at our door we may not be left with those who are rejected. Let us welcome the sweet visitation of Jesus Christ, our sole source of salvation in the heavenly light of the Gospel, which, as has been said, is the rule of Christians, the rule of life, and the rule of redemption.

Repeatedly he insisted on the absolute uniqueness of the Christian gospel and the folly of looking to anyone other than Christ for help, reminding his readers of the apostolic affirmation that "there is salvation in no one else" (Acts 4:12).

> If we put our faith and trust in anyone other than Jesus Christ for eternal life, . . . we are still in the darkness of night. . . . Therefore, my brothers and sisters, let us walk in the light of day, in the light of the holy Gospel. . . . Let us not go to any other than the heavenly Father through Jesus Christ and in Jesus Christ, as his word commands us, and we shall be children of God in him and through him, children of grace and of light, children of spirit and of life.

Extrabiblical tradition was also inadmissible unless it was consonant with God's word:

> Let us know that men and their doctrines are nothing, except insofar as they are corroborated and confirmed by the word of God. But Jesus Christ is everything; he is fully human and fully divine; and every man is nothing, except in him; and every word of man is nothing, except in his word.

Finally, Lefèvre discussed certain objections to the translation of the Bible into the language of the people. To those who argued that the translator was liable to pervert or lose the sense of the original text, and thus to lead simple people astray by his translation, he replied that there was no danger of this when the original text was carefully followed and the temptation to provide elegant paraphrases shunned. To the complaint that there were many difficult and obscure places in the Gospels that simple people could not understand, and that therefore a translation might lead such persons to erroneous interpretations, he rejoined that, by the same logic, the evangelists should not have given the Gospels to the Greeks in Greek, or later to the Latins in Latin, since there are obscure passages that both Greeks and Latins find difficult to understand. The primary necessity was belief, in accordance with Christ's command to "believe the Gospel" (Mark 1:15).[71]

It was, moreover, a fact of history, Lefèvre observed, that those who have fallen into error have not been persons ordinarily regarded as simple and common, but highly educated men of great subtlety and ability like

---

71. In the preface to his Latin commentary on the Gospels Lefèvre explained the relationship between believing and understanding in the following way: "When the Lord commands us, as the text says, to believe the Gospel, not to understand it, should we make it our aim to understand it? Why not? But in such a way that believing comes first and understanding afterwards; for he who believes only what he understands does not yet believe properly and sufficiently." Rice, p. 438.

Arius, Eunomius, Photinus, and Sabellius. Understanding of the truth did
not come by human skill but by the free grace of God.

> Every person must know how vain it is to try to make a blind man
> understand the beauty, excellence, and magnificence of the physical sun.
> So much the more is it impossible to express in writing, or to cause others
> to understand in writing, the beauty, excellence, and glory of the Gospel,
> which is the word of God, the shining of the true spiritual sun by which
> all beauty, excellence, and glory, and all transcendental goodness is com-
> prehended, and which cannot be known unless it manifests itself within
> the inner eye of the spirit, just as the physical sun cannot be known unless
> it manifests itself within the exterior eye of the flesh. But as the physical
> sun communicates itself by itself and by its own natural goodness, so also,
> only much more so, does the spiritual sun communicate itself by itself
> and by its own supernatural goodness, inasmuch as it is inestimably more
> beautiful and excellent than the physical sun, and sometimes communicates
> itself more completely and spiritually to simple persons, insofar as they
> are more humble and lowly, rather than to clerics who are less humble
> and more exalted, as is acknowledged by the word of our Lord when he
> says in the Gospel of St. Matthew, "I thank thee, Father, Lord of heaven
> and earth, that thou hast hidden these things from the wise and understand-
> ing, and revealed them to babes."[72]

Furthermore, any who wished to forbid or obstruct the giving of the
Gospel to the people in their own language could not escape the fact that
Jesus himself spoke against them. Lefèvre cites three passages: 1) "Woe
to you teachers of the law! for you have taken away the key of knowledge;
you did not enter yourselves, and you hindered those who were entering"
(Luke 11:52)—a text that would be frequently cited by the Reformers who,
life Lefèvre, understood "the key of knowledge" to mean the word of God;
2) "Go into all the world and preach the Gospel to every creature" (Mark
16:15); and 3) "Teaching them to observe all that I have commanded you"
(Matt. 28:20). "And how," Lefèvre asked, "will they preach the Gospel
to every creature, how will they teach them to observe all that Jesus Christ
commanded, if they are quite unwilling that the simple folk should see and
read the Gospel of God in their own language?"[73] He might also have
reminded his critics that the Vulgate to which they were so deeply attached
was itself a translation originally intended, as the name indicates, for the
benefit of the common people.

The second part of Lefèvre's French translation of the New Testament,
containing the Pauline Epistles, the Catholic Epistles, the Acts of the
Apostles, and the Apocalypse (in that order), was published five months
later on 6 November 1523. Like the first part, it was introduced by a hor-

---

72. Matthew 11:25. This biblical reference provides ample justification for Lefèvre's argument; but is there perhaps an echo of the *idiota* concept here? See pp. 12f., 50 above.

73. Rice, pp. 449ff.

tatory epistle addressed "to all Christian men and women." Lefèvre began by calling attention to St. Paul's assertion in Romans 15:4 that "whatever was written in former days was written for our instruction, that by steadfastness and by encouragement of the Scriptures we might have hope." This, he said, meant that, "instructed by the Holy Scriptures all our trust should be in God;" consequently "it is not at all surprising that those who are touched and drawn by God desire the true and life-giving doctrine which is nothing other than Holy Scripture." He recalled that some thirty-six years previously Charles VIII had been animated by this desire and that it was at his request that the whole Bible was translated into the vernacular by Jean de Rély, "his confessor, a learned theological scholar, who was elevated to episcopal dignity." Rély's translation was largely a revision and modernization of Guyart des Moulins' *Bible historiale* of the end of the thirteenth century. Lefèvre had enjoyed the firendship of Rély, who died in 1499, and had dedicated his edition of Aristotle's *Nicomachean Ethics* to him (in 1497). Lefèvre built on his work without discarding his own independence of judgment and research.[74] Now in his turn Lefèvre enjoyed royal support as he worked at providing the French people with a new and more reliable translation of the Bible.

The holy and vital doctrines of the New Testament are all comprised in the single term "gospel," Lefèvre asserted. These doctrines, he declared, "are not doctrines of men but doctrines of Jesus Christ, doctrines of the Holy Spirit, who is the Spirit of Jesus Christ speaking in and through men," namely, the apostolic authors of the New Testament writings. The appeal with which he concluded this preface is filled with the confident expectation of spiritual renewal:

> Who, then, is the person who will not reckon it a thing right and consistent with salvation to have this New Testament in the language of the people? What is more necessary for life—not the life of this world, but the life everlasting? . . . It is, indeed, essential to have it, to read it, to treat it with reverence, to have it in one's heart, and to hear it, not just once, but regularly in the assemblies of Jesus Christ, which are the churches where all the people, both simple and learned, should gather to hear and honor the holy word of God. And it is the intention of our gracious king, most Christian in heart as well as name, in whose hand God has placed so noble and excellent a kingdom, that the word of God should be purely preached throughout his kingdom to the glory of the Father of mercy and of Jesus Christ his Son. This consideration should encourage all the citizens of his kingdom to profit from true Christianity by listening to and believing the life-giving word of God. And blessed be this hour when it comes. And blessed be all men and women who help to make this a reality, not

---

74. See S. Berger, *La Bible française au moyen âge* (Paris, 1884); also C. A. Robson, "Vernacular Scriptures in France," *The Cambridge History of the Bible*, vol. 2 (Cambridge, 1969), pp. 436ff.

only in this kingdom, but throughout the whole world, so that what was said by the prophet may be everywhere fulfilled: "O give thanks to the Lord, for he is good, for his mercy endures for ever, from the east and from the west, from the north and from the south" (Ps. 106:1–3). Therefore all bishops, curés, vicars, teachers, and preachers ought to move the people to possess, to read, and to meditate on the sacred evangelical writings.[75]

Mid-February 1524 saw the publication in Paris of Lefèvre's French translation of the Psalms. In the prefatory epistle, addressed, once more, "to all Christian men and women," Lefèvre spoke of the necessity for the worship of God to be offered in spirit and in truth (John 4:23) and reminded his readers of St. Paul's assurance that "because we do not know how to pray as we ought" the Holy Spirit helps us in our weakness (Rom. 8:26). He declared that his purpose in translating the book of Psalms into French was "that men and women who speak and understand this language might be able to pray to God with greater devotion and deeper feeling." In the primitive church, he advised them, Christian people were instructed to pray to God in no other way than by God's word the Scripture; and the Psalter, filled as it was with holy praises, petitions, and canticles, was particularly well suited to this purpose. To approach God otherwise than Scripture taught could lead only to superstition. St. Paul insisted that the worship of God should be in a language understood by all (1 Cor. 14:19). In the early church, moreover,

> St. Jerome saw to it that in his country of Dalmatia all persons, great and small, priests and others, offered no prayer to God except in the Dalmatian language. Why, then, [Lefèvre asked] should not the people of this kingdom and of every other nation pray in the language of the country, thus understanding the prayers they pray and the thanks they render to God and the requests they make of him?[76]

Lefèvre's next publication was an edition of the Psalms in Latin—actually a corrected Vulgate text with summaries at the head of each Psalm. The introductory letter was addressed to Jean de Selve, the distinguished diplomat and first president of the Parlement of Paris. Lefèvre described the reading of Holy Scripture as "a happy pilgrimage of our mind to God." "Who would deny," he inquired, "that this is truly a drawing near to God

---

75. Rice, pp. 457ff. It is interesting and significant that the same emphasis recurs, in our own day, in the *Dogmatic Constitution on Divine Revelation* issued by the Second Vatican Council, as the following quotation shows: "Therefore, all the clergy must hold fast to the sacred Scriptures through diligent sacred reading and careful study. . . . This sacred Synod earnestly and specifically urges all the Christian faithful . . . to learn by frequent reading of the divine Scriptures the 'excelling knowledge of Jesus Christ' (Phil. 3:8)." *The Documents of Vatican II* (New York, 1966), p. 127.

76. Rice, pp. 469f.

when we hear him speaking in Scripture?'' For Holy Scripture is indeed the utterance of God. Lefèvre described the Psalms as ''a sacred hymnology,'' and he expressed the wish that in reading them attention should not be paid to him but to David, ''the instrument of the Holy Spirit,'' and to ''the Father of mercies and Christ himself from whom the Psalms have come by divine inspiration.'' That Christ was the true focus of the Psalms was evident from Christ's assertion that everything written about him in the law of Moses and the prophets and the Psalms should be fulfilled (Luke 24:44), and also from the fact that the Psalms are so frequently quoted in the New Testament (Lefèvre lists fifty-nine places). The christological understanding was, indeed, the proper key to Scripture.

> The word of God [Lefèvre explained] is an immense light, which is received not by human but by divine illumination. O how beautiful it is for man to die to himself and for God to live in him, for man to be in subjection and for God to reign, for man to be humbled and for God alone to be exalted![77]

After this Lefèvre completed a Latin commentary on the Catholic Epistles, which was ready about Christmastide 1524,[78] though its actual publication was delayed until July 1527, when Andreas Cratander brought it out in Basel. The dedication was to the chancellor of France, Antoine Duprat, who subsequently became archbishop of Sens (1525), was made a cardinal (1527), and on the death of Briçonnet (1534) annexed the bishopric of Meaux to his other high offices. In the prefatory letter, once again, is the clearest evidence of Lefèvre's fervent devotion to the gospel of Christ and of his insistence on the absolute uniqueness of that gospel as the way of salvation for humankind. After citing biblical passages that speak of the complete supremacy of Christ over the whole of creation (Ps. 68:35; Eph. 1:20ff.; Phil. 2:9–10), he quotes the affirmation of St. Peter that ''there is salvation in no one else, for there is no other name under heaven given among men by which we must be saved'' (Acts 4:12). The contemplation of this truth leads him to exclaim:

> O words most powerful for salvation! O that they might be engraved by the finger of God on the minds of those who are to be saved! O truth that shall never injure anyone, never deceive anyone! He it is whom the Catholic Epistles proclaim as the sole author of salvation. He it is whom our commentary preaches, so that all whom it reaches may participate in such wonderful salvation and grace—salvation and grace which in him and through him are to be revealed to those who have and shall have this faith, and which exceed all mortal sense and comprehension.

---

77. Ibid., pp. 471ff.

78. *Commentarii in Epistolas Catholicas*. The interpretation of the somewhat problematic phrase at the conclusion of the prefatory letter regarding the time when it was written is discussed by Rice, p. 478, and Herminjard, II:37.

Lefèvre then made a strong plea for the widespread promotion of this gospel by the leaders of the people (which indicates the strategy of the dedication of Duprat):

These epistles and this commentary desire this faith and this salvation for our most Christian king, and for you [Duprat] and the leaders and all the inhabitants of the kingdom, indeed, to speak more christianly, all people everywhere, especially those who lovingly follow Christ and his holy word, which is the eternal Gospel of peace. Nor should kings, rulers, parliaments, and governments hesitate to permit the word of God to circulate freely in their kingdoms, dominions, territories, and jurisdictions: indeed, they should rather promote this, for it will result in their being held in so much the more honor and esteem. This is what Christ commands, whether through the Gospels, or through Paul, or through Peter, as well as through other men enlightened by the inspiration of the Holy Spirit.

Lefèvre took care to point out that to promote the gospel was at the same time to promote respect for authority and orderliness in society; and he cited a selection of scriptural texts that enjoin submission to rulers, obedience of children to parents, and respect for orderly standards (Matt. 22:21, Rom. 13:1–2; 1 Tim. 2:1–2; Titus 3:1; 1 Pet. 2:13–14). "The sacred pages are full of these holy instructions and teachings of eternal life: why then," he challenged, "should not all who hold high office promote them with enthusiasm?"

Lefèvre took the opportunity to praise the French king for the manner in which he had encouraged the provision and distribution of the word of God in his domain, and to urge Duprat to use his influence to press things still further. He spoke of the great praise the king would deserve before both God and men if he was diligent to appoint faithful ministers of the word of God in every one of the dioceses of his kingdom.

May it therefore be your glory, you who are the king's Mercury, herald, and interpreter [he exhorted Duprat], to direct the royal heart to this course of action and to spur on him who is the noblest born, prepared as he already is to pursue a bold path. For, to put it briefly, the word of God is the stability, the solidity, and the strength of the whole commonwealth.[79]

A second edition of Lefèvre's French translation of the Psalms was published in Antwerp on 20 June 1525 by Martin de Keyser (who in December 1530 would also produce Lefèvre's translation of the complete Bible in a single volume) with the addition of a "concluding exhortation," in which Lefèvre warned that "no one should speak disparagingly against Holy Scripture, since to do so would be blasphemy against the Holy Spirit, who is its author."[80]

---

79. Rice, pp. 478ff.

80. Ibid., pp. 487ff.

THE EPISTLES AND GOSPELS
FOR THE CHRISTIAN YEAR

Despite the intensity of the opposition, Lefèvre's confident anticipation of a new day of conquest for the gospel remained unshaken. The remarkable industry and productiveness of these few years at Meaux, during which he continued unremittingly to devote his energies to the translation and exposition of the biblical text, are to be explained not just in terms of his natural propensity for hard work, but more particularly by his awareness of the clamant spiritual needs of his nation and his determination to do all in his power to promote the renewal for which he was looking. Especially significant in this connection was the appearance in 1525 of a volume printed in French by Simon du Bois in Paris with the title *Epistles and Gospels for the Fifty-Two Weeks of the Year*.[81] The work did not bear the name of an author. The withholding of the author's identity may have been a precautionary measure made expedient by the Sorbonne's 1523 edict forbidding the publication of any French translations of the Scriptures; but it is just as likely that the mention of the work's author or authors was regarded as inappropriate since it was not offered as a contribution to academic scholarship but was designed rather for regular use in the parish ministry among the general populace.

Certainly the professors of the Sorbonne, by whom the book was condemned in November 1525, were under no illusions regarding its provenance, for they described it as "according to the use of the diocese of Meaux." Lefèvre's archenemy Béda was saying the same thing, though in more specific terms, when the following year he designated "Jacques Lefèvre and his disciples" as its authors, while dismissing the work itself as neither Holy Scripture nor the Word of God but an invention of Lefèvre. The work does indeed bear the hallmark of Lefèvre—that is not in dispute. Each Epistle and Gospel, set out in the French language, was followed by a homiletic exhortation, also in French. In addition to the fifty-two Sundays a few of the main commemorative days were included, namely, Christmas, St. Stephen, St. John, Circumcision, Epiphany, Purification, and Ascension, and also the Monday and Tuesday in Easter Week and the Monday and Tuesday after Pentecost. The noticeable reduction of the

---

81. A second edition was brought out some five years later, and two further editions, one printed by Pierre de Vingle in Lyon in 1531 or 1532 and the other by Etienne Dolet in the same city in 1542, are known, both of which include some supplementary passages and sermons not found in du Bois' edition and with *Sundays* instead of *Weeks* in the title. See *Jacques Lefèvre d'Etaples et ses disciples: Epistres & Evangiles pour les cinquante & deux sepmaines de l'an*: Fac-similé de la première édition Simon du Bois, avec introduction, note bibliographique et appendices, par M. A. Screech (Geneva, 1964); *Jacques Lefèvre d'Etaples et ses disciples: Epistres et Evangiles pour les cinquante et deux dimenches de l'an*: Texte de l'édition Pierre de Vingle, édition critique avec introduction et notes, par Guy Bedouelle et Franco Giacone (Leiden, 1976).

number of such days was doubtless a consequence of Lefèvre's fear of feeding superstition by encouraging the observance of numerous saints' days. The exhortations were brief, simple, practical, and evangelical in tone. They were composed by four of Lefèvre's younger colleagues, under his close supervision and subject to his correction. This information we owe to one of the four, Jean Le Comte de la Croix, who shared with Lefèvre the town of Etaples as his birthplace, where he was born in 1500; he was Lefèvre's disciple both in Paris and in Meaux. Le Comte produced a similar collection of Homilies in 1549, when he was in Switzerland serving as pastor in Grandson. It was in the dedicatory epistle of this work, addressed to the civic leaders of Berne and Fribourg, that he spoke of the production of the earlier volume in Meaux; he did not, however, give the names of his three collaborators.[82]

The theologians of the Sorbonne lost little time in finding fault with the contents of the *Epistles and Gospels*. On 6 November they censured forty-eight propositions extracted from the exhortations, denouncing them variously as heretical, scandalous, odious, false, rash, impious, erroneous, schismatic, and as "Lutheran." They condemned the propositions as "favoring the heresy of Luther," "derived from the workshop of Manicheus and Luther," "concurring with the errors of the Manicheans and Lutherans," "close to the error of the Bohemians[83] and Lutherans," and "favoring the errors of the Waldenses, Wycliffites, and Lutherans." These forty-eight condemned propositions are of special interest because they allow us to see clearly those aspects of the theological position held by Lefèvre and his disciples in 1525 that were regarded as offensive by the traditionalists. The particular doctrines that were condemned by the Parisian professors may be summarized under the following headings:

(1) The sinner is justified by faith alone in Jesus Christ and good works do not in any way contribute to his salvation.

(2) Salvation does not rest within our power, but comes to us by the grace and goodness of God alone.

(3) Jesus Christ is the sole mediator between God and men, and therefore it is futile to invoke angels or saints to intercede for us.

(4) Anything other than the word of God in Holy Scripture is not to be preached, taught, or believed in the church.[84]

The Parisian theologians objected that to affirm that "faith alone is required and is sufficient for the remission of sins and for justification per-

---

82. See Bedouelle and Giacone, op. cit., pp. xxviiff.

83. I.e., Hussites.

84. These are the four main heads that repeatedly come up for censure. Some lesser issues involved questions concerning ecclesiastical rites and festivals and Lefèvre's substitution, based on the textual evidence available to him, of "Bethabara" for "Bethany" in John 1:28 (Gospel for Advent IV).

niciously turns the faithful away from achieving their own salvation through pious works''; that to maintain that ''no satisfaction other than the death of Christ is required by sinners deceives those who have sinned with a rash and futile hope''; that to disallow the invocation of angels or other creatures ''derogates from the veneration of the holy Mother of God, of angels, and of the other saints,'' and ''by propounding faith or trust in Christ as alone necessary excludes the help of the saints and the observance of the divine laws from being necessary for salvation''; and that to declare that the word of God is everything and all else nothing, and that nothing should be preached to the people that is not contained in Holy Scripture is ''insulting to the Church and its reverend theologians and preachers.''

After listing the condemned propositions, they summarized their censures in the concluding judgment:

> The aforesaid book contains the errors already noted, wickedly detracting from good works and contending that satisfaction for sins is not necessary for salvation and that human laws and ecclesiastical sanctions are of no consequence, schismatically rejecting also the cult of the saints and their holy days, together with catholic expositions of Holy Scripture, under pretext of the same divine Scripture which it twists throughout to a heretical sense; it is no small stumbling-block to the faithful populace; it encourages schisms which can hardly be eliminated; and it obviously recalls the heresies of the Manicheans, Waldensians, Wycliffites, and Lutherans; it is manifestly lacking in self-consistency, as for example in its constant insistence that nothing is to be preached to the people except the Gospel, while no exhortation to the people, or almost none, contained in the said book is consonant with the Gospel, but rather contrary to it: indeed, they are diabolical inventions and fabrications of heretics that are contained in the aforesaid book. Therefore this book will deservedly be burned in the presence of the populace to whom, whether read or preached, it has been disseminated, together with all similar writings; and those responsible for its composition or who caused it to be read or preached to the populace must make reparation for the offense by publicly execrating and condemning it and especially the errors listed above.[85]

---

85. The text (Latin) of this judgment is given by Bedouelle and Giacone. op. cit., pp. liiif., and Screech, op. cit., p. 51. For the text of the condemned propositions (French) and the *censurae* (Latin) see Screech, pp. 41ff. Bedouelle and Giacone subscribe the *censurae* on the pages where the condemned propositions occur in the exhortations.

The text of the passages cited for censure in the Sorbonne document shows some variations of wording when compared with the text of the first edition of Du Bois. These verbal differences are not in themselves particularly significant and might be regarded as attributable to a copyist, made perhaps with the intention of clarifying slightly the censured propositions extracted from their context. But the differences extend also to the page references given in the censure, and this poses a problem that is not so readily explicable. It must be counted improbable that there was a still earlier printed edition of the *Epistles and Gospels* of which no copies survive, and indeed of which there is no record. More probably, as Bedouelle and Giacone suggest, the Sorbonne professors had the manuscript or some preliminary, virtually identical document, such as printer's proofs, before them (p. xxi; cf. Screech, pp. 22f.). Whatever the answer, the authenticity of the text we possess is not affected or in dispute.

The bias and misrepresentation of this judgment are plain to anyone who has read the exhortations in the condemned work. It is marked by an unwillingness even to attempt to understand what Lefèvre and his circle were saying with such earnestness to the theologians and to the church as a whole. Lefèvre, quite simply, was reaffirming the principle that he had sought to honor throughout the course of his intellectual and spiritual pilgrimage by calling on his generation to return to the source. For him now, as we have said before, there was only one source that mattered, because it was supreme, namely, the word of God as revealed in Holy Scripture. The essence of his challenge was that the church should compare its teachings and practices with the dominical and apostolic doctrine of the New Testament and submit to the pristine authority of that source. But the theologians of the Sorbonne in particular, and ecclesiastical officialdom in general interpreted this as a threat to their dignity and an assault on the establishment. They reacted in much the same way as did the religious leaders in Jerusalem when they tried to silence St. Paul by denouncing him as one "who was teaching men everywhere against the Jewish people and law and temple, . . . a pestilent fellow, an agitator among all the Jews throughout the world, and a ringleader of the sect of the Nazarenes, who even tried to profane the temple" (Acts 21:28; 24:5-6). Does this, then, make Lefèvre a heretic? According to Screech, "Yes, certainly, in the eyes of the Sorbonne who without doubt would have censured St. Paul himself."[86] Lefèvre's accusers were content, as Bedouelle and Giacone observe, to take refuge in a contradictory position, saying in effect: "This book teaches that nothing should be preached to the people except the Gospel, and yet none of the exhortations contained in it is found to be consonant with the Gospel!"[87]

Lefèvre and his collaborators did not deny the importance of good works, especially as the fruit and evidence of evangelical faith in the life of the Christian; they did deny the teaching that good works are in themselves meritorious and contribute to the justification and salvation of the sinner. They did not maintain that satisfaction for sins was unnecessary for salvation; they did maintain that the sinner was unable to make such satisfaction, while affirming the absolute perfection and adequacy of the satisfaction made by Christ on the cross. They did not hold that human laws and ecclesiastical sanctions were of no consequence; they did hold that they cannot take precedence over the gospel and that if they should be found discordant with the teaching of the New Testament they were harmful rather than beneficial. They did criticize the cult of the saints, but only because they saw this as threatening the sole and unique mediatorship of Jesus Christ and as fostering false expectations in the minds of the worshipers. They

86. Screech, op. cit., p. 16.

87. Bedouelle and Giacone, op. cit., p. liv.

did not despise catholic expositions of Holy Scripture, but were intent only on affirming that all noncanonical writings should be subject to the rule of, and to correction by, the biblical canon—a position maintained by the catholic Fathers themselves! They were not Manicheans. Their doctrines of grace, faith, and justification did indeed have close affinities with the teaching of Wycliffe, Hus, and Luther, but they were derived directly from the New Testament, not from these or other men. They were not schismatics: they were working within the church as its loyal members, and their objective was the good of the church. While criticizing what they considered to be erroneous beliefs and unscriptural practices, they labored constantly for the renewal of the church by preaching the gospel of divine grace and by calling on the church to return to the integrity of its origin in the New Testament. Their zeal was not destructive or self-seeking; it was evangelical, activated by concern for the glory of God and the triumph of his truth, and with it the infinite blessing of their fellow men. But history shows that even in the church there are those who place their own aggrandizement above the glory of divine truth, and Lefèvre and his friends had plenty of evidence that this was still so in their day.

Flight and Return

THE DEPARTURE FROM MEAUX

In 1525 the situation became critical. In March, Zwingli dedicated his book *True and False Religion* to the king of France, and in doing so appealed to the king to silence the adversaries of the gospel at the Sorbonne, who

> . . . denounce propositions which are derived from Holy Scripture as impious, heretical, and blasphemous, whereas I do not know any doctrine more blasphemous than that which they teach themselves. Silence them, Sire, for fear lest by allowing them to utter against Christ everything that comes to their lips you should incur his wrath.

He urged the king not only to protect and encourage men of true sanctity and learning but also to appoint them to influential positions throughout his kingdom. To do so would ensure a harvest of peace and prosperity for the French nation. Even if the situation were considered from the merely pragmatic viewpoint, the reading of his book would show, Zwingli said, how kings and nations prosper and are blessed when they undertake the reform of manners in accordance with the Word of God.[1]

At a time when rulers took pleasure in projecting an image of themselves as scholar-princes, it was not uncommon for authors to dedicate their works to them with encomiastic and hortatory addresses in the hope either of gaining their favor and patronage or of persuading them to promote a particular cause or line of action. (It was a practice that Calvin, for example, would follow by dedicating the first edition of his *Institutes* to this same king and his commentary on the Catholic Epistles to Edward VI of England.) What likelihood there was of Zwingli being able to influence the French king to foster the evangelical cause by means of this dedication it is impossible to say; but as things turned out, it was not the most propitious moment to

---

1. Herminjard, I:350f.

make such an approach, for in the previous month Francis had been defeated at Pavia and carried off to Spain as the prisoner of Charles V.

Now, with the king off the scene, the opposition in Paris gathered momentum. The faculty of the Sorbonne submitted to the Parlement a statement of objectionable teachings attributed to Pierre Caroli, who had disregarded their order to desist from preaching in Paris.[2] Caroli had trumped this order by flourishing a letter from the king in his support! Now the Parisian theologians condemned as Waldensian, Bohemian, and Lutheran the doctrines with which they found fault. They took exception, for example, to Caroli's opinion that anyone, whether or not he had a doctorate or some other degree, could be a minister of scriptural truth, indeed that a poor saintly woman could have a better understanding of the Bible than priests and prelates inflated with their own importance; that we are saved by faith and not by works and fasting, because the grace of God depends not at all on the works and merits of people but solely on his infinite goodness; that true faith is not belief merely in historical facts but personal trust in and appropriation of the promises of God; that man-made temples are not essential for the worship of God; that the blessing and sprinkling of holy water effect nothing; that the lighting of candles and tapers does not increase the glory of God; and that nothing removes us further from the knowledge of God than the veneration of images.[3] Caroli, as previously mentioned, escaped from the French capital and found refuge with the king's sister.

Roussel described the increasing boldness of the adversaries of the evangelical movement in a letter written from Meaux on 25 September 1525 to Farel in Strasbourg:

> The captivity of our king has aroused such self-assurance in our opponents that they are persuaded the victory is now theirs. Their objective is the complete nullification of the word of God, for they are unwilling to tolerate the way it has spread among the populace and is bearing no little fruit.

Roussel informed Farel that a number of persons had already been thrown into prison and that others had been compelled to make public recantations. At the same time he deplored the turpitude of some who, through wishing to be regarded as Christians, by their inconstancy had hindered the advance of the gospel, and to avoid bearing the cross had allowed others to endanger their lives. He described the enemies of the evangelicals as innumerable and very powerful, in fact as holding in their hands absolute powers of life and death, thanks largely to a papal bull (of 20 May 1525) conferring on the judges appointed by the Parlement—"Quercus and Clericus[4] and two counsellors of not dissimilar ilk"—full authority to take whatever action

---

2. See pp. 143f. above.

3. Herminjard, I:378ff.

4. That is, Guillaume Duchêne and Nicole Le Clerc.

they might think necessary without there being any right of appeal from their decisions.[5]

Plans were formulated with all speed for rounding up and arraigning the evangelical leaders in the diocese of Meaux. An order for the burning of Lefèvre's French translation of the New Testament was issued at the end of August, and early in October the Parlement published an edict requiring Lefèvre, Roussel, and others to be brought to judgment in Paris. On 6 November, as we have seen,[6] the Sorbonne censured teachings extracted from the "exhortations on the Epistles and Gospels according to the usage of Meaux." The king tried to intervene from Spain, sending to the Parlement on 12 November an injunction to stop the persecution. He mentioned specifically Lefèvre, Caroli and Roussel, whom he commended as "persons of great knowledge and learning," and deprecated the hostility shown to them, and to Lefèvre especially, by the Parisian professors. He reminded the Parlement that the Sorbonnists had previously (in 1523) assailed Lefèvre with accusations and calumnies of which he had been completely cleared, and for this reason and also because of Lefèvre's high international reputation he demanded that he should not be subjected to their slander and molestation and that the proceedings should be suspended until his return to France.[7] It was felt, however, that the king's message from his Spanish prison could be safely disregarded, and the Parlement, persuaded by Lefèvre's enemies of the need to take immediate action against the heresy that was spreading in France, went its own way.

What were Lefèvre and his companions to do? Death awaited them if they stayed in Meaux. The alternative was to take refuge elsewhere with the intention of returning as soon as possible—which in effect would mean when the king had been restored to France—to resume the work of renewal they had been so assiduously promoting. They chose the latter course. Indeed, some two or three weeks before the latest of the royal interventions, Lefèvre, Roussel, and others who were still at liberty had fled the country.

LEFÈVRE IN STRASBOURG

Lefèvre and Roussel were welcomed and given hospitality in Capito's home in Strasbourg, where subsequently Michel d'Arande was able to join them. Strasbourg was the city to which Martin Bucer had come as a fugitive two and a half years earlier; he was destined to exercise a remarkable influence there. The refugees from France were pleased to find here what they judged to be a model community, revitalized in manners and ministry, of the kind they had been striving to establish in Meaux. Roussel wrote

---

5. Herminjard, I:389ff.

6. See pp. 164ff. above.

7. Herminjard, I:401ff.

favorably of the situation at Strasbourg in a letter sent to Briçonnet before
the end of the year. The diligence with which the word of God was preached
resulted in "wholesome food, unmixed with pharisaic chaff and leaven,"
being available to the people for much of each day.

> From the fifth to the sixth hour in the morning services for the offering
> of common prayer are held in the different churches; and this is repeated
> at the seventh hour. At the eighth hour or thereabouts there is a sermon
> in the main church, when songs translated from the Hebrew Psalter into
> the common language are sung and it is delightful to hear the wonderful
> blending of the men's and women's voices. There is another sermon at
> four o'clock in the afternoon, with singing preceding and following the
> sermon. . . . And though this might seem an excessive number of services,
> yet there is never one without a large attendance of people intensely eager
> for the divine word. There is nothing I would strive after so much as the
> supplying of this need in the hearts of our own people.

Roussel also admired the efficient manner in which scholars of distinction
were basing the instruction of their students on the knowledge of the original
languages of the Old and New Testaments.

Further, he wrote approvingly of the loving concern for the poor that
he found in Strasbourg. No destitute persons there lacked provision for their
daily needs. Funds for this were made available from the public purse by
the civil authorities, with the help of collections among the people and contributions to the poor-boxes placed in the churches—all without compul-
sion. Begging was strictly forbidden. The ministry of each parish, moreover,
was provided for partly by public funds and partly by earnings of the clergy
from secular occupations. Images had been removed from the churches,
and no other name was permitted to compete with the name of Christ, for
"Christ alone is worshipped, and only in conformity with his own word."
It was true that there were persecutions, but God used these to test those
who were his.[8]

At about the same time Roussel wrote in a similar manner to Nicholas
Le Sueur in Meaux; however, he mentioned that Lefèvre, who had been
using the cover-names "Coracinus" and "Antonius Peregrinus" to con-
ceal his identity, was nonetheless careless about keeping his identify secret.[9]
Consequently, the place where they had taken refuge was likely to become
known to their persecutors. Although they might wish to be better concealed,
they were not inactive, for they diligently occupied themselves with the
demanding task of translating the Bible into French. Roussel was working
from the original Hebrew and Greek texts, and he mentioned Lefèvre's per-

---

8. Ibid., pp. 403ff.

9. *Coracinus* is a diminutive form of *corax*, Greek and Latin for "raven"; Antonius
Peregrinus means "Antony the pilgrim." Roussel was using the cover-name "Joannes Tolninus"
for himself, and refers cryptically to Briçonnet as "Joannes Marcus" (John Mark).

sistence in struggling with the Hebrew of the Old Testament, despite his friends' attempts to persuade him to desist because of the difficulty of the undertaking caused by his inadequate knowledge of Hebrew.[10] (Lefèvre's translation of the New Testament, as we have seen, had been completed and published in two parts in 1523.)

THE RETURN TO FRANCE

The prospects for the French evangelical movement brightened considerably with the release of Francis I and his restoration to France in the spring of 1526, and the way rapidly opened up for Lefèvre and his friends to resume their ministry in their own country. In Strasbourg Capito's home had been a center for the meeting of evangelical scholars and leaders from different parts of Europe, and Lefèvre and his companions must have been tempted to remain where such congenial and stimulating company was to be found. But they did not hesitate to seize the opportunity now provided to return to France. Lefèvre traveled by way of Basel, where he had the pleasure of meeting with Erasmus and Ecolampadius. It was not to Meaux, however, that he went back, for the king had called him to Blois, near Orléans. There he was assigned the responsibility of putting the royal library in order and serving as tutor to Charles, the youngest of the royal princes, then only four years old. This may seem a strange appointment for an elderly man, but it was in fact designed to allow him ample time to pursue his own scholarly labors, now almost solely concentrated on the production of the French Bible. Nonetheless, he fulfilled his duties as tutor and librarian so acceptably, a contemporary author tells us, that he won the king's heart and could have obtained a position of no small authority at the royal court had he not esteemed honors and dignities so lightly.[11]

Soon after Lefèvre returned to France, Pierre Toussain, one of the younger evangelical scholars, wrote to Ecolampaduis from Malesherbes on 26 July 1526, giving his personal assessment of the situation as it was developing. A native of Metz, Toussain had pursued his studies in Basel, Cologne, Paris, and Rome, and in the previous year had spent some time with Erasmus in Basel. After leaving that city in October 1525, he had suffered imprisonment and torture at Pont-à-Mousson. Now at liberty again, he told Ecolampadius that his persecution had been so severe that he had frequently despaired of his life. On being released, he had found refuge in the home of the Baroness d'Entragues, whom he described as a "protectress of Christ's exiles." Because of his expectation that "the Gospel of Christ would soon prevail throughout France," and with the hope of per-

---

10. Herminjard, I:408ff.

11. See the quotation from Bergamo's *Supplementum chronicorum* (Paris, 1535) given by Rice, p. 499.

suading the king to reverse the sentence pronounced against him by the Sorbonne (a proceeding of which we have no information), he planned to live once more in France with the royal approval and protection.

Toussain informed Ecolampadius that he had had frequent conversations with the Duchess of Alençon (the king's sister) and that she had received him with the greatest possible kindness.[12] "We spoke much," he wrote, "of the promotion of Christ's Gospel, which is the constant theme of her prayers, and not hers only but the king's also." He added that the queen mother, too, was not hostile to these aspirations. News had reached him, he continued, that the bishop of Meaux (Briçonnet) had recently been preaching the word with little sincerity, "more anxious to please men that God." Indeed, Toussain seemed now to number Briçonnet among the "false prophets," of which, he said, "the court has many." About Marguerite, however, he had no misgivings: she was "so well instructed in the Lord, so well schooled in Holy Scripture, that she cannot be torn away from Christ." He complained of those who, "under the guise of religion, with their long vestments and shaven heads," hunted for high ecclesiastical office, and then, once they had obtained it, led the assault on "those whom the world calls Lutherans" and shunned nothing so much as the company of persons who had been brought into disgrace for the name of Christ. But this, he observed, was only to be expected of the court, "that most dangerous harlot"; and so he urged Ecolampadius to entreat the Lord to raise up prophets for them in France "who have a spirit of courage, not fear."

Apparently Toussain did not now regard Lefèvre as a prophet of this kind, for he continued as follows:

> I have spoken with Lefèvre and Roussel,[13] but Lefèvre lacks courage. May God strengthen and embolden him! Let them be as judicious as they wish, let them wait, defer, and dissemble: the Gospel cannot be preached without the cross! When I see these things, my dear Ecolampadius, when I see the king and the duchess so eagerly intent on the promotion of Christ's Gospel, as though nothing were more important, and then see those whose sole business ought, according to the grace given them, to be its promotion delaying to speak out, I cannot hold back my tears. "It is not yet time, the hour has not yet arrived," they say.[14]

Toussain, however, was unduly harsh and unfeeling in his criticism of Lefèvre. Though no flamboyant demagogue, Lefèvre, as we have already seen, was certainly not lacking in courage and constancy. Moreover, he was seeking all along to influence the royal leaders to set forward the cause of the gospel in France: he saw his presence at court as an advantage, not

---

12. "Without doubt in Agoulême"; Herminjard, I:445.

13. Again presumably in Angoulême, where Lefèvre had been in mid-June.

14. Herminjard, I:444ff.

to himself but to the gospel. Unlike Toussain, he was now an old man; he retained the vision but not the vigor of youth; he was certain that in the years that remained to him his own main task was to make the Scriptures available to the French populace in their own language, and it was at this, with the royal encouragement, that he was assiduously laboring. In any case, Toussain had no justification for forming so severe a judgment: it was only a few short weeks since Lefèvre's return to France—and even less since they had met and spoken together—and it was inexcusable to interpret the desire to "make haste slowly" as a symptom of cowardice. Toussain's attitude had perhaps been exacerbated by the persecution he had recently endured, but he evidently had a propensity for making exaggerated and less than charitable judgments of other people.[15] Besides, he himself had not been slow to accept the protection and hospitality offered him by the Baroness d'Entragues, and he was now attempting to return to France by the same means that had served Lefèvre, namely, under the safeguard of the royal goodwill, and with the same conviction that the gospel was about to conquer the country; otherwise, he told Ecolampadius, he would go instead to Germany. How, then, did he show himself any more courageous, or less cautious, than Lefèvre, whose longings and labors had the one objective of the victory of the gospel in France? Moreover, as even Toussain's letter testified, the situation at court, despite the favor of the king and his sister, was far from easy, crowded as it was by unscrupulous place-seekers who had little concern for sincere religion; and yet Toussain himself soon gave proof of his willingness to accept a court appointment, without, apparently, feeling it incongruous for him to do so.[16]

Roussel expressed the hopes and difficulties mentioned above in a letter he wrote from Amboise a month later, on 27 August 1526, to Farel in Strasbourg. "Things are going somewhat more favorably for us than previously," Roussel reported, "and hope is increasing that the fury of our enemies will be restrained and a measure of liberty restored to us." The perils and obstacles were still daunting, however: "I am fulfilling the office of preacher in the court of the duchess" (that is, Marguerite d'Alençon), Roussel continued, "but not without envy and great danger to my life; but God supplies strength." It was far from being an easy situation in which he found himself, and if there was any cause for surprise it was that he did not return forthwith to Strasbourg; "for, believe me, if I had paid attention to my friends I would hardly have lived among our people for a single week."

Writing again on 7 December, this time from Saint-Germain-en-Laye, Roussel told Farel that Prince Robert de la Marck of Sédan[17] and his two

---

15. See ibid., III:4, 9; Bedouelle, op. cit., p. 111.

16. See Herminjard, II:3f.

17. Robert II, comte de la Marck, prince de Sédan, duc de Bouillon, seigneur de Florange, de Jametz, et de Saulcy.

sons had embraced the evangelical faith and were eager for Farel to come
to them in Sédan and minister there. He assured Farel that he would be
treated as a member of their household and, as an added inducement, gave
him the news that they were willing to set up a printing press for his use.[18]
Roussel's appeal was supported two days later by Pierre Toussain who wrote
from Paris urging Farel to seize this opportunity for advancing Christ's
kingdom in a new area.[19] But Farel was unresponsive to these and other
appeals to return and minister in his homeland. He had made up his mind
to preach and minister in Switzerland, hoping, it may be, that the advance-
ment of the gospel there would have beneficial repercussions for the
evangelical cause in France.

Yet the invitation to minister in Sédan seemed to present him with
everything that he had long desired: a golden opportunity for evangelism
in his own country, the support and patronage of an aristocratic household,
and a press for disseminating the Christian message by means of the printed
page. Was it really too late for him to change his mind? Whatever the answer
to that question, in Switzerland, as previously in France, he soon met with
opposition and rejection. At Neuchâtel, the city in which he would later
play so prominent a role, he found it necessary to wear a priestly vestment
and to resort to various other subterfuges in order to gain a hearing; but
after a while the denunciations of certain persons who recognized him
resulted in his being prohibited from preaching because of the disturbance
his public utterances had caused in Basel and Montbéliard. Accordingly,
he was forced to leave Neuchâtel and made his way to Aigle, a city under
the jurisdiction of Berne. Perhaps he then thought regretfully of his refusal
to go to Sédan. But perhaps not, for the indications are that he had come
to the conclusion that there was now no prospect of success for evangelism
in France.

HOPE FOR RENEWAL IN FRANCE

Others, in addition to Lefèvre, were more hopeful than Farel and continued to believe that, by God's ordering, there could still be a bright day
for the gospel in France. Capito in Strasbourg, for example, dedicated his
commentary on the prophet Hosea to Marguerite in March 1528—with the
intention of commending and intensifying her encouragement of the French
evangelical movement.

> I have received no mandate [he wrote] to urge you to persevere courageous-
> ly in the course on which you have entered, nor even to warn you against
> the temptations which come like a battering-ram to demolish the walls

---

18. Herminjard, I:458ff.

19. Ibid., pp. 462f.

of your faith, surrounded as you are by idle gluttons who simulate piety for the love of gain and whose influence can weaken and pervert little by little those who ought to remain the faithful servants of Christ. What makes me hesitate most of all from assuming this undertaking is the knowledge that there are men close to you better able to fulfill it. Need I name Michel d'Arande, whose eloquence is so earnest, his piety so remarkable, his faithfulness so scrupulous in performing the duties of his bishopric?[20]

He mentioned also the presence of Gérard Roussel, "whose most judicious discernment is allied to the liveliest zeal for the glory of God," and of course Lefèvre:

Moreover, whenever you desire it, and I know that you desire it very often, you can converse with that lovable, learned, and pious old man Lefèvre d'Etaples, whose earnest spirit, tempered by a geniality appropriate to his age, expounds with grace and charm the mysteries of our faith when he is requested to do so.[21]

Nor had Martin Bucer, also in Strasbourg, written off France as a lost cause for the gospel. In July 1529 he dedicated his commentary on the Psalms to the Dauphin, François de Valois, who was then eleven years old, in the hope that through the crown prince he might succeed in exerting some influence on the course of events in France. Bucer observed that thanks to those who had been entrusted with his instruction, "men no less remarkable for their judgment than for their sanctity," the young prince was already acquainted with the truths of religion and the art of just government. He then added this exhortation:

All good men are looking to you to restore, like another David, the ark of the covenant to its place and to achieve a total renewal of the affairs of the kingdom which the misfortunes of the time have prevented your father from undertaking and accomplishing. Your religious real, so rare in these days, leads one to hope that the anticipations of so many pious men will not be disappointed.

Bucer expressed the hope also that his work on the Psalter would win the favor of the Dauphin's youngest brother, the Duke of Angoulême, who was the king's third son, because of the tuition he had recently been receiving from "the most pious and learned old man Jacques Lefèvre" in the book of Psalms.[22]

---

20. Michel d'Arande was now bishop of Saint-Paul-Trois-Châteaux in the Dauphiné.

21. Herminjard, II:119ff.

22. Ibid., pp. 194ff. Lefèvre had prepared "explanations" of the Book of Psalms for the royal children in 1528, and in 1529 a Latin-French vocabulary of the Psalter and a textbook "for the instruction in grammar of Monseigneur d'Angoulême and Madame Magdaleine his sister, [royal] children of France."

As the aging Lefèvre worked away at his biblical translation, however, the prospects for effective ecclesiastical renewal began to look less propitious. The king, anxious to patch up his relationship with the Vatican, gave some the impression that he was sympathetic to the claims of the antievangelical faction. He had taken no steps to countermand the ban that had been imposed by the Parlement on the publication of French translations of the Scriptures, though this struck at the work on which Lefèvre was engaged, making it necessary for him to find a printer outside of France. Farel's skepticism seemed, if anything, to be confirmed. On 10 May 1529 he wrote from Aigle to Capito with the news that Pierre Toussain had been invited to minister in Metz. "I would rejoice," he said, "if his preaching Christ there produced any fruit; but I cannot see what progress can be made among the French under so insane a sovereign who has allowed the New Testament to be forbidden to the populace, with the result that there remains no way of making the truth known."[23] Lefèvre, as we have shown, did not share this view, even though there might seem cause for discouragement. The king's attitude was ambivalent: the demands of practical politics conflicted with the claims of genuine religion; yet he had made Lefèvre welcome at Blois, where he was free to devote himself to his evangelical projects, and in particular to the work of translating the Old Testament into French. And so, undaunted, and certain of what he had to do, Lefèvre pressed on with his task.

The pessimism of some evangelicals regarding the situation in France was reflected further in Ecolampadius's letter of 4 May 1530 to Zwingli:

> It is getting too late [he wrote] for France to turn to Christ, for persons who arrived here at Easter brought the news that the bishops and theologians are extremely hostile to those who profess Christ, and that the king is not merely silent about this but actually threatens the most learned Gérard Roussel and Jacques Lefèvre and others with burning if they do not dissuade his sister from the beliefs they have induced her to embrace.[24]

The first part of this report was accurate enough, but not the latter part about the king's readiness to put the evangelical leaders to death, which was probably a mistaken inference from his failure to dissociate himself from the bishops and theologians. As we have said, he was playing a diplomatic game, and, despite apparent coolness to the evangelicals in public, there is no question that he continued to be well disposed to Lefèvre and his colleagues in private. Erasmus would appear to have given a truer description of the situation when, on 11 August, in a letter to Conrad of Stadion, the bishop of Augsburg, he asserted that the French king had forbidden anyone to write either against or in favor of Lefèvre.[25] It did not

---

23. Ibid., pp. 179f.

24. Ibid., pp. 249f.

25. Allen, IX:10.

suit the king at this juncture to convey the impression that his sympathies were with the evangelicals. There were strong personal reasons for his behavior, as we shall soon explain.

LEFÈVRE AT NÉRAC

At the end of May 1530 Marguerite wrote on Lefèvre's behalf to her cousin Anne de Montmorency, marshal of France and grand master of the king's household, telling him that Lefèvre was anxious to leave Blois because the climate was adversely affecting his health and requesting de Montmorency to seek the king's permission for him to do so. She assured him that Lefèvre had completed the work assigned to him as librarian: "He has put the royal library in order, classified the books, and drawn up a complete inventory which he will give to whomever the king pleases."[26] The permission was readily given and Lefèvre moved from Blois to Nérac in the southwest where for the remaining years of his life he enjoyed the peace and hospitality of Marguerite's home.

If the king was disposed to burn Lefèvre rather than allow the continuation of his spiritual influence on his sister, it is inexplicable that he should have been willing for him now to go and live at Marguerite's court in Nérac as her close friend and mentor. That the king was not in fact personally hostile to Lefèvre and his beliefs is confirmed by the report passed on to Luther by Bucer, in a letter of 25 August 1530, that the gospel was making good progress in France. Bucer advised Luther, however, that the unfortunate contention over the eucharist (between the Lutherans and the Swiss evangelicals) was proving such a hindrance that, if unresolved, the progress of the gospel in France would be seriously hampered, whereas if it were settled there was good hope that within a short while Christ would be received by the people: "for," Bucer pointed out, "the king is not opposed to the truth, and now that he has received back his children he will cease to be so dependent on the Pope and Caesar." He spoke of the unfailing support given by "that most Christian heroine" the king's sister, and asserted that "a great number have already come to the truth," adding that "in a certain region of Normandy so many have now professed the Gospel that the enemies have begun to call it 'little Germany.' " It was at the behest of the Queen of Navarre[27] that those involved in the eucharistic dispute were exhorted to treat the settling of their differences as a matter of urgency.[28]

The mention of the return of the king's children indicates another consideration, and a very powerful one, that has to be taken into account if

---

26. Herminjard, II:250f.

27. Marguerite d'Angoulême, whose first husband the Duke of Alençon had died on 11 April 1525 (overwhelmed, it was said, with grief as he had been held chiefly responsible for the defeat at Pavia), had been Queen of Navarre since 30 January 1527, the date of her marriage to Henri d'Albret, King of Navarre.

28. Herminjard, II:271f.

we are to understand the caution that marked his relationships with the
evangelicals in his kingdom during the years following his release from
captivity. The children referred to were his two older sons, François and
Henri, whom he had been compelled to leave in Spain as hostages (that
is why during this time Lefèvre had been tutor of the youngest son). The
manner in which the king conducted himself had to satisfy the Spanish king
and also, in view of the circumstances of his capture, the Pope, before he
could hope to receive his sons back; and it was only after they had been
held by the Spaniards for four and a half years that they were permitted,
in July 1530, to return home. Understandably, then, these were years in
which Francis I was particularly careful not to do anything in public that
might be prejudicial to the restoration of his children. Now that he had
received them back the future looked brighter again for the evangelicals.

Farel's critical attitude toward the evangelicals who remained in France
did not change, however. In the summer of 1531 he complained in a letter
to Zwingli that his frequent invitations to godly persons to come and serve
the cause of the gospel in Switzerland had fallen on deaf ears: "The charms
of France hold them captive to such a degree that they prefer to die without
fruit and to lie low in silence under tyrants rather than to profess Christ
openly."[29] But such a condemnation must be judged quite unfair. It carried the stamp of Farel's impetuous nature; and one may well wonder
whether those who felt it right to stay in France might not with greater reason
have reproached Farel for abandoning his native land. What justification
was there for him to assert that they were "dying without fruit" and failing to profess Christ openly, especially as there was much evidence to the
contrary?

The optimistic expectancy that continued to animate the spirit of Lefèvre
and his colleagues in France received further vindication of a spectacular
kind in the remarkable response to the preaching of Roussel in, of all places,
Paris during the Lenten season of 1533. He preached under the patronage
and sponsorship of Marguerite and her husband the King of Navarre, whose
court was then located in the palace of the Louvre. Not only did the huge
and enthusiastic audiences seem to signal a victory for the evangelicals,
but the aftermath also gave every appearance of a shattering defeat for their
opponents. Faced with this new development in the heart of the capital city,
the theologians of the Sorbonne lost no time in preferring charges of heresy
and "Lutheranism" against Roussel. Marguerite in turn intervened strongly
on his behalf by writing to her cousin Anne de Montmorency. She appealed
to him to use his influence as grand master of the royal household to persuade the king to take action against "those whose only concern is to speak
evil," who were busy planning Roussel's destruction. She declared her
readiness to vouch for Roussel's personal integrity and doctrinal soundness.[30]

---

29. Ibid., p. 356.

30. Ibid., III:52f.

BÉDA BANISHED

The deputation appointed by the Sorbonne to present to the king the articles intended to establish the heresy of Roussel received an unpleasant shock when the king ordered the arrest not of Roussel but of four leaders of the opposition, including Noël Béda, the arch-enemy of the evangelicals. Convicted of *lèse-majesté*, they were sentenced to be banished from Paris and forbidden to live within thirty leagues of the capital.

The excitement occasioned by this remarkable turn of events is graphically conveyed in two accounts given by persons who were in Paris at the time. The first is in a letter sent on 28 May 1533 by Peter Siderander (Schriesheimer), who was then completing his studies in Paris, to Jacques Bédrot, his professor of Greek in Strasbourg. Siderander explained that the king of France had been in Paris for some months, but that after the pre-Lenten festivities known as the Bacchanalia had withdrawn to Picardy. The king of Navarre had, however, remained in the capital with Marguerite his queen, and at his invitation Gérard Roussel had preached every day throughout Lent in the royal palace with such acceptance that the location had to be changed three times to accommodate the thousands who thronged to hear him. Angered by this development, a number of the Sorbonne theologians had been so rash as to denounce the French king in public as a promoter of Lutheranism and heresy and to incite a demonstration against the evangelicals. Shortly after Easter the king of Navarre had placed the agitators under house arrest and Béda was forbidden to leave the precincts of the Collège de Montaigu. When their conduct was reported to Francis, he sentenced them to banishment.[31]

The second account comes from a letter written some three months later, on 23 August, to Martin Bucer in Strasbourg by Johannes Sturm, who had been teaching rhetoric and dialectic at the Collège Royal since its opening in 1530. Sturm, who had been won over to the side of the evangelicals by Bucer's writings and Roussel's preaching, gave a more detailed account of the sequence of events that led to Béda and those convicted with him going into exile. After mentioning that Lefèvre was in Aquitania (at Nérac), "where he defends himself against the tyranny of the theologians," he described the remarkable popular response to Roussel's preaching and the attempts of his Sorbonne adversaries to silence him. Rebuffed in turn by the king, the chancellor (Antoine du Prat), the bishop of Paris (Jean du Bellay), and the First President (Pierre Liset), they had slandered the royal personages, using the city's pulpits for their rabble-rousing purposes and placarding public places with libels and pictures and

---

31. Ibid., pp. 54ff. Given twenty-four hours to leave Paris and ordered to remain at a distance from each other, they were forbidden to infringe their banishment under penalty of death, to preach or speak at any kind of assembly, or to communicate in any manner whatever with each other either directly or indirectly, until such time as the king might order otherwise.

dramatic satires that were particularly insulting to Marguerite. The sympathy of the majority was now with Roussel.[32]

A couple of months after the writing of this letter the king of France met with Pope Clement VII in Marseilles—a consultation that understandably was expected to have crucial consequences for the evangelical movement in France. In another letter to Bucer, written in mid-October, Sturm spoke of the anxiety with which he awaited the outcome of the meeting, and of the manner in which his feelings alternated between hope and misgiving. The animosity toward Marguerite as the patroness of the evangelical cause was now kept alive by less public methods. A startling manifestation of this hostility had been a recent presentation at the College of Navarre of a play in which Marguerite, Queen of Navarre, was lampooned as a woman who, together with a priest called Megera—a thinly veiled reference to M. Gérard (Roussel)—had handed herself over to the teaching of the devil. The principal of the college was arrested and others were expected to join him in prison. These developments encouraged Sturm to view the situation more optimistically, and he promised Bucer that he would write more fully about this incident and send him the text of the scurrilous play.[33]

Near the end of the same month Calvin wrote a somewhat fuller account of the event in a letter addressed to François Daniel and his other friends in Orléans. He also informed them that "certain factious theologians" had perpetrated "another outrageous act, equally malicious, though not so audacious": they had actually confiscated from the booksellers copies of a small book of verse entitled The Mirror of the Sinful Soul[34] composed by Marguerite, with the intention of placing it on the list of prohibited reading. The first edition, published by Simon du Bois at Alençon in 1531, did not carry the name of the author (though a second edition, which appeared in 1533, did); but Marguerite admitted her responsibility for the work to her brother the king, who ordered its examination to determine whether it was in fact religiously offensive. Nicholas Cop, rector of the University of Paris and son of the king's physician, pronounced judgment in her favor in an oration before the professors of the faculties of the four colleges of arts (medicine, philosophy, theology, and law), berating those who had presumed to attack the book and praising Marguerite as "the mother of all virtues and good literature." He complained that the book had been condemned without the knowledge or approval of the university (that is to say, by the theological faculty independently of the other faculties). Nicole Le Clerc, one of the Sorbonne theologians and curé of the parish of Saint-André-des-Arcs, was held primarily to blame, and he now made a speech

---

32. Ibid., pp. 72ff.

33. Ibid., pp. 93ff.

34. Le miroir de l'âme pécheresse.

in which he effusively extolled the integrity of the king as an energetic defender of the faith, denying that he belonged to the number of those who were conspiring against king and university, asserting that the action taken had been in fulfillment of the function delegated to him by the university (the carrying out, namely, of the rulings of the Parlement of July 1521 and March 1522 forbidding the publication of any religious works not first examined and passed by the faculty of theology), and protesting that nothing had been further from his mind than to promote a movement hostile to the Queen of Navarre, "a woman distinguished both for sanctity of morals and also for purity of religion." Her book, in no way comparable (he declared) to such obscene publications as *Pantagruel* by Rabelais, had been placed among suspect works only because it had been published without first consulting the faculty. He had simply been performing the duty assigned to him; consequently, if there was any blame, it belonged to them all. Pronouncement was then made that the book was not under suspicion and that the university should apologize to the king for any semblance to the contrary.[35] Le Clerc could count himself fortunate that he had managed to take shelter under a technicality.

THE KING'S ATTITUDE

Very soon, however, the king gave every appearance of turning against the evangelicals. Influenced, no doubt, by his conference with the Pope, he declared his determination to halt the advance of Lutheranism in his kingdom. Accordingly, he wrote to the Parlement from Lyon on 10 December 1533 expressing his displeasure that in Paris, the capital city of his realm, where the leading university of Christendom was located, "this accursed heretical Lutheran sect" was spreading, and announcing his intention to use all his power to stamp it out and to impose the extreme penalty on anyone, without respect of persons, who was found propagating it. Promoters of heresy were to be sought out and brought to trial. The king also wrote to the bishop of Paris ordering him to cooperate with those delegated by the Parlement to give effect to his wishes. He desired no delay and sanctioned the use of whatever force might be necessary. Moreover, he supplied both the Parlement and the bishop with copies of the papal bull enjoining the extirpation of the Lutheran sect in France.

Francis I also mentioned the flight from Paris of the university's rector, Nicholas Cop, to avoid arrest and arraignment on account of certain objectionable doctrines propounded in the address he had delivered before the university in October, following his appointment as rector. It is generally believed that the address betrayed the thought and terminology of Jean Calvin, then a young man twenty-four years of age, with whom Cop was

---

35. Herminjard, III:106ff.

friendly and who escaped with him in disguise. To show that his will was not be be trifled with, the king demanded that any who had assisted Cop to escape should be thrown into prison.[36]

In the middle of the following January Bucer wrote to Ambrose Blaarer (Blaurerus) in Constance, informing him of the severe persecution set in motion by the French king. He referred in particular to Nicholas Cop's rectorial oration, which had aroused the rancor of the theologians because he had included in it "a few things concerning justifying faith," and describing how a price had been placed on the fugitive's head for the purpose of bringing him back dead or alive. The king, he said, had issued an edict that anyone who was convicted of being a Lutheran was forthwith to be burned at the stake. According to reports some 300 persons had already been arrested in Paris. Bucer also gave Blaarer news of the "herodian marriage" of the king's second son, Henri Duke of Orléans, to Catherine de' Medici, the niece of Pope Clement VII, who himself had solemnized the marriage in Marseilles on 27 October 1533.[37]

In a letter of 19 February 1534 to John Choler in Freiburg, Erasmus also spoke of "the savage treatment being meted out to the Lutherans in Paris as the result of the promulgation of a terrible edict": numbers had been imprisoned and others, fearing for their lives, had fled. He related, further, that Béda and his colleagues had been recalled and had returned to Paris in triumph.[38]

Yet things were not as contrary to the evangelicals as they seemed, for the French king was still playing, in the main, a political game. To please the pope, he had taken action against the "Lutherans," without, however, resorting to the extremes he had threatened. A secret alliance with the German princes who favored Protestantism made it convenient for him to deal more mildly with the French evangelicals. A letter from Oswald Myconius in Basel to Bullinger, dated 28 February 1534, throws some interesting light on the situation. Myconius recounted a conversation on the previous day with a nobleman of evangelical persuasion who had told him that not everyone knew the reasons for the king's actions, insisting that, despite appearances to the contrary, he was not ill disposed to the gospel. Political considerations dictated that his sympathies should seem to coincide with those of the Vatican. The king, according to Myconius's informant, had prevented Béda from burning four prisoners in Paris, including Roussel, and had actually made Béda look a fool by arranging a debate between him and the prisoners and thus exposing the weakness of Béda's position. Bullinger's response was less than enthusiastic. Writing on 12 March, he described Francis as "an impure, profane, and ambitious man"

---

36. Ibid., pp. 114ff.

37. Ibid., pp. 129ff.

38. Allen, X:357.

whose dissimulation was dictated not by Christian principles but by his desire
to become the master of Italy.[39]

Bullinger's judgment may not have been wide of the mark. But a further letter from Myconius, written on 8 April 1534, conveyed news that
apparently confirmed his noble informant's assessment of the situation. He
had just heard, he told Bullinger, that "wonderful things are happening
among the Parisians." The king's return to Paris early in February from
a visit to the German Protestant patron, Philip, Landgrave of Hesse, had
brought the restoration of peace to the capital and revived the hope of a
bright future for the gospel in France. An Augustinian preacher was pro-
claiming the gospel to great crowds of people in a church close by the
Louvre,[40] and in the Louvre itself a bearded Italian Carmelite, whom the
pope had appointed almoner to his niece Catherine de' Medici, was freely
preaching Christ. What was more, the pope's niece was under the guidance
of Marguerite, and persons of high rank were daily attending the sermons.
And there were others, including academics, diplomats, and physicians,
who had openly identified themselves with the evangelicals. On the very
day of writing, Myconius had received news that Roussel had been set free,
while Béda had been arrested and imprisoned by order of the king.[41] Subsequently, Béda was sent again into exile for the rash and derogatory manner
in which by his words and actions he had insulted the king's majesty.

Further interesting information is found in a letter from Myconius to
Joachim Vadian in St. Gallen, written toward the end of May that year.
Myconius gives an account of a conversation in Marseilles between
Guillaume du Bellay, seigneur de Langey (brother of Jean du Bellay, bishop
of Paris), and the pope when the pope was meeting with the French king
(that is, in the preceding October or November). Myconius described
Guillaume du Bellay, a distinguished diplomat and statesman, as "an exceptionally learned man, who favors the purity of the Christian faith, but
who would wish the old profession of religion, valued for its apostolic
seriousness, to be restored with a measure of moderation." As a prominent member of the royal entourage, he had had the opportunity of speaking with the pope about the state of the church and various abuses that might
need to be corrected. The pope admitted that there were some aspects of
the mass with which he was not happy. Still more remarkable was du
Bellay's revelation that at their first session the pope had proposed to Francis
I the preparation of a military expedition for the purpose of violently compelling the Zwinglians and Lutherans to submit to the papal obedience, but
that the French king had refused to have any part in such a venture. Francis
pointed out that the Zwinglians and Lutherans based their case on the appeal

39. Herminjard, III:145ff.

40. Presumably, Saint-Germain l'Auxerrois.

41. Herminjard, III:160ff.

to Scripture, and that consequently to resort to force of arms against them would make it appear that the papal trust was not in Scripture but in military strength. He was prepared to lend his support only to the convening of a council made up of the best and most learned men for the purpose of determining what was and what was not in accord with the true faith of the church; and the king had resisted every attempt of the pope to persuade him to change his mind. Francis, it was said, was constrained by the treaty he had entered into with the Landgrave of Hesse and the Elector of Saxony; but the moderating influence of his sister and his own not unfriendly attitude toward the renewal of the church in France also help to explain his unwillingness to support the violent measures proposed by the pope.[42]

But just at this juncture, when a comparatively smooth and untroubled course seemed to lie ahead for those who were intent on advancing evangelical religion, their hopes were shattered, not by the scheming of their opponents but by the ill-considered action of certain extremists within their own ranks. On the night of 18 October 1534, placards displaying coarse denunciations of the mass and depicting pope, cardinals, and priests as vermin, liars, and blasphemers, were posted on the walls of the capital and of a number of other French cities by fanatical activists. One was even audaciously affixed to the door of the king's bedchamber in the palace at Amboise, where Francis I was currently residing. The king was incensed and affronted both by the inflammatory nature of the placards and also by the temerity that had violated the privacy of his own home. The Parlement was alarmed and arrests, imprisonments, and executions followed in quick succession. Conrad Gesner described the flood of persecution that was now let loose in a letter from Strasbourg to Bullinger on 27 December:

> Placards composed in French and, according to reports, printed in Neuchâtel were posted up by certain irresponsible persons. Many say that Farel[43] and a certain Augustinian monk are the authors. The theme was against the abuse of the mass, and the presence of the Lord's body in the eucharist was denied. During the one night they were affixed in Paris and Orléans and to the door of the royal bedchamber. The result is war: there have been innumerable arrests—some 300 or more, it is rumored. People are being tortured by new and unheard of methods in the most ghastly fashion: they are burned, their tongues are torn out, their hands are first cut off. There are endless lists of names of those whose arrest is wanted.

Because houses were being searched, evangelical writings that hitherto had eagerly been sought and purchased were hurriedly destroyed or thrown into the Seine.[44]

---

42. Ibid., pp. 183ff.

43. Incorrectly, it seems; see ibid., pp. 225f.

44. Ibid., pp. 235ff.

On 6 March 1535 Johannes Sturm wrote from Paris to Philip Melanchthon in Wittenberg explaining the calamitous reversal of the fortunes of evangelical Christians in the capital city produced by the affair of the placards:

> From the most excellent and agreeable situation that prudent men had brought about for us we have fallen, thanks to the stupidity of utterly mindless persons, into the greatest calamities and disasters. Only last year I wrote to tell you how well established we were becoming and what high hopes we had because of the king's moderation. At that time ours was a spirit of joyfulness, but wild men who are close to us have deprived us of that favorable prospect.

Deploring a situation in which the enemies of the gospel had regained control, Sturm spoke of the arrests, the tortures, the burnings, and the increasingly perilous conditions that were causing even innocent persons to tremble.

But there was also some news of a more reassuring nature, for Sturm told Melanchthon that Barnabas de Voré, seigneur de la Fosse, a trusted envoy whom Francis I was using in his negotiations with the Germans, had spoken to the king in enthusiastic terms about Melanchthon.

> Without being asked, he declared that he was your disciple. He expounded the whole rationale of your life and religion. The king listened most attentively and, as though not satisfied with hearing you praised, he decided that, if possible, and if you should be willing to come, he would hear you in person.

Sturm confidently expected that a visit from Melanchthon would do much to restore the prevailing tumultuous situation to a state of tranquility and toleration, and enable the evangelical cause to regain momentum, especially as the king's attitude toward this wave of violence was one of hesitancy, though his anger was fully justified. Sturm assured Melanchthon that the king, who was well aware of the evils within the church and of the need for their correction, was anxious to have the counsel of men like Melanchthon, and in fact was so strongly drawn toward him that there was reason to believe that apart from him a satisfactory resolution of the present troubles would not be achieved. Consequently he used his most impassioned powers of persuasion to convince Melanchthon that it was his duty to come to Paris.[45]

A few days later Sturm wrote to Bucer, enclosing a copy of his letter to Melanchthon, and appealing to him likewise to meet the French king for the purpose of healing a desperate situation:

> It rests in your and Philip's hand whether we live with the Gospel or for it are most cruelly put to death. That is why I beg you to see to it that

---

45. Ibid., pp. 266ff.

he is not driven to exasperation who is willing, with the help of your judgment, for his extensive kingdom to be moulded, strengthened, and guided. Never have I been able to realize that the heart of the king is in God's hand more than at this present time, when even with the flames burning he is thinking of the need for the renovation of religion. What we have always longed for, what we have never been able to obtain, this he now offers of his own accord, namely, a peaceful changing of those things which are false in the Christian religion.

As evidence of the prevailing confusion, Sturm reported that even while good men were being so brutally treated Béda had been sent again into exile. He told Bucer that just three days previously Béda, bare-footed, had publicly confessed his guilt and acknowledged the justice of his punishment for speaking against the king's person and writing untruthful letters and pamphlets. Assuring Bucer that the king was anxious for him to come to Paris, Sturm concluded: "Let me say just this, my dearest Bucer, that you should desert neither the Gospel nor those who, on account of the Gospel, for the glory of Christ, are awaiting the extremes of torture."[46]

Both Melanchthon and Bucer responded by affirming their complete willingness to come to Paris and confer with the French king; and in June the king himself wrote to Melanchthon to tell him that he earnestly desired him to come and assist in the retoration of ecclesiastical harmony and that a cordial welcome awaited him. Melanchthon had taken the opportunity to send some articles he had written, and Sturm advised him that they had been approved by the king almost in their entirety.[47]

The evangelicals had further cause for encouragement in the person of the new pope, Paul III. Elected on 6 October the previous year, following the death of Clement VII, Paul was said to be "more fair-minded and considerably better than his predecessors." He was reported to have written to Francis I to express his complete disapproval of the cruelty of torture. That this was indeed his attitude is confirmed in the contemporary *Journal d'un bourgeois de Paris,* which states that when the pope was informed of "the execrable and horrible justice which the king was meting out in his kingdom to the Lutherans" he wrote to say that, though he believed Francis I was acting with good intentions, yet "God the Creator, when he was in this world, used mercy rather than condemnation"; he declared, further, that "to cause a man to be burnt alive was a cruel death, and a way more likely than not to make him renounce the faith." Accordingly, the pope desired him to moderate his fury and the rigor of his justice; and from then on the king pursued a gentler course and ordered the Parlement to proceed with less severity, with the result that a number who had been imprisoned were released and savage penalties ceased to be enacted.[48]

---

46. Ibid., pp. 271ff.

47. Ibid., pp. 300ff.

48. Ibid., pp. 306ff.

Farel evidently shared Sturm's hopes of a beneficial outcome from a consultation between the king of France and Bucer, Melanchthon, and other German theologians, for he too did everything he could to persuade the latter not merely not to turn down the king's invitation, but to go with the positive expectation of gaining the most bountiful harvest from the meeting. "Christ well knows," he told Guillaume du Bellay, "that I desire the welfare of the king and his kingdom so earnestly that I never preach without offering up prayer for the king."[49]

As things turned out, however, neither Bucer nor Melanchthon came to Paris for the proposed consultation—the former for personal reasons and the latter because Frederick, the Elector of Saxony, refused permission for him to do so.[50] Both wrote to the king explaining their reasons for being unable to meet with him, and subsequently Sturm informed Bucer, in a letter of 18 November 1535, that the king, then in Dijon, was much pleased with what he had written and had decided to send Guillaume du Bellay to the Diet of Schmalkalden (which assembled the following month). The king fully understood both his and Melanchthon's reasons for not coming to Paris. "Never was the cause of the Gospel better placed than it is at present in France," Sturm said, "if only we can take advantage of this opportunity." He begged Bucer to do his utmost to win the king to the evangelical faith so that great numbers of good men might live in France without fear. "God is my witness," he affirmed, "that I look for nothing else than the progress of the Gospel."[51]

It is evident, then, that at the end of 1535, when Lefèvre's life was drawing to its close, the evangelicals in France and their friends elsewhere in Europe, far from regarding the advance of the gospel on French soil as a lost cause, were confidently looking for the crowning of their labors with a rich and plentiful harvest.

LEFÈVRE'S LAST DAYS

This historical survey has served to demonstrate that during the last dozen years of Lefèvre's life, despite bewildering changes of fortune and in the face even of severe setbacks and persecutions, the French evangelicals found good reasons for holding to their expectation that the conquest of

---

49. Ibid., pp. 357ff.

50. This prohibition was effected by the maneuvering of the English king, Henry VIII, who, anxious to prevent any allegiance between the Germans and the French and eager himself to have a place in the Schmalkaldic League, presented himself in the unaccustomed guise of a friend of Protestantism through the mediation of his diplomatic emissary Robert Barnes. Ironically, Barnes, the former Augustinian prior and no more than a pawn in the political game being played by Henry, would later be burned at the stake by Henry because of his evangelical convictions.

51. Herminjard, III:363ff.

France by the gospel would become a reality in their day. Though no longer at center stage, Lefèvre was in the closest association with the royal family, and he too continued to be of the same mind. And these hopes, as we have seen, were shared by others who were watching the situation sympathetically from beyond their borders. Even Farel had been stirred to reconsider the pessimism with which he had viewed the possibility of spiritual renewal in his native land. The harm done to the cause by the affair of the placards, which at the time had every appearance of being fatal, was being mended during Lefèvre's last days by the French king's wish to establish good relations with the German princes who supported the Protestant movement; and the new pope's disposition had proved to be unexpectedly mild. Moreover, there was the constant factor of the steady patronage and courageous advocacy of the evangelicals and their aspirations by the king's sister. Also encouraging was the manner in which evangelical reform was progressing elsewhere in Europe.

A dozen years later, the very thing that had been looked for in France came to pass in England, when a youthful king, Edward VI, espoused the evangelical cause and the whole country was opened up to the preaching of the gospel under the leadership of the archbishop of Canterbury and his fellow bishops. Even before that, William Tyndale, who was put to death in the same year that Lefèvre's life ended, went to the stake with a vision and a prayer that very soon afterward began to be fulfilled—an order was given for a copy of the Bible in English (the fruit, mainly, of Tyndale's faithful work of translation) to be placed in every parish church throughout England. Lefèvre, who had similarly labored to make the Bible available to all in French, died with the same vision for France. But the course of events in France would take a different turn from that in England.

Early in 1536 Lefèvre departed this life at Nérac in the palace of Marguerite and her husband the King of Navarre. According to a contemporary record, he uttered these words as he lay dying: "I leave my body to the soil, my soul to God, and all my goods to the poor." There is a story that as death approached Lefèvre passed through a period of distress, lasting some days, before recovering a calm and assured frame of mind. He is said to have described himself as "the most wicked man on earth" and to have asked: "How can I stand before the judgment-throne of God, I who, after teaching in all purity the Gospel of his Son to so many persons who have suffered death for it, have always avoided death though my age is such that, far from fearing it, I ought to desire it?" Farel, who had been won to the evangelical faith by Lefèvre, wrote some sentences to the same effect on the back of a letter sent to him by Michel d'Arande in which "the passing of that godly old man" was mentioned.[52]

This story is accepted by some who are antipathetic to Lefèvre as

---

52. See ibid., pp. 399f.; Bedouelle, op. cit., pp. 133ff., particularly note 59.

evidence that all along he had been a dissembler, that he consulted only his own safety, and that he died a self-confessed hypocrite. But this interpretation does not take into account the affirmation that this experience of anguish was no more than a passing phase and that he breathed his last in the full peace and liberty of the Christian hope. Bedouelle, in fact, questions the authenticity of the story, which he regards as belonging to a "literary genre," fashionable in the seventeenth century, which recounts the last words of notable men. It is his contention that Lefèvre's last days remain unknown to us.[53] Yet it is possible that the story is true, at least partially, and we cannot deny that it is not unusual for a good person, facing death, to be overwhelmed with a sense of failure and remorse as he looks back on his life. An experience of this kind, distressing as it is, is quite the opposite of a demonstration of hypocrisy or self-trust. Rather, it is evidence of self-despair, which is the obverse side of the gospel. And it is a passing phenomenon that should not be judged apart from the testimony of the whole of a person's life and character. If there is one thing that can be affirmed with certainty, it is that Lefèvre's life was in no way marked by lack of integrity and courage. To the contrary, there is a quite exceptional consistency in his single-minded dedication to the principle of authenticity throughout the whole of his life. He was never one to lower his standards or to be content with anything that was less than genuine for the sake of preserving his own ease and security. The temporary mood of despair, then, if indeed it happened, was uncharacteristic and should be attributed to physical rather than spiritual causes. That this is a right assessment is confirmed by an examination of his biblical writings, which bear ample witness to the depth and genuineness of his personal faith.

That Lefèvre's attitude toward death and judgment was one of perfect trust, free from fear, is very plain from a number of passages. The basis of this confidence was not self-assurance or even his love for God but rather the perfection of God's love for him, which he spoke of as a precious jewel:

> O inestimable pearl, which alone offers us the perfect trust that is in God and from God! But if it is imperfect, it is partly distrustful, and there is an admixture with one's trust of the fear of judgment, both particular and universal, on the last day. Then one is terrified of the day of death and the last day because of the fear of judgment and punishment. And this kind of love is imperfect, and this fear is still servile, befitting not sons but either slaves or persons not yet perfectly free, or who do not understand their liberty and the perfect goodness of their Lord who adopts them as sons.[54]

Such unhesitating trust made it possible to instruct others that "the forgiveness of our sins, our adoption as children of God, the assurance and

---

53. Bedouelle, loc. cit.

54. CE, on 1 John 4:17.

certainty of life eternal, proceed solely from the goodness of God" through faith in "our blessed Saviour and Redeemer Jesus,"[55] and that thanks to God's love "we have complete confidence in him and the certainty of the forgiveness of our sins and of eternal life, and we have no fear of the day of judgment or of being condemned for our sins."[56]

It was Lefèvre's clear conviction that final perseverance is the consequence not of human effort but of divine grace and the indefectibility of God's saving work, as the following homiletical passage shows:

> The apostle teaches us that we must await from God the completion of every good work that has been begun, saying that it is for him to make perfect the work he has begun, which is without doubt the work of faith; for Jesus Christ says in the 6th chapter of St. John "This is the work of God, that you believe in him whom he has sent." And Jesus Christ also is called the author of faith [Heb. 12:2]. It is also for God to give us perseverence in this faith until the day of Jesus Christ. . . . Therefore we can easily understand that man of himself can perform no good thing, and that all those who boast of their ability are in error and blaspheme against God, since they attribute to themselves what is proper to God, from whom comes the ability for us to do any good thing. . . . The apostle was able rightly to judge of the Philippians that God would provide grace to cause them to persevere to the end.[57]

Lefèvre's perspective as a Christian, then, was not one of doubt and uncertainty about the everlasting security of the recipients of divine grace. If a dark period of a few brief days intervened in his old age this should be seen as out of character with the firmness of his faith and ascribed to the dissolution of his faculties as death drew near. His life, like his exposition of Holy Scripture, had for long years been christocentric: it is by this consideration that he must be judged, not by an alleged passing spasm of despair during the ebb tide of his powers.

CHRISTIFORMITY

If there is a single word to sum up Lefèvre's profound spirituality it is the term *Christiformity,* that is, conformity to, or transformation into, the likeness of Christ. This term, though not common, occurs in Nicholas of Cusa's work *Learned Ignorance,* as we have noticed earlier,[58] and it is possible that Lefèvre picked it up from Cusanus. Another possibility is

---

55. EG, Epistle for the Monday in Easter Week (Acts 10:34ff.).

56. EG, Epistle for the First Sunday after Pentecost (Trinity Sunday); (1 John 4:8ff.).

57. EG, Epistle for the Twenty-second Sunday after Pentecost (Philippians 1:6ff.).

58. See pp. 46f. above.

that he discovered it in a Latin translation of Pseudo-Dionysius, a version of whose works he had published in 1499.[59] But the word is occasionally found from the ninth century onward in some British writings and also in Thomas Aquinas and his teacher Albert the Great[60] in the thirteenth century. Such speculative derivations are of little importance, however, since the concept behind the term as it is used by Lefèvre is completely consonant with the apostolic teaching of the New Testament. The source or seed from which it sprang may well be, as Bedouelle suggests, St. Paul's exclamation in Galatians 4:19: "My little children with whom I am again in travail until Christ be formed in you!"[61] But it is from other passages that he develops the concept, and he does so in such a way as to make it in a special sense his own.

By 1512, when his commentary on St. Paul's Epistles was first published, Lefèvre had clearly formulated the principle. The notion of Christiformity may reasonably be seen as an extension and a deepening of the theme of the imitation of Christ familiar to him from the teaching of Thomas à Kempis and the Brethren of the Common Life. But Christiformity, for Lefèvre, is more than the copying of Christ; it is the formation of the believer into the likeness of Christ. The constitution of Christians as the body of Christ implies and requires their Christiformity. This is the thrust of Lefèvre's comments on Colossians 3:1-4:

> As many as come to Christ die in his death and rise again in his resurrection; for they do not rise unless they have first died. In this way they are made *christiform* [*Christiformes*], so that they may constitute his body. For it is necessary that the members of the whole body should be conformed to the head; otherwise we should have a monstrosity. This sort of conformity in other things is called relationship and proportion, but in the body of Christ it is *Christiformity* [*Christiformitas*]. When therefore they rise in the resurrection of Christ they also live by the life of Christ.[62]

Lefèvre is referring to the present existence of Christians in union with Christ; the experience of Christiformity is a process of growth in Christ-likeness. Thus Lefèvre explains the assertion of 2 Corinthians 3:18 that

---

59. In the *Ecclesiastical Hierarchy*, VII.ii and the *Divine Names*, I.iv (Migne, PG, III; 594 and 553/554 respectively) the Latin rendering of χριστοειδής is *christiformis*, though in the edition brought out by Lef `evre the Greek term is translated by the expression *Christi species*.

60. The adverb *christiformiter* is used by both Thomas Aquinas (*Summa Theol.*, III, Q.64, Art.6, Ob.3; Q.82, Art.5, Ob.3: III, Suppl. Q.36, Art.5) and Albert (*Eccl. Hier.*, 7.3, p. 765b20)

61. The Vulgate reads: "Filioli mei, quos iterum parturio, donec formetur Christus in vobis." In commenting on this verse, however, Lefèvre does not propound the theme of Christiformity. Bedouelle, op. cit., p. 228.

62. PE, ad loc.

"we all, with unveiled face, beholding the glory of the Lord, are being transformed into the same image from glory to glory" as the reality of being made *christiform*.[63]

In his commentary on Romans 8:26–29, where St. Paul says that when we pray the Spirit "helps us in our weakness" and speaks of Christians as predestined by God "to be conformed to the image of his Son," Lefèvre writes:

> No one tastes this sweetness of prayer except he in whom the Spirit of God dwells. But God dwells in those who in this world strive to conform themselves to Christ as he was when he lived in the world, and who will be conformed to his glory. For glory in this world is to be made like Christ as he was when he lived in this world, just as glory in the world to come will be to be made like the glorified Christ. This is the conformity of the Son of God with which God glorifies his own, whether in this age or the next. For is it not glorious to be conformed to Christ, indeed to be *christiform*?[64]

Later in the same epistle (13:12–14), St. Paul exhorts the Christians in Rome to "cast off the works of darkness," to conduct themselves "becomingly as in the day," and to "put on the Lord Jesus Christ"; Lefèvre summarizes this passage as a summons to "lead the *christiform* life" (*Christiformem vitam gerentes*), so that "we may also be seen to have put on Christ Jesus."[65]

This leading of the *christiform* life is not something superficial: it is described by Lefèvre as internal as well as external, hidden as well as seen. He explains, when writing on Colossians 3:12–17, that the various forms of discipline sanctioned in the church are in themselves of no worth; but if they are used to focus attention on Christ instead of on oneself they may help to make one "conformed to Christ according to the infirmity of the flesh," which is outward conformity to Christ. "Inner *Christiformity*" (*interior Christiformitas*), however, is promoted "by following not the doctrines of men but our exemplar in heaven," so that we may have "heavenly imitation." "Happy is the man," he declares, "who is able worthily to imitate Christ and to become *christiform* both inwardly and outwardly."[66]

It is the anointing with the oil of the Holy Spirit that makes Christiformity not only a possibility but a reality of the Christian experience. Thus Lefèvre expounds 1 Peter 2:9ff.:

> All who come to Christ are anointed with the oil of the Spirit so that they may be *christiform*. Christ indeed is both king and priest. We are anointed with that true oil so that we may all partake of Christ, who receives this

63. *Christiformes*. PE, ad loc.

64. *Christiformes*. PE, ad loc.

65. PE, ad loc.

66. PE, ad loc.: . . . *Christum imitari et intus et foris fieri Christiformis.*

name from chrismation. . . . He is Christ in the absolute sense, we by participation of Christ; and we have all been anointed with the internal and spiritual unction so that we may all become spiritual kings and priests with an anointing so much more real than that with which the kings and priests of the old law used formerly to be anointed. . . . O the wonderful dignity of Christians in Christ![67]

Christiformity is for Lefèvre the sum total of the Christian life. It comprehends all that Christians should be and do. It is to this effect that he comments on Ephesians 5:1ff.:

Our whole good consists in the imitation of Christ; for his life is our example. His love is the form and source of our love, so that because of him who loved us we in turn should so love that we prefer to die rather than offend a neighbor or a member of Christ, in whom Christ has been formed,[68] and who lives by the Spirit of Christ. Where this imitation of Christ is, where this love is present (for Christ is total love), not only will there not be fornication or any impurity, baseness, foolish talk, levity, and the seeking of this world's pleasures, but, as befits the saints and their converse with each other, they will not even be named.[69]

Again, when writing on 1 John 3:16, he observes that "there is nothing more important than the imitation of what Christ has done for us, namely, his laying down his life for us": those who imitate Christ must be prepared to do the same, not only for their friends but also for their enemies, for the divine love knows no limits of time or space.[70]

In this present life, however, Christiformity, though earnestly sought, is ever incomplete. It should indeed be progressive, so that there is an increasing conformity to the likeness of Christ; but this process of sanctification is brought to completion only eschatologically. The sum of this doctrine is stated in 1 John 3:2–3: "Beloved, we are God's children now; it does not yet appear what we shall be, but we know that when he appears we shall be like him, for we shall see him as he is. And every one who thus hopes in him purifies himself as he is pure." Lefèvre offers the following commentary:

This is the will of the Father, that his pilgrim sons should imitate his Son when he was a pilgrim, that they should suffer harsh and adverse things, that they should be pious, gentle, patient, obedient to God in all things unto death, even if need be the most distressing death, always bearing their cross, . . . and that equally with Christ they should gain a depar-

---

67. CE, ad loc.

68. This concept, *in quo Christus formatus est*, strongly echoes the thought and language of Galatians 4:19.

69. PE, ad loc.

70. CE, ad loc.

ture to the joys of immortality, exalted at last from the prison of this world
to the kingdom of light, made *christiform*,[71] knowing God face to face,
no longer through a veil, or through shadows and figures, but just as we
are known to God.[72] . . . Let us conform ourselves to him, not indeed that
we can do so of ourselves, but solely by his grace, placing our hope entirely
in him; for if, not thanks to ourselves but thanks to the love of God for
us for Christ's sake, we hold this hope of our future state and of glorious
conformity to Christ, we will sanctify ourselves in this world just as he
is holy. . . . Just as Christ lived in this world as our example, so we also,
as we are enabled by grace, ought to live in imitation of him in this world.[73]

This emphasis on the grace of Christiformity casts further light on
Lefèvre's spiritual perspective and devotional intensity. All along, the
impulse of his scholarly labors had been the concern for authenticity. During the last quarter-century of his life, his singleness of purpose expressed
itself in his dedication to the cause of ecclesiastical renewal through the
call to return to the New Testament as the source of Christian faith, the
preaching of the evangelical message, the restoration of sane exegesis, and
the translation of the Bible into the language of his fellow countrymen. The
vital religion he desired for himself he desired also for the whole of France,
indeed for all humankind. Nor did he doubt that God would raise up leaders
to carry forward the work he had been promoting and to bring in the day
of renewal for which he looked. An event toward the end of his life gave
evidence once again of the firmness of his expectation. Calvin, who, as
we have seen, avoided arrest by escaping from Paris in disguise, made a
special journey to Nérac in the spring of 1534 for the purpose of meeting
and consulting with Lefèvre. Not yet twenty-five years of age, Calvin was
given a cordial welcome. The only record of anything that was said as they
conversed with each other is the information given by Beza (in his life of
Calvin) that the old man predicted that his youthful visitor would be used
as an instrument for establishing the kingdom of God in France.

Though Geneva was destined to become the center of his ministry,
Calvin did indeed carry on the work Lefèvre had begun. After the visit
to Nérac, Calvin joined his cousin Pierre Robert Olivétan in the labor of
revising Lefèvre's French translation of the Bible.[74] During the succeeding
years his toil was unremitting in the public exposition of the sacred text,
the publication of commentaries on almost every one of the canonical books

---

71. *Christiformes effecti*, i.e., in eschatological fullness.

72. Cf. 1 Corinthians 13:12.

73. CE, ad loc.

74. Lefèvre's translation of the entire Bible "would continue to be the basis, for three
centuries, of the French translations of Holy Scripture, Roman Catholic as well as Protestant." Pierre Courthial, "Esquisse d'une histoire de la théologie 'réformée' en France," *La
Revue Réformée* 134 (1983):56.

of both Old and New Testaments, and the formulation of evangelical theology, perhaps encouraged by his meeting with Lefèvre.

In this twentieth century the voice of Lefèvre is beginning to be heard and heeded anew within the ranks of both Protestantism and the Roman Catholic Church. It is not unreasonable to hope that even today, by the witness of his life and writings, this one dedicated little man, Jacques Lefèvre d'Etaples, who traveled a road that led him from pagan philosophy to evangelical faith, has something important to say to us.

Select Bibliography

For a detailed bibliography of Lefèvre's editions of the works of other authors and of his own writings see Rice, *Prefatory Epistles*, pp. 535ff.

The following texts have recently been republished:

Jacobus Faber Stapulensis. *S. Pauli epistolae XIV ex Vulgata, adiecta intelligentia ex graeco, cum commentariis.* Faksimilie-Neudruck der Ausgabe, Paris, 1512. Stuttgart, 1978.

Jacques Lefèvre d'Etaples. *Quincuplex Psalterium.* Fac-similé de l'édition de 1513. Geneva, 1979.

Jacques Lefèvre d'Etaples. *Hecatonomiarum libri.* Texte latin des *Hécatonomies* de Lefèvre d'Etaples, en parallèle avec la traduction latine de Platon par Marsile Ficin. Ed. Jean Boisset et Robert Combès. Paris, 1979.

Jacques Lefèvre d'Etaples et ses disciples. *Epistres & Evangiles pour les cinquant & deux sepmaines de l'an.* Fac-similé de la première édition Simon du Bois, avec introduction, note bibliographique et appendices par M. A. Screech. Geneva, 1964.

Jacques Lefèvre d'Etaples et ses disciples. *Epistres et Evangiles pour les cinquante et deux dimenches de l'an.* Texte de l'édition Pierre de Vingle. Edition critique avec introduction et notes par Guy Bedouelle et Franco Giacone. Leiden, 1976.

Jacques Lefèvre d'Etaples. *Le Nouveau Testament.* Fac-similé de la première édition Simon de Colines, 1523. Ed. M. A. Screech, avec introduction. 2 vols. Paris, 1970.

Barnaud, Jean. *Jacques Lefèvre d'Etaples, son influence sur les origines de la Réformation française.* Cahors, 1900.
——————. "Jacques Lefèvre d'Etaples," *Etudes théologiques et religieuses* 11 (1936):3ff., 98ff., 135ff., 203ff.
——————. "Lefèvre d'Etaples et Bédier: Les premiers assauts donnés à la Réforme française," *Bulletin de la Société de l'Histoire du Protestantisme français* 85 (1936):251ff.
Bedouelle, Guy. *Lefèvre d'Etaples et l'Intelligence des Ecritures.* Geneva, 1976.
——————. *Le Quincuplex Psalterium de Lefèvre d'Etaples: Un guide de lecture.* Geneva, 1979.
Bedouelle, Guy, and Franco Giacone. "Une lettre de Gilles de Viterbe (1469–1536) à Jacques Lefèvre d'Etaples (c. 1460–1536) au sujet de l'affaire Reuchlin," *Bibliothèque d'Humanisme et Renaissance* 36 (1974):335ff.

Bentley, Jerry H. "Erasmus' *Annotationes in Novum Testamentum* and the Textual Criticism of the Gospels," *Archive for Reformation History* 67 (1976):33ff.

_____. "Biblical Philology and Christian Humanism: Lorenzo Valla and Erasmus as Scholars of the Gospels," *The Sixteenth Century Journal* 8, no. 2 (1977):9ff.

Berger, Samuel. *La Bible au seizième siècle: Etudes sur les origines de la critique biblique.* Paris, 1879; reprint Geneva, 1969.

_____. "Le procés de G. Briçonnet," *Bulletin de la Société de l'Histoire du Protestantisme français* 44 (1895):7ff.

Briçonnet, Guillaume, and Marguerite d'Angoulême. *Correspondance (1521–1524).* Edition du texte et annotations par Christine Martineau et Michel Veissière avec le concours de Henry Heller. 2 vols. Geneva, 1975, 1979.

Brush, John W. "Lefèvre d'Etaples, Three Phases in his Life and Work," in *Reformation Studies: Essays in Honor of Roland H. Bainton.* Ed. F. H. Littell. Richmond, 1962, pp. 117ff.

Cameron, Richard. "The Attack on the Biblical Work of Lefèvre d'Etaples, 1514–1521," *Church History* 38 (1969):9ff.

_____. "The Charges of Lutheranism brought against Jacques Lefèvre d'Etaples (1520–1529)," *Harvard Theological Review* 63 (1970):119ff.

Carrière, Victor. "Lefèvre d'Etaples à l'Université de Paris (1475–1520)," in *Etudes historiques dédiées à la mémoire de M. Roger Rodière.* Arras, 1947, pp. 107ff.

_____. "Libre examen et tradition chez les exégètes de Préréforme (1517–1521)," *Revue d'histoire de l'Eglise de France* 30 (1944):39ff.

Chantraine, Georges. "Josse Clichtove: témoin théologien de l'humanisme parisien: Scholastique et célibat au XVIe siècle," *Revue d'Histoire Ecclésiastique* 66 (1971):507ff.

Chrisman, Miriam U. *Strasbourg and the Reform: A Study in the Process of Change.* New Haven, 1967.

Copenhaver, Brian P. "Lefèvre d'Etaples, Symphorien Champier, and the Secret Names of God," *Journal of the Warburg and Courtauld Institutes* (1977):189ff.

_____. *Symphorien Champier and the Reception of the Occultist Tradition in Renaissance France.* The Hague, 1978.

Crespin, Jean. *Histoire des Martyrs.* Geneva, 1554.

Craven, W. G. *Giovanni Pico della Mirandola: Symbol of his Age.* 1981.

Dagens, Jean. "Humanisme et évangélisme chez Lefèvre d'Etaples," in *Courants religieux et humanisme à la fin du XVe et au début du XVIe siècle.* Colloque de Strasbourg, 1957; Paris, 1959, pp. 121ff.

_____. "Hermétisme et Cabale en France de Lefèvre d'Etaples à Bossuet," *Revue de Littérature comparée* 45 (1961):5ff.

Dankbaar, W. F. "Op de grens der Reformatie: de rechtvaardigingsleer van Jacques Lefèvre d'Etaples," *Nederlands Theologisch Tijdschrift* 8 (1953–54):327ff.

Debongnie, Pierre. *Jean Mombaer de Bruxelles, abbé de Livry, ses écrits et ses réformes.* Louvain, 1927.

Doerries, Hermann. "Calvin und Lefèvre," *Zeitschrift für Kirchengeschichte* 44 (1925):544ff.

Dorez, L., and L. Thuasne. *Pic de la Mirandole en France.* Paris, 1897.

Douen, O. "La Réforme française: est elle fille de la Réforme allemande?", *Bulletin de la Société de l'Histoire du Protestantisme français* 30 (1881):57ff., 122ff.

Doumergue, Emile. *Jean Calvin: Les hommes et les choses de son temps,* vol. I. Lausanne, 1899, pp. 79ff., 539ff., 542ff.

Eberling, Gerhard. "Die Anfänge von Luthers Hermeneutik," *Zeitschrift für Theologie und Kirche* 48 (1951):172ff.

Erasmus, Desiderius. *Opus Epistolarum Des. Erasmi Roterodami denuo recognitum et auctum.* Ed. P. S. Allen, 11 vols. Oxford, 1906–1947.

Farel, Guillaume. *Du vray usage de la croix de Jésus-Christ suivi de divers écrits du même auteur.* Geneva, 1865. This collection includes Farel's *Epistre à tous seigneurs et peuples et pasteurs.*

_____. *Guillaume Farel (1489–1565)*. Biographie nouvelle écrite d'après les documents originaux par un groupe d'historiens, professeurs, et pasteurs de Suisse, de France, et d'Italie. Neuchâtel/Paris, 1930.

Ganoczy, Alexandre. *Le Jeune Calvin: genèse et évolution de sa vocation*. Wiesbaden, 1966.

Garin, Eugenio. *Giovanni Pico della Mirandola, vita e dottrina*. Florence, 1937.

Gosselin, Edward A. *The King's Progress to Jerusalem: Some Interpretations of David during the Reformation Period and their Patristic and Medieval Background*. Malibu, 1976.

_____. "Two Views of the Evangelical David: Lefèvre d'Etaples and Theodore Beza," in *The David Myth in Western Literature*. Ed. Raymond-Jean Frontain and Jan Wojcik. West Lafayette, Indiana, 1980.

Graf, Charles-Henri. *Essai sur la vie et les écrits de Jacques Lefèvre d'Etaples*. Strasbourg, 1842; reprint Geneva, 1970.

_____. "Jacobus Faber Stapulensis: ein Beitrag zur Geschichte der Reformation in Frankreich," *Zeitschrift für die historische Theologie* 21 (1852):3ff., 165ff.

Hahn, Fritz. "Faber Stapulensis und Luther," *Zeitschrift für Kirchengeschichte* 57 (1938):356ff.

Heller, Henry: *Reform and Reformers at Meaux, 1518–1525*. Unpublished doctoral thesis, Cornell University, 1969.

_____. "Marguerite of Navarre and the Reformers of Meaux," *Bibliothèque d'Humanisme et Renaissance* 33 (1971):271ff.

_____. "The Evangelicism of Lefèvre d'Etaples: 1525," *Studies in the Renaissance* 19 (1972):42ff.

_____. "The Briçonnet Case Reconsidered," *Journal of Medieval and Renaissance Studies* 2 (1972):223ff.

Herminjard, A. L. *Correspondance des réformateurs dans les pays de langue française recueillie et publiée avec d'autres lettres relatives à la Réforme et des notes historiques et biographiques*. 9 vols. Paris, 1866–1897.

Holban, Marie. "François du Moulin de Rochefort et la querelle de la Madeleine," *Humanisme et Renaissance* 2 (1935):26ff., 147ff.

Hufstader, Anselm. "Lefèvre d'Etaples and the Magdalen," *Studies in the Renaissance* 16 (1969):31ff.

Hughes, Philip Edgcumbe. "Jacques Lefèvre d'Etaples (c. 1455–1536): Calvin's Forerunner in France," in *Calvinus Reformator*. Potchefstroom, 1982, pp. 93ff.

_____. "The Jewish Cabala and the Secret Names of God," *Philosophia Reformata* 21 (1956):81ff.

_____. "Pico della Mirandola: 1463–1494. A Study of an Intellectual Pilgrimage," *Philosophia Reformata* 23 (1958):108ff., 164ff.; 24 (1959):17ff., 65ff.

Imbart de la Tour, P. *Les origines de la Réforme*. 4 vols. Paris, 1905–1935.

Jourda, P. *Marguerite d'Angoulême, duchesse d'Alençon, reine de Navarre*. 2 vols. Paris, 1930.

Jourdan, George V. *The Movement towards Catholic Reform in the Early Sixteenth Century*. London, 1914.

Kieszkowski, Bohdan. *Giovanni Pico della Mirandola: Conclusiones sive Theses DCCCC, Romae anno 1486 publice disputandae, sed non admissae*. Texte établi . . . avec l'introduction et les annotations critiques. Geneva, 1973.

Kittelson, James. "Wolfgang Capito, the Council, and Reform Strasbourg," *Archive for Reformation History* 63 (1972):126ff.

_____. *Wolfgang Capito: from Humanist to Reformer*. Leiden, 1975.

Kristeller, Paul Oskar. *Renaissance Thought and its Sources*. Ed. Michael Mooney. New York, 1979.

Kunze, Horst. *Die Bibelübersetzungen von Lefèvre d'Etaples und von P. R. Olivetan verglichen in ihren Wortschatz*. Leipzig, 1935.

Laune, Alfred. *La Traduction de l'Ancien Testament de Lefèvre d'Etaples*. Le Cateau, 1895.

_____. "Lefèvre d'Etaples et la traduction française de la Bible," *Revue d'Histoire des Religions* 32 (1895):56ff.

_____. "Des secours dont Lefèvre d'Etaples s'est servi pour sa traduction de l'Ancien Testament," *Bulletin de la Société de l'Histoire du Protestantisme français* 50 (1901):595ff.

Levi, Anthony. "Humanist Reform in Sixteenth Century France," *The Heythrop Journal* 6 (1965):447ff.

Lovy, R. J. *Les origines de la Réforme française: Meaux, 1518–1546.* Paris, 1959.

Lubac, H. de. *Exégèse médiévale: Les quatre sens de l'Ecriture.* 4 vols. Paris, 1959–1964.

_____. *Pic de la Mirandole.* Paris, 1974.

Maitre, H. B. "Les 'Théologastres' de l'Université de Paris au temps d'Erasme et de Rabelais (1496–1536)," *Bibliothèque d'Humanisme et Renaissance* 27 (1965):248ff.

Mann, Margaret. *Erasme et les débuts de la Réforme française (1517–1536).* Paris, 1534.

Massaut, J. P. *Josse Clichtove: L'humanisme et la réforme du clergé.* 2 vols. Paris, 1968.

_____. *Critique et tradition à la veille de la Réforme en France.* Paris, 1974.

McNeil, David O. *Guillaume Budé and Humanism in the Reign of Francis I.* Geneva, 1975.

Moore, W. G. *La Réforme allemande et la littérature française: Recherches sur la notoriété de Luther en France.* Strasbourg, 1930.

Oberman, Heiko A. *Forerunners of the Reformation: The Shape of Late Medieval Thought, illustrated by key documents.* New York, 1966.

Pannier, J. "De la Préréforme à la Réforme: A propos les deux dernières publications de Lefèvre d'Etaples (1534)," *Revue d'Histoire et de Philosophie religieuses* 15 (1935):530ff.

Payne, John B. "Erasmus and Lefèvre d'Etaples as Interpreters of Paul," *Archive for Reformation History* 65 (1974):54ff.

Pico della Mirandola, Giovanni. *Opera Omnia.* Basel, 1572. (The second of the two volumes in this edition contains the writings of Pico's nephew, Gian Francesco.) See also the texts published in the Edizione Nazionale dei Classici del Pensiero Italiano, ed. E. Garin (Florence, 1942 onwards); and the entry under Kieszkowski.

Proosdij, C. van. *Jacques Lefèvre d'Etaples, Voorganger van Calvijn.* Leiden, 1900.

Renaudet, Augustin. *Jean Standonck: Un réformateur catholique avant la Réforme.* Paris, 1908.

_____. *Préréforme et Humanisme à Paris pendant les premières guerres d'Italie (1494–1517).* Paris, 1916; 2d ed. 1953.

_____. "Un probléme historique: la pensée religieuse de J. Lefèvre d'Etaples," in *Humanisme et Renaissance.* Geneva, 1958, pp. 201ff.

Rice, Eugene F., Jr. "The Humanist Idea of Christian Antiquity: Lefèvre d'Etaples and his Circle," *Studies in the Renaissance* 9 (1962):126ff.

_____. "Humanist Aristotelianism in France: Jacques Lefèvre d'Etaples and his Circle," in *Humanism in France.* Ed. A. H. T. Levi. Manchester, 1970, pp. 132ff.

_____. "Jacques Lefèvre d'Etaples and the Medieval Christian Mystics," in *Florilegium historiale, Essays in honor of Wallace K. Ferguson.* Ed. J. G. Rowe and W. H. Stockdale. Toronto, 1971. pp. 89ff.

_____. "The Patrons of French Humanism, 1490–1520," in *Renaissance Studies in honor of Hans Baron.* Ed. A. Molho and J. A. Tedeschi. De Kalb, Illinois, 1971, pp. 687ff.

_____. *The Prefatory Epistles of Jacques Lefèvre d'Etaples and Related Texts.* New York/London, 1972.

_____. "The *De Magia Naturali* of Jacques Lefèvre d'Etaples," in *Philosophy and Humanism: Renaissance Essays in honor of Paul Otto Kristeller.* Ed. E. P. Mahoney. Leiden, 1976.

Riesco, Jose. "Jacobus Faber Stapulensis, Reformador parisiense, Humanistica y Filosofo," *Salamanticensis* 17 (1970):569ff.

Rossi, Paolo. "The Legacy of Ramon Lull in Sixteenth-Century Thought," *Medieval and Renaissance Studies* 5 (1961):182ff.

Sabatier-Plantier, H. de. *Origines de la Réformation française: J. Lefèvre d'Etaples.* Paris, 1870.

Salley, Claudia-Louise. "Jacques Lefèvre d'Etaples, Heir of the Dutch Reformers of the Fifteenth Century," in *The Dawn of Modern Civilization: Essays . . . presented to honor*

Albert Hyma. Ed. K. A. Strand. Ann Arbor, 1962, pp. 73ff.

Secret, F. "Les Dominicains et la Kabbale chrétienne," *Archivum Fratrum Praedicatorum* 27 (1957):319ff.

_____. *Les Kabbalistes chrétiens de la Renaissance.* Paris, 1964.

_____. "Notes sur quelques kabbalistes chrétiens," *Bibliothèque d'Humanisme et Renaissance* 36 (1974):67ff.

Smalley, Beryl. *The Study of the Bible in the Middle Ages.* Oxford, 1952.

Spicq, Ceslas. *Esquisse d'une histoire de l'exégèse latine au Moyen Age.* Paris, 1944.

Stauffer, Richard. "Lefèvre d'Etaples: artisan ou spectateur de la Réform?", *Bulletin de la Société de l'Histoire du Protestantisme français* 113 (1967):405ff.

Taverney, P. *Doctrines réformatrices et influences luthériennes à Paris et à Meaux.* Lausanne, 1934.

Thorndike, Lynn. *A History of Magic and Experimental Science.* 8 vols. London, 1923-1958.

Tyler, A. E. "Jacques Lefèvre d'Etaples and Henry Estienne the Elder, 1502-1520," in *The French Mind: Studies in honour of Gustave Rudler.* Ed. W. Moore, R. Sutherland, and E. Starkis. Oxford, 1952, pp. 17ff.

Veissière, Michel. "Le groupe évangélique de Meaux à la lumière de quelques travaux récents," *Bulletin de la Société d'Histoire et d'Art du diocèse de Meaux,* 24th year, 1973.

_____. "Guillaume Briçonnet, abbé rénovateur de Saint-Germain-des-Près (1507-1534)," *Revue d'Histoire de l'Eglise de France* 60 (1974):65ff.

Viénot, J. "Y a-t-il une Réforme française antérieure à Luther?", *Bulletin de la Société de l'Histoire du Protestantisme français* 62 (1913):97ff.

Victor, Joseph M. "The Revival of Lullism at Paris, 1499-1516," *Renaissance Quarterly* 28 (1975):504ff.

_____. *Charles de Bovelles, 1479-1553: An Intellectual Biography.* Geneva, 1978.

Villain, Maurice. "Le message biblique de Lefèvre d'Etaples," *Recherches de Science Religieuse* 40 (1952):243ff.

Weiss, N. "Martin Luther, Jean Eck, et l'Université de Paris d'après une lettre inédite, 11 septembre 1519," *Bulletin de la Société de l'Histoire du Protestantisme français* 66 (1917):35ff.

_____. "Réforme et préréforme: Jacques Lefèvre d'Etaples," *Revue de Métaphysique et de Morale* 25 (1918):647ff.

_____. "Guillaume Farel: ses premiers travaux," *Bulletin de la Société de l'Histoire du Protestantisme français* 68 (1919):179ff.

Wiriath, R. "Les rapports de Josse Bade Ascensius avec Erasme et Lefebvre d'Etaples," *Bibliothèque d'Humanisme et Renaissance* 11 (1949):66ff.

Index